LET YOUR LIGHT SHINE

Secrets in the Shadows

by
LUCIA MUIR

Email: luciamuirauthor@gmail.com

Approximate Word Count 95,958

SYNOPSIS

This book is a memoir of Lucia's life journey, born into the religion of Jehovah's Witnesses that she discovered has many traits of a cult organization.

The story begins with her memories as a small child and how she was treated as a scapegoat from an early age.

Read how the religious instruction affected her time at school, adolescence and what led to her disfellowship at the age of sixteen.

Lucia's disappointment of discovering the hypocrisy and unethical behaviour within a religion where her parents sought refuge, believing their promises of life everlasting while hoping the sect would be the answer to all their problems.

Lucia describes how her life changed after leaving the organisation and the difficulties of going out into the world without further education, qualifications and minimal social skills.

Read how her naivety attracted predators that she had to deal with alone while living a difficult life without her family. She also explains why she returned to the Jehovah's Witnesses on two occasions.

This book will show you how someone can go through many trials and tribulations but they can emerge from it as a knowledgable stronger person.

Lucia now believes that its not what happens to you in life, but how you perceive your experiences that can either destroy you or make you successful. The choice is yours.

ACKNOWLEDGMENTS

In memory of my parents who raised me with a spirituality even though I did not agree with it's teachings or views.

In memory of Aunt Mary who I had some wonderful times with and who gave me a little insight into what it would be like to have a birthday and Christmases.

To my Uncle Vernon who had the courage to debate even though it meant that he was shunned by his sister.

To Patrick my second husband who encouraged me to explore other spiritualities.

To the influential people that I met on my spiritual journey that opened my mind to new possibilities.

To Hattie Lovell who has been a lifelong friend and had the strength and courage to leave the religion and build her own life.

In memory of Vivien who taught me to play the piano, that brought therapeutic music into my life.

In memory of Ann Sheldon who was like another mother to me, but also gave unconditional love.

To Tom Shelden and his children who have given me love, support and unconditional love throughout my life.

To Clarissa who has given me an abundance of love, support and help since my arrival in Cornwall.

To Steven Hassan for helping me understand religious cults through his publications

To William Bowen the founder of Silent Lambs for his help and encouragement.

To Amazon publishing for helping me produce this book.

INTRODUCTION

Dear Reader,

Today is Sunday. When I reflect on memories of this day in childhood and adolescence it was certainly an active one. In the morning we would preach door to door from half past nine in the morning, return home for lunch two hours later and then prepare for our religious meeting. On alternate weekends we attended the Sunday morning meeting (as two congregations had use of the hall) so that we could visit Carl my autistic brother who resided in a hospital approximately twenty miles away. In later years we would visit my eldest brother and his wife for dinner before returning home. During the 1960s and 1970s, Sunday was considered a day of relaxation for most after working all week, but this is not the case when one becomes a member of, or is raised within the Jehovah's Witnesses. My parents devoted most of their lives to this religion, believing that Armageddon could arrive at any time and bring an end to the present world we lived in but only Jehovah's Witnesses would survive.

Today is also the fifth anniversary of my father's death and I did not realise my mother would also pass away suddenly six weeks from this moment. I have mixed feelings about her passing and as you read my life story you will understand why, Recruitment into this religion has ruined many aspects of our lives. This book will explain how and why my parents were recruited and how it affected their lives. The title I have chosen for this book is the instruction my mother would call out to me each day whenever I left the house.

Many people view Jehovah's Witnesses as kind, helpful, happy people who are always smiling. As you read on, you will gain more insight into their lives 'behind closed doors' and the harsh reality behind the smiles.

TABLE OF CONTENTS

CHAPTER 1

RECRUITMENT

My parents married at eighteen years of age. Neither of them had easy childhoods living through the trauma of a second world war, especially as their parents decided not to evacuate them. My mother's childhood affected her mentally and emotionally and she depended heavily upon my father. Kevin, my eldest brother was born five months after their marriage and eighteen months later, Carl, my second brother entered the world. My parents rented a 'bed-sit' (now known as a studio flat) which my mother described as a gloomy, grubby place. They spent many evenings at the cinema to spend time away from this place. One evening on their return home, my mother placed eight-month-old Carl into his cot and she was shocked to hear him humming the tune of the *National Anthem* played each night at the cinema after the closing credits of the movie. As time passed, he sang various pieces of classical music with the ability to imitate the sounds of each instrument and this amazed my parents. They wondered whether Carl would become a 'genius' musically as he seemed advanced in certain abilities for one so young.

By the time Carl reached the age of two, he spoke sentences that did not flow smoothly as the words came out rather jerkily. He developed severe tantrums and bouts of frustrated rage, with the strength to throw a mattress off a bed. My parents owned a heavy oak dining table that Carl would upturn, tipping all food and crockery onto the floor. He removed all his clothes, ran out of the house and around the neighbourhood. Carl had violent rages towards my mother, sinking his teeth into her arms and face so hard that she bled. My father had to work each day and could not be there to assist her. By the time Carl reached the age of six, he had more strength than her and was uncontrollable.

After consulting the General Practitioner, Carl was eventually diagnosed with severe autism and committed to a residential hospital for the mentally handicapped. It was devastating for my mother to part with her six year old son, but as well as biting her and himself, he also attacked others, including Kevin; a bus conductor on public transport; and one of the elders at the Kingdom Hall. Commuters on public transport stared at my mother as she sat there with bleeding bite-wounds on her arms. Carl could no longer communicate with anyone and retreated into his own world. The hospital staff were able to monitor him and prescribed daily medication to keep him calm him and lessen the bouts of violent behaviour.

A short time after my brother moved to the hospital, Vivien, a Jehovah's Witness, called at my parents' home. My mother described Vivien as a kind lady who spoke about God and read scriptures from her Bible that answered questions my mother had about a hope for the future. She needed to hear this after her separation from Carl.

Many people wonder why religious members continuously call at homes, but there will come a time when a householder has an emotional crisis and needs someone to talk to and then they will often be prepared to listen.

CHAPTER 2

EARLY CHILDHOOD.

I was born in a small town in Kent U.K., four years after Carl was admitted to the residential hospital. My parents had attended the meetings of Jehovah's Witnesses for a while and were eventually recruited. My birth, according to my mother, was a difficult one. My due date was on her birthday, but from that day on she had five days of false contractions and eventually a difficult labour. My parents resided in a prefabricated residence next to local woodland and when her labour began, my father left home to fetch the local midwife. He left in haste, forgot his keys and locked himself out, so my mother had to get out of bed and open the door to let them in. My head was apparently about to emerge and I am sure this short walk to the door helped me on my way! After the birth, my mother refused to look at me after her horrendous labour, so my father said: "if you don't want her, I will keep her". He cared for me until she changed her mind and as he walked around the room with me, my mother saw a small tuft of my hair above the shawl and changed her mind. When she eventually held me, she told me she thought I was a beautiful baby and cried for days, afraid something awful may happen to me, because of her initial rejection.

I have a few vague memories of being a toddler, but nothing related to religion at this time. My sister Waverley arrived eighteen months after me and my mother adored her as the labour was apparently quicker and easier, despite giving birth to a baby weighing a hefty nine pounds! My mother, at four feet and eleven inches tall, was a small woman. Kevin had reached twelve years of age and was my parent's 'blue eyed boy'.

At the age of six, I had complications from two childhood illnesses. I developed meningitis from mumps and was admitted to an isolation ward in a local hospital for three weeks. I recall my first examination when a nurse removed all my clothes and left me naked upon the hospital bed alone. Two male student doctors entered the room and seemed a little embarrassed as they conversed and gazed out of the window until a doctor arrived to discuss my case. It was a horrendous illness and the treatment was painful and terrifying. Members of my family and a few members of our religion visited me. Brenda was a pretty lady who gave me a fairy doll wearing a white dress trimmed with silver tinsel. It looked like the dolls that sat on top of Christmas trees and I loved it. Even at six I was aware that Jehovah's Witnesses would probably disapprove of this doll and surprised Brenda had given it to me. All visitors to the ward were instructed to wear gowns and masks, and they kept their visits short.

Although my stay in hospital was a traumatic one, I was in one way, relieved to be away from the situation at home. My abuser was a family member (who I hasten to add was NOT my father) This family member bullied me after I disclosed his inappropriate sexual behaviour with Waverley to my parents. He had behaved this way on many occasions, visiting our bedroom during the night and while babysitting when my parents were out. He invited Waverley or I upstairs on the pretence of helping him make his bed and on one occasion, when he and Waverley were gone for a while, I crept upstairs and witnessed his actions. I recall a time when my parents were away overnight and he insisted we slept in our parents bed with him.

The atmosphere at home was highly sexual as my parents had an extremely fiery and passionate relationship. They were not discreet when demonstrating their physical affection for one another, so my siblings and I witnessed regular inappropriate behaviour between them. I would sometimes watch them to try to work out if it was the same type of attention I received from him. My parents explained the love they had for one another was completely different to the love they had for us but I found this confusing. When my mother saw me watching them, she accused me of being 'perverted' and did not ask me why I was watching them. She was also overly-affectionate with Kevin who was forbidden to experiment sexually with girls his own age as any courtship within the religion had to be strictly chaperoned.

I assumed that these restrictions may have been the reason my abuser turned his attention to Waverley and I. When I caught him behaving this way with her, I decided to disclose. There were three reasons for this – firstly, the abuse I received had become painful and I was concerned he may be causing her pain. Secondly, I had someone else to back up my disclosure, as before it would have been my word against his, as I sensed they would not believe me. Thirdly, I may have been a little jealous that Waverley, who was considered the favourite daughter, was also receiving this 'special attention' as he had explained it was his way of showing 'love'. When I disclosed, my father listened and asked Waverley to accompany him upstairs to demonstrate what he had done.

My father wanted to be sure of this and later that day he had a long whispered conversation with him. From that moment on, he was no longer allowed to babysit for me but I did not understand why they took me out with them, but still left Waverley at home with him.

In hospital I had time away from this situation, but wondered if he had continued this behaviour with Waverley as she enjoyed being the favoured child.

I assumed this type of behaviour occurred in all families and I occasionally instigated 'sexual play' with childhood friends assuming they were accustomed to it. One summer afternoon Waverley and I were in the garage of a neighbourhood boy who was near my age and I hugged and kissed him. Waverley left the garage first and I returned home to find her in the garden talking to my mother as she sat upon the doorstep. Waverley told my mother about the activity in the garage and as I slowly approached them, my mother narrowed her eyes and called me a 'dirty little girl' in a cruel tone of voice. I stared accusingly at the family member who crouched behind her as he was the one who taught me this behaviour. He glared at me but said nothing.

At infant school, my parents told my teachers to keep me out of morning assemblies so that I did not join in with hymns and prayers at the start of each day. My parents had taught me that anyone outside our religion prayed to the Devil and only our religion worshipped the 'true' God. Kevin visited my school each morning and we sat alone in the classroom reading the bible. Each day he told me to read John chapter eight verse forty-four : "*You are from your father the Devil and you wish to do the desires of your father. That one was a murderer when he began and he did not stand fast in the truth, because truth is not in him. When he speaks the lie, he speaks according to his own disposition, because he is a liar and the father of the* *lie".*It seemed he was trying to convince me that I was a liar. My mother had told our relatives they were having problems with me lying. On reflection I realise that these rumours were spread to protect the family member fearing that I may reveal the abuse to others.

After disclosure to my parents, the family member bullied me mentally and physically. Waverley enjoyed being the 'favoured child' and sided with him. On occasions she also participated in his bullying. He enjoyed the *Doctor Who* television series and we were allowed to watch these episodes before going to bed. While Waverley and I were in bed, he would scare us by playing 'tricks' and I recall one occasion when he tied cotton thread around the light switch so it appeared to turn the light off after he left the room. He drew illustrations of horrific faces, creating paper masks to scare us and after viewing the *Dr Who* episodes, he succeeded. I had frequent nightmares about monsters in our bedroom and there were many dreams where I leapt down all thirteen stairs in slow motion to escape from them.

At six years of age, a few months after my last hospital admission, I developed what is known as an eye 'squint', which can be a complication from measles. Waverley and I had recently recovered from this illness. My parents arranged for me to have eye surgery at a local eye hospital, and I recall feeling quite nervous about it. My abuser enjoyed relating horrific stories of how the doctors would remove my eye during the operation.

The day arrived when my parents left me at the hospital and I sat upon a bed in the ward watching other children listening to a story read by one of the nurses. The nurse eventually approached me explaining she had read a story about fairies and asked if I believed in them. I gazed at the floor and slowly shook my head, wishing that I could believe in them although our religion forbade it. My mother's behaviour was contradictory, as she told us fairy stories. One that remained in my memory was about a white daisy that wished it had pink-tipped petals like the others. The other daisies did not consider it as pretty as them and excluded it from their friendship circle. One day, a fairy visited the daisy and gave it a magic pill to hold within its petals overnight while all the flowers slept. The following morning, the daisy was delighted to find she had pink tipped petals and was then accepted by the others, living happily ever after. My mother drew an illustration of this story for me to keep. I loved hearing this as a child; but on reflection, the moral is – when a person is different they will be disliked and excluded by others. However if a person makes the effort to be like others in a group they will be accepted and happy. My mother purchased coloured crepe paper to construct fairy wings and skirts for Waverley and I to wear while playing in the garden.

When the day arrived for my eye surgery I nervously laid upon a trolley as they wheeled me to the elevator by a comical man, who tickled my feet and joked with me. In the elevator, the nurse administered an anaesthetic to the back of my hand and I remembered no more until I awoke with extreme pain in my head covered with bags of ice. It was difficult to sleep, however the pain had gone by the next day and I was introduced to other children in the ward with various eye problems. An older girl 'mothered' us and praised me for eating my dinner, stating she was proud of me. I noticed that one of her eyes was permanently closed and a nurse inserted ointment into it every few hours. The white of my eye was completely bloodshot and my parents commented on this when they visited. After three days in hospital, I returned home. My parents were instructed to insert medicated ointment into my eye three times a day. I also had regular eye exercises where my father instructed me to follow his finger in all directions while keeping my head as still as possible. They took me to the local opticians who prescribed spectacles for me and as they could not afford to purchase a stylish pair, I wore free National Health spectacles that resembled those worn by the movie character *Harry Potter*. His character has now made them a stylish fashionable accessory, but during my childhood, they were considered ugly!

I was teased by other children at school for being different because I was excluded from morning assemblies to avoid their worship. I had also acquired spectacles and they added another reason for ridicule. Some children referred to me as 'four eyes' and when boys began the popular game of 'kiss chase', they chased the pretty girls with long hair and ribbons, but avoided those with short hair and spectacles! At the end of each school day, we placed our chairs upon the tables before leaving the classroom to help the cleaners. We were told to recite a prayer before leaving and on one occasion a 'substitute' teacher asked me why I did not pray with the other children. I replied that I was not allowed to, and she insisted that I prayed. I felt embarrassed about this, so I placed my hands in the prayer position and moved my mouth to give the impression I was doing as she instructed. They sang the words of the prayer: "*Hands together softly so, little eyes shut tight, Father just before we go, hear our prayer tonight. We are all God's children here, this is what we pray, guide us when the dark is near, and through every day. Amen*". Upset about this, I informed my parents who immediately visited the school and explained to the teacher why I had refused.

A few days before Mothers Day, our teacher guided us through the process of creating a flower from coloured tissue paper for our mothers. She advised us to take them home and hide them until Sunday. I enjoyed creating the flower and happily skipped home with it. I hid it in my room and happily told my mother I had a surprise for her on Sunday. She guessed I had made something for Mother's Day and explained that we did not celebrate it, as only Jehovah God should be honoured. I asked her if I should throw the flower away and she replied that it would be better for me to give the flower to her straight away rather than wait until Sunday.

Memories of attending religious meetings as a small child are vague, but I do recall that Waverley and I were often taken out of the main hall for a sharp smack on our legs for fidgeting or misbehaving. On one occasion, my father walked out of the hall carrying Waverley and in distress I called out that he was taking her out to spank her. She had actually asked to visit the lavatory and my father blushed with embarrassment and the congregation members laughed. Accompanying my parents on the preaching work became more of a problem after our neighbour's small terrier dog bit me when I reached out to stroke her. I then feared all dogs and when one appeared at a householder's door, I would literally climb my father's leg in an attempt to avoid it while he tried to continue preaching to them. This continued for a few years until, as an older child, I participated in the preaching work alone and although still wary of dogs, I no longer feared them. I was an extremely observant child and while my parents preached to various householders, I would study them closely. I observed their clothes and grooming. If their feet were bare I would study the shape of their feet, toes, nails and the way they stood. If they were cooking their Sunday dinner, I would take in the aroma and try to work out the type of meal they were having. When children stood at the door with their parents, we would often stare at one another. Each home we visited had a unique aroma and energy about it and I sensed that some of them were welcoming, while others were not.

My mother was an extremely attractive woman with a wild and free spirit. As a small child, she had fantasies about being a movie star as she loved Hollywood musicals. My father was flattered that she chose him as her husband and in the early days of their relationship, he was extremely jealous, reacting violently toward any man who even glanced her way. He was what one would call conservative, as he dressed in smart suits, shirts and ties most of the time. My father wore denim overalls when working in a lead manufacturing company but would bathe immediately on his return home. My mother's clothes were highly creative and trendy, I remember her brown leather dress that she trimmed with coloured beads. Her waist-length dark brown hair and Romani appearance complemented the way she dressed. I watched her as she sat on the doorstep painting a pair of high-heel shoes with many colours to give them a psychedelic appearance. My mother yearned to own a dress covered in sequins like actresses in her favourite movies. She purchased a black petticoat and strands of black sequins and during the evenings we spent at home, she had sewn sequins onto the garment one by one while she watched television programs. A few years passed until the petticoat was completely covered. Silver sequins were added around the chest area and along the shoulder straps. My mother wore it while visiting the supermarket as she enjoyed people looking at her as though she were a famous movie star.

On many occasions the elders in our congregation had intense discussions with my father about my mother's attire, instructing him to tone down her appearance, however she refused to cooperate. My mother loved my father, telling others in the congregation that she wanted to 'stand on the rooftops and shout it out'. My mother embroidered his name in gold lurex thread surrounded by a heart on a tight pink sweater and wore it to religious meetings. This caused further complaints.

One afternoon when Waverley and I were very young, my mother put on black tights and a red leotard to walk through the high street of our home town. A man stopped her in the street and asked if she was aware she was causing a sensation. She conversed with him for a while and I stood beside Waverley's pushchair. On our return home, my mother warned me never to tell my father about this or I would be punished. I said nothing. The controversy over my mother's attire was an ongoing battle for years, but her wild and free spirit fascinated me. It was in complete contrast to other mothers I met within our community. Unfortunately, she had mental health problems and told my father that if he travelled more than two miles away from her, she would panic. When he did venture out alone, he did not travel far, however he once revealed there were occasions when he rode his bicycle ten miles into town without her knowledge. My mother had fluctuating moods, as she could be loving and affectionate towards us, but her mood could suddenly change into anger, hysteria, aggression and violence.

I do not know the full history of her upbringing, but she revealed that her own mother had violent rages. On reflection, it seemed my grandmother projected her own guilt (from past occurrences I chose not to reveal) and mental health problems onto my mother, placing her in the scapegoat role. Some of her childhood memories haunted and tormented her throughout her life. She regularly ingested tranquillisers prescribed by general practitioners to help her cope with agoraphobia and refused to venture into town unless my father accompanied her. Women of past generations would refer to emotional and mental health issues as 'their nerves' however nowadays there are medical terms for these problems.

I recall a time when my mother unexpectedly packed a suitcase and left home. This was out of character for someone who would not travel far without my father. He took Waverley and I to Brenda's home while he searched for her. Brenda's family was middle-class, her daughter Tracey was a year older than I, and her son Clark three years older. My mother admired Brenda's beauty and appearance, capturing many photographic images of her that she kept in a photograph album. During our stay, Brenda washed Waverley and I, then placed us in her double bed to sleep. My father returned in the early hours of the morning and looked extremely worried as he had not located her. On our return home, we found my mother in the lounge talking to Brother Strong, one of the elders. My parents were fond of him and often consulted him when they had problems. Brother Strong sat opposite her with an open bible on his lap and I watched my father drop to his knees in front of her, placed his head in her lap and sobbed loudly. I found this bewildering as our father rarely cried, but we were reassured by Brother Strong that all would be well and he suggested we both went to our bedroom. My parents were very affectionate with one another the following day and I heard my father promise it would never happen again. I asked my mother the reason she left him years later and she would not explain.

My mother also experienced a horrendous side effect from tranquillisers prescribed by the general practitioner that apparently caused hallucinations of gigantic spiders in the bedroom. My father often caught spiders for her when they appeared, but after her description of them, even he was reluctant to find them! It was not until my mother saw one of them separate into two halves and disappear into the wall, that she realised it was the medication. A female member of our congregation recommended a homoeopath and herbal medicines. She advised my mother not to trust the general practitioner again. From that moment on, there were frequent family visits to Great Ormond Street Hospital in London with hours of travelling and sitting in a waiting room while my mother attended her appointments. Homoeopathic medicines were expensive but my father would try anything that would help her.

Our first visit to Cornwall was in the late 1960s. My father decided to visit on impulse, with no planned accommodation. On reflection, I wonder whether the visit was connected to my mother's new treatments as the woman who recommended homoeopathy also spoke of Cornwall as a beautiful healing place. It was exciting travelling three hundred miles overnight in my father's three-wheel car. The vehicle did extremely well to complete the journey, but while we were there it had difficulty tackling the steep hills.

After we arrived my father spoke to residents and found accommodation in a guest house owned by a Spanish lady named Rosella. Our apartment overlooked Fowey harbour and after settling in, Kevin volunteered to search for the local Kingdom Hall as my family always attended religious meetings no matter where they were. Members of the Cornish congregation were warm, friendly and welcoming which delighted my parents. Elsie and Enid, who were twin sisters, approached us after the meeting and invited us back to their cottage for tea and lemon buns. Elsie worked as a cook in Fowey castle, and baked wonderful buns and cakes. Fascinating ornaments filled their home and they had an interesting story about how they acquired each one. Elsie and Enid loved card games and we were invited to their home each year for fun evenings of partner whist and they taught us to play the popular Cornish game Euchre. My mother fell in love with Cornwall and maybe my father hoped these visits would help to heal her anxiety and mental health problems. Vacations to this wonderful place also provided me with an escape from family problems, as life seemed happier for us all while we were there.

At the age of seven, I received my first assignment for a six-minute talk as a new member of the Jehovah's Witness Ministry School. I admired brothers who gave long talks to the congregation while standing behind a rostrum. I expressed a desire to stand there and give a talk myself in the future but my mother told me that women were not allowed to address the congregation as it is not their place to do so. They could only converse with one person on the platform who played the role of a householder on a given subject. This disappointed me. I also noticed when an elder or ministerial servant was not present to offer a prayer within a group of Witnesses, the woman had to cover her head with either a scarf or a hat when praying as a sign of submission and being in a lower position than a male. I was a little nervous about my first talk, but my mother assisted in writing a script for me and bookmarked scriptures in their translation of the Bible and we rehearsed several times. When the time arrived, six short minutes seemed much longer, but on completion, all congregation members applauded as they did for anyone on their first assignment. An elder then provides feedback and counsel where one is praised for good points and offered alternative suggestions on aspects where improvement is needed.

Being a Jehovah's Witness since birth, meant that I never celebrated a birthday. However on my eighth birthday Aunt Mary, my mother's youngest sister paid us an unexpected visit. She had no children of her own because of a debilitating arthritic problem and she worried she would not be physically capable of caring for them. I loved her dearly as we were alike in many ways and had a close connection. Aunt Mary entered our home carrying a large white cardboard box saying she had a surprise for me. She opened the box to reveal a stunning pink and white birthday cake fresh from the local baker's shop. I still recall the wonderful smell of it to this day. My parents sat in silent disapproval at the dining table, but I could not contain my excitement as she placed eight pink candles onto the cake and proceeded to light them. Mary sang *Happy Birthday* and I blew out the candles. She then cut a slice of cake for me which tasted wonderful. She offered some to my parents and they refused with a serious expression. My neighbourhood playmate Kitty was in her garden and I invited her in to see the cake and share some. When our plates were empty, my parents instructed Waverley, Kitty and I to play in the garden. I knew they were about to have a serious conversation with Mary and I felt sad for her, as it had been given with love. After their discussion this was never repeated. I do, however, appreciate that day and will always be grateful to her, cherishing the memory of my first birthday cake.

Jean, one of our neighbour's children on the other side of the garden from Kitty, had a large garden birthday party on a warm summer's day. She was a year older than I and all the neighbourhood children were invited except for Waverley and I. Her parents knew we did not celebrate birthdays. Waverley and I stood by the fence and watched the children playing games in Jean's garden. I sensed Mr and Mrs Mc Cellan felt sorry for us as they quietly conversed when they saw us. They were in a dilemma whether to invite us as they knew it may upset our parents but eventually they did. Our mother was preoccupied with something in the house, so we slipped quietly into the garden and joined the games. She eventually realised we had disappeared and stood in our garden glaring at us through the fence. We were in no hurry to return as we knew that she would scold us, so she had to wait for our return when the party was over. Waverley and I received a stern lecture from my father on his return from work and of course, I received the blame for not setting an example as the older child, but it was worth it as we had a wonderful time.

My family regularly attended the Tuesday evening religious book study at Vivien's spacious Victorian house. Jacob, one of her lodgers, began to attend this and meetings at the Kingdom Hall. He was a quiet, gentle man who wore brown suits and his hair was shaved close to the scalp. He reminded me of a monk in some ways. The congregation's members gossiped about him wearing sheer ladies tights beneath his trousers as they were visible around his ankles and between the straps of his brown leather sandals. Jacob seemed approachable and easy to converse with, so I asked him why he wore them. He explained to me that as a little boy his father was cruel to him and his mother was a kind and loving person. Wearing ladies tights reminded him of his mother and had comforted him since she passed away. At the age of eight, I understood his explanation, however adults within our congregation only whispered about it. They would not want to understand as it was against their rules. The elders eventually discussed the matter with Jacob and he refused to stop wearing them and eventually stopped his bible studies and attendance at meetings.

Waverley would do whatever was required to be liked by most people and at a young age she quickly learnt how to be favoured. She sided with my abuser after my disclosure, and from their actions it became apparent I was given the blame for speaking out. My parents placed great emphasis on the appearance of 'a happy family' to make us look good so that it reflected well on our religion. Waverley knew this and copied my father by always wearing a smile in public. With her large blue eyes, long eyelashes, cheeky smile and dimples, most people immediately warmed to her. I received the blame for many things and was placed in the role of the family 'scapegoat', therefore I became an unhappy child. I refused to wear a fake smile, so people did not immediately like me. I refused to give an outward appearance of being happy when it was not true. It was understandable why at times I intensely disliked Waverley who was viewed as the favoured child and we had many fights and disagreements during our childhood. She was extremely competitive and I learnt there was little point in competing, as no matter how I tried they would view me as the 'bad' child.

Waverley and I once played a game of 'doctors and patients', where I gave her two pills that I found inside a rent payment book. I grew concerned about this and I told my parents who could not identify the pills. They took her to the hospital for a stomach pump. Years later when Waverley related this story to her second husband in my presence, she stated that I intentionally tried to kill her. If that were the case, I would not have alerted anyone.

Waverley developed a limp at the age of six and as she was a 'comical' child, my parents thought she may be limping in jest. It gradually became more pronounced and after consulting a doctor who sent her for x-rays at the hospital, we discovered she had a soft hip bone. Waverley was admitted to hospital where she underwent surgery and her leg was placed in traction for six weeks. She returned home with iron callipers to keep her foot off the ground and any weight off her leg so the hip bone could heal. Waverley was a 'fighter' and did not let callipers deter her from learning to run, playing football and continuing door to door preaching where she sold many publications. Waverley was what some would describe as a 'tomboy'. Girls often act this way to become a 'son' for their father's approval. Some children at our school were afraid of her callipers as she threatened to kick them if they upset her. A female class member of mine who was a well-known bully had caused many problems for me and it amazed me to see her cry and cower in the headmasters office when Waverley threatened to wait for her outside the school gates. I was grateful to her for this as I had no further problems with this girl from then on. One of the boys in Waverley's class pushed her in the playground and she fell, breaking a bone in her arm. I returned home from school and saw her sleeping on the couch with an arm in plaster after returning from hospital. I had been so worried about her and cried because she had been through so much. No matter what had occurred in Waverley's life, she continued to smile and appear a happy child. Unfortunately, the more my parents favoured her, the more angry and miserable I became in reaction to it.

The special treatment I received from Aunt Mary for my birthday led to another impulsive action at school. Each morning during the school assemblies, the teacher asked if there were any birthdays. I began attending these when the morning worship was less frequent. One or two pupils stood at the front of the hall to hear a chorus of Happy Birthday sung by all the children. No one stood up that day. I waited a while and out of curiosity, impulsively rose to my feet and walked to the front of the hall. The children sang to me, but instead of enjoying the experience, I felt a little guilty. My form teacher checked her register for my details when we returned to class and discovered that it was not my birthday and laughed. Tracey was present in the hall and she approached me during the morning break to let me know she would tell my parents about this. Some of the children overheard her and told her to leave me alone as I had done nothing wrong. At our next religious meeting she immediately approached my parents and when they questioned me, I explained that I wanted to see what it felt like to have the whole school sing to me. They were annoyed, but I do not recall receiving punishment for it.

One Easter holiday, Aunt Mary brought Waverley and I two chocolate rabbits housed in long pink boxes. The chocolate moulds were wrapped in shiny pink foil displaying the figure of a rabbit. Waverley and I were excited to receive these and my parents thanked her and put them aside, explaining we would have them after dinner. When Mary left, my parents spent the next few days contemplating whether or not we should have them, as rabbits were a Pagan symbol that disturbed their consciences. We waited patiently for their decision and eventually they decided we could not have them after all. Waverley and I watched as my mother melted them in hot water and poured the chocolate liquid into the kitchen sink. This angered and upset me so much that I visited the local shop with some of my pocket money and purchased a hollow milk chocolate Easter egg. I aggressively consumed it before returning home. We were instructed not to tell Mary they had melted the rabbits as it would have upset her. My mother however adored hot cross buns. She loved the spices in them and could not resist buying some when they arrived just before Easter. When she took them home she would but the crosses off the top before consuming them. She said the belief that Jesus died upon the cross was a false teaching. I wondered why she could eat the hot cross buns but we were not allowed a chocolate rabbit as we could have removed the wrapping. Each Christmas, holiday Mary purchased a gift for Waverley and I. My parents allowed her to bring them to us on Boxing Day and we were excited about this. She would ask us what we would like and made an effort to either get what we wanted or something similar. It was difficult to understand why my parents allowed us to have some things and not others.

My parents were married on the twenty-first of December which is also known as Winter Solstice and close to the Christmas holidays. My father often joked about it being the shortest day of the year and the longest wedding night! They visited a restaurant each year for a celebratory meal, surrounded by diners having pre-Christmas celebrations. I watched my mother preparing to go out for the evening. I was in awe of her physical beauty, how she applied her cosmetics and looked beautiful and stylish in long evening dresses. Jehovah's Witnesses allowed wedding and anniversary celebrations, so we would purchase gifts for my parents that day and in return, my mother gave her immediate family gifts, explaining that it was their anniversary gift to them. Kevin's future wife Linsey disapproved of this, commenting that my mother had used their anniversary for a Christmas celebration.

We often visited cousin Carmel at this time of year and she had a tall, beautifully decorated Christmas tree that stood next to her couch. I sat beside it while the adults conversed and gazed deep into the tree, through the tinsel, baubles, and fairy lights, sensing another world within it. I thought how wonderful it would be to live within a world that was like a Christmas tree.

When my father transported us to religious meetings, Waverley and I counted Christmas trees in the windows of houses and shops on either side of the road, while looking through the back windows of my father's car. We counted more than one hundred and fifty trees on our ten mile journey and they made the homes look so warm, inviting, and magical. My mother warned us that the Devil would make everything sparkly, glamorous and exciting to lure us into his world.

The worst time in my opinion was on Christmas morning, as we had to go out on the preaching work. Most of the residents would be at home with their families, children enjoying gifts, mothers preparing Christmas dinner and fathers relaxing if they were not visiting the local Inn. With all this activity going on, the last thing they wanted were religious people calling at their homes. I recall one man shouting angrily at my father while pointing at Waverley and I, stating we should be at home opening gifts and enjoying ourselves. It was more embarrassing if we happened to call at the homes of children we knew from school! We had no birthday or Christmas celebrations and some people assumed we did not receive gifts.

I remember a time when my mother unexpectedly purchased two new dolls and small perambulators from her mail order catalogue. Waverley and I were delighted when the parcels arrived and when they were unwrapped and assembled, my mother instructed us to walk up and down the garden with them. One of our neighbours happened to be out in her garden, and my mother explained to her that we received gifts at any time of year and did not have to wait for Christmas or birthdays. Although I enjoyed the surprise, it seemed the gifts had been purchased with an agenda.

My family attended a religious convention in London where we stayed in a local guest house. It was owned by a lovely woman who cared for us in the way a grandmother would. I was seven at this time and our parents told us to be on our best behaviour (as the owner was aware we were Jehovah's Witnesses) so that it would reflect favourably on the religion and could encourage her to join.

We also attended a religious convention in Birmingham as it was the first one to release new publications. My father wanted to be the first in his congregation to purchase them; two books were for children, a pink one entitled 'Listening to the Great Teacher' and a gold one entitled 'My Book of Bible Stories'. On arrival at the campsite, Waverley and I were quite ill with a severe cough known as croup which became worse at night. One of the sisters invited us into her camper van and gave us a cough mixture to ease it. There were other families at the campsite and in the evenings they sat around a campfire singing songs and conversing, but Waverley and I were in bed by then and missed out on this. I do not recall much about the convention, but after purchasing the new books, we all posed for a family photograph holding the newly released literature. I still have this image in my possession today.

Kevin loved Reggae music and often played his vinyl records at home. He was frequently scolded for the volume of his music, the risqué lyrics and his 'suggestive dancing'. He loved the 'skinhead' craze and their attire of jeans, braces and 'Bovver Boots'. These did not fit the conservative image of a Jehovah's Witness! The only time he was allowed to play his music at high volume was when Waverley and I misbehaved at the Kingdom Hall. We would be spanked with my father's slipper on our return home, so Kevin gleefully turned his record player up to full volume so the music drowned out our cries late at night.

He had many teenage friends in our congregation and they sat together at the back row of our Kingdom Hall. I recall sitting in the back seat of a car with a few of his friends on one occasion, listening to their conversation. One of the young men spoke about a young sister he liked for her personality and not her looks. Another brother commented that a sister he knew had 'a nice pair of personalities'! He then related that one sister gave him a hug and 'pressed her necessity up against him'. Although I was a small child, I knew only too well what they meant. I looked at a teenage sister with a shocked expression and she seemed uncomfortable about their conversation.

At district conventions, Kevin collected contact details from attractive young sisters and my parents also hosted occasional teenage parties for him. My mother appeared and acted younger than her age, wore glamorous attire and joined them at the parties as she loved to dance. Waverley and I were in our bed and stayed awake listening to the music and laughter, wishing we were with them. One of the young sisters visited the upstairs lavatory and we called her to our room, asking for stories. She obliged, even though she would rather have returned to the party.

A few of Kevin's girlfriends visited our home, but their courtships were strictly chaperoned. One of his girlfriends, a quiet young woman, had short, curly blonde hair and when she smiled, she would not show her teeth. She lived a long way from us in Scarborough and Kevin wanted to visit her for a weekend. He had a disagreement with my father who would not allow him to go, but Kevin stated that he was eighteen years of age and they could not stop him. I do not however remember him going there.

We visited Cornwall for the third time when I was eight years of age. We had grown to love the brothers and sisters in the local congregation as they were warm, friendly and different compared to our own. A new family had moved to Cornwall from Manchester and joined the congregation. Their son Gavin was of similar age to Waverley and his sister Lynette a year older than me. Their parents befriended mine and visited the campsite where we stayed. The four of us played together in the fields while our parents conversed in the caravan. I recall Gavin sitting in his father's car and said he would not let me join him unless I told him I loved him. He was a comical little boy with ginger hair, freckles and crooked teeth. His father had a gentle soothing voice that my mother loved and she got on well with both of them. The Jehovah's Witness elders in Cornwall did not seem as strict as in Kent and the children there seemed happier; it was a pleasure to associate with them.

CHAPTER 3

OLDER CHILDHOOD

As I mentioned previously, my brother Kevin met many teenage girls at religious conventions. A few of his girlfriends visited us and each of them were unique in appearance. One was very attractive with long black hair, thick eyeliner and in some aspects resembled our mother. Waverley and I liked her and she had been a friend of Kevin's for some time but would have liked a relationship with him. He was not interested as he disliked her facial cosmetics and said she was not his 'type'. I found it interesting that he did not take to a woman who resembled his mother as this conveys an important message.

Kevin eventually met Linsey from a congregation about twenty miles away. She was also a cousin of my friend Josie as their fathers were siblings.

My parents were close friends of Josie's family and she was the eldest of twelve children. Her father was disabled with a condition known as muscular dystrophy and often needed a wheelchair. Josie's mother loved having children so after giving birth to Josie, she had further children every two years! Josie's family lived in various rental properties as it was difficult to find one large enough for them all, but eventually they found a beautiful Victorian town house with large rooms that was ideal for them. Josie's father's occupation was clockmaker and antique dealer. Their home was full of fascinating furniture and unusual chiming clocks. The large basement kitchen had a huge oak dining table and Josie's mother was a fabulous cook. Waverley and I stayed overnight on many occasions and there were four girls in each double bed, while the boys slept in a large bedroom across the hall. I cannot remember exactly where Waverley and I slept but we managed to fit in somewhere! All twelve children were named after bible characters. All the girls had 'old fashioned' faces, long wavy brown hair and wore vintage style clothes. Their mother had shorter dark brown hair and the only cosmetics she wore were powder rouge and lip colour. It was like travelling back in time whenever we visited their home. The older girls assisted in caring for younger siblings and when the boys were older, they helped to lift their father in and out of his wheelchair. They were hard workers and well behaved, following the religious rules they were taught.

Josie's cousin Linsey had seven siblings and her mother was not a Jehovah's Witness. Their father insisted they attended religious meetings despite her disapproval. I heard from Linsey that she used to watch Kevin from a distance as he walked around the convention hall, little black address book in hand, collecting telephone numbers from young sisters. She told her friend that she would never consider having a relationship with someone like him!

Linsey seemed a lovely, quiet, homely girl at sixteen years of age who was completely different to my mother as she wore no facial cosmetics and dressed modestly. Linsey had an eye disease which meant her sight would gradually deteriorate and there was nothing medically that could help her. Although Kevin and Linsey were chaperoned, I saw a huge amount of kissing and petting between them. I felt uncomfortable when I had to sit in the back seat of my father's car with them and he would adjust his rear-view mirror to keep an eye on them, telling them to tone down their affections.

Linsey told me that my mother became jealous of their relationship and she found her intense affection towards Kevin disturbing and inappropriate. I remember those days. On one occasion when I was about to enter our bathroom, I caught Kevin and Linsey heavy petting. My parents asked them to babysit for Waverley and I (as they left me at home when Linsey was present). We were allowed to stay up late as they thought it would prevent them both from getting carried away in their affections. This did not make sense as our presence did not stop them! Kevin would fetch a blanket from his bed to make Waverley and I comfortable and sleepy on the couch instructing us to watch television. He and Linsey would go into the kitchen where they engaged in kissing and petting. On a few occasions they were on the couch under a blanket and Kevin instructed us to face the television and not to turn around. I did not reveal his behaviour with Linsey to my parents, as I had learnt how hot tempered, violent and nasty he could be. Linsey occasionally stayed overnight and slept in our double bed with us. I enjoyed her being there as Kevin treated me better when she was around.

One afternoon while Kevin was out working, Waverley and I found his love-letters in a cardboard shoe box under his bed. We read them and found quotes from the Song of Solomon in the Bible and giggled about it. On reflection I am surprised I took the risk as when he vented his rage, he would drool uncontrollably and his saliva would spray everywhere as he shouted at us. This would be frightening for young children to experience. On one occasion Kevin hit me so hard I had finger welts on the side of my body for some time.

My father would wait for him to return when he went out in the evenings, and he often returned later than his curfew, which caused disagreements between them. It was not long before Kevin and Linsey got engaged to be married and I was relieved that he would soon move out of the family home. He was annoyed when he discovered we found his letters were read by us and then he found that we had used his 'sleeping' hat for our snowman. He wore it in bed to keep his hair in place. On reflection and after the research I have done, his behaviour had possible traits of autism that seems to be present in my other male siblings. There are however different levels of this and I will explain this further as my story continues.

From the age of seven when my front adult teeth emerged, they began to protrude which may have been caused by using a pacifier as a toddler. My siblings and children at school teased me about them and closing my mouth could be problematic at times. My father arranged an appointment for me to visit an Orthodontist at the local hospital to correct this problem. We discovered after examination I would need four teeth removed and a wire retainer fitted to push my front teeth back to straighten them. I was nervous about the extractions as I had a bad experience with chloroform at the age of six. My father insisted I had this done and although nervous, I agreed to go ahead as I no longer wanted the name of 'Bugs Bunny'! I had already refused to wear my spectacles after being called 'four eyes', however cruel children will often find a reason to tease others. The Orthodontist and his assistant commented that they would make me 'beautiful' and I reacted with a disbelieving expression! I cooperated with the local dentist when the time came to remove four teeth and breathed in the awful chloroform as quickly as possible. My father was impressed by this as he was expecting a struggle. After recovery time, I returned to the hospital where the Orthodontist made impressions of my teeth. It was difficult not to choke with a mouth full of a substance that felt like clay and tasted of mint! On the next appointment my retainer was fitted. It was a small plastic plate with thick wire attached and I wore this for three years. I visited the Orthodontist regularly to have the wires tightened and although it was a painful process, I followed their instructions and was pleased with the end result.

Kevin purchased a sapphire and diamond ring for Linsey and they planned a celebratory dinner with my parents at a restaurant. When Linsey arrived, she looked older than sixteen with her hair up and discreetly applied facial cosmetics. We were surprised at how beautiful she was, as she usually seemed reluctant to dress in this way. I did not realise they originally planned to marry her on the fourth of December 1971, but the date was brought forward by two months. According to Linsey's sister, Kevin told my parents he was in danger of committing fornication if he had to wait any longer. The wedding arrangements were very exciting for us as it would be the first time Waverley and I were bridesmaids. Linsey had four sisters, so there would be six bridesmaids in total. The colour was yellow and white. Our dresses were created from wool and each of us had a yellow and white poncho, white tights and shoes. My mother purchased white hair bands and trimmed them with a frill made from white netting and yellow flowers. Linsey knew a lady who was talented at knitting and crochet. I was a little disappointed by this as I had visualised a long satin dress like the ones I had seen my friends wear when they were bridesmaids. Waverley still wore callipers, so my parents arranged for her white shoes to be fitted to a new set.

Just before the wedding, my parents attended a hospital appointment with Waverley and the consultant told them her hip bone had healed and she no longer had to wear them. We were delighted at this news and on our return home, Waverley walked slowly to Kevin without her callipers and as he picked her up to hug her, she wrapped her legs around his waist. It took her a while to learn to walk correctly without them and she had regular physiotherapy appointments. My parents purchased another pair of shoes for her to wear on the wedding day.

The day of the wedding arrived. Kevin was twenty years of age and Linsey only seventeen. A young black brother who was a close friend of Kevin's, had stayed overnight at our home as he had the role of 'best man'.

When we arrived at the Kingdom Hall, the bridesmaids walked up the centre aisle behind Linsey and her father to the tune of a Kingdom song 'Love's Excelling Way' which is often used for weddings and sang at meetings. The ceremonies are kept simple, a talk is given about love and marriage and Kevin and Linsey repeated their vows. When that is done, they always seize the opportunity to preach to any relatives who are non-believers. I sat in the front row enjoying the smell of my bouquet of yellow and white carnations.

After the ceremony we stood on the entrance steps of the Kingdom Hall and posed for a photographer. I stood proudly with the other bridesmaids and I heard a voice gently calling my name. I glanced in the direction of the voice and saw my aunt Mary smiling and she waved gently to me. I could tell she was proud of us all. Kevin and Linsey had stated they wanted no children at their wedding reception except for those of immediate family. We were disappointed, as it meant our childhood friends were unable to attend. Rosie had volunteered to play the piano to entertain the guests in our local Co-op Hall. I enjoyed the day, especially the thought that Kevin would no longer be living at home and I would be free of his bullying. I sensed Linsey was a good-hearted person and I was concerned how he would treat her after the 'honeymoon period' was over. Kevin, aware of my wariness of dogs, told me he would purchase a large St Bernard to stop me from visiting his home.

By the summer of 1972, my mother was due to give birth to our younger brother. We had a well-spaced family of almost three generations, as my two eldest brothers were born when my mother was eighteen and twenty years of age. Waverley and I were born when she was thirty and thirty-one and she had my two youngest brothers at forty and forty-one. There was a space of eighteen months between each pair of children. According to my mother, Kevin was a planned pregnancy before marriage to force their parents into allowing them to marry as they disapproved. Kevin arrived five months after their marriage and when anyone asked about his date of birth, my mother told them he was born a year later so as not to arouse suspicion.

When she began labour with my younger brother, I recall that her contractions began on the due date at five o' clock in the morning. After a few hours, the midwife visited to check on her. I remember that towards the end of my mother's pregnancy, her hands and feet were swollen, caused by pre-eclampsia. The midwife listened for the baby's heartbeat and contacted the doctor who arrived quickly. He also listened and then they contacted the hospital requesting an ambulance. They did not explain why to my mother, but advised her to go in. We later discovered they could not hear the baby's heart. Kevin and Linsey arrived to stay with Waverley and I. We cried as the ambulance took our mother away, as we were worried. Kevin also cried, but Linsey told him not to be silly and that all would be well. The next day my father returned home with the sad news our baby brother had died three days before his birth. My mother's womb had been trying to eject the foetus when she thought her baby was arching its back inside her. She endured hours of difficult labour to give birth to a deceased child and they did not show her the foetus after its birth as it had already begun to decompose. My mother told us they left her in the labour room where she heard other mothers giving birth to their babies that cried, when all she could remember was the silence of her own.

My mother was then placed in a ward with mothers and their new babies which was extremely distressing for her. I watched as my father and members of our congregation cleared our home of all baby clothes and items that were stored in readiness. He brought her home as soon as possible to get her out of the maternity ward as this made her situation worse. I will never forget the weeks that followed the birth while my mother grieved for her baby, particularly when her breasts began to lactate. The elders from our congregation continued to preach to her and promised that if she stayed faithful, she would see her child again in the 'new system'. This may have helped her in some ways but she soon had a nervous breakdown, because she was so desperate for her baby and afraid she may be tempted to abduct one. My mother was admitted to a psychiatric hospital for over a week while my father cared for us. When we visited her, she attempted to smile as she welcomed us with tear-stained, black eyes where her mascara had smudged. She eventually returned home, but it took a long time for her to recover from this traumatic experience. She mentioned electric shock treatment given to patients in order to rid them of traumatic memories they found too unbearable to live with. I was aware my grandmother had this and I believe my mother may have had it during her stay at the hospital. Throughout her life she often spoke of our little brother and how her arms ached for him, however she strongly believed that one day he would be returned to her on a paradise earth.

Kevin and Linsey's first daughter was born six months after my still-born brother. My father was so excited to see his first grandchild and as soon as Kevin told us she had arrived, he wanted to visit immediately. My mother did not want to go as she knew her grandchild would resemble the son she lost. My parents had a disagreement about this, but my father still insisted on visiting. He transported us to the home of Linsey's mother as that was where the birth took place. We all met Merea, my new niece, but my mother sat in the car. Kevin went out to her to persuade her to come in but without success. A few weeks passed by before she felt emotionally strong enough to meet her new granddaughter.

We would visit Carl at the residential hospital every other Sunday afternoon. Before arriving at the hospital, my parents visited the Candy Box shop to purchase bags of potato crisps and confectionery for Carl. When Waverley and I were older, we walked from the residential villa to the visiting hall while my parents transported Carl in the car. Many patients were visited by their family members in the hall who sat at tables with them. Waverley and I were wary of patients who wandered around alone as there was an unpredictable energy about them. My mother fed Carl with food and confectionery during our visits. We were amazed how he ate with such speed with little time to unwrap one piece of confectionery before he finished the previous one. After his feast, my mother tried to hug and interact with him. There were some visits where he let her and on others he would push her away. If Carl was in a good mood, we could all interact with him and it was wonderful to see him smile and laugh. Occasionally he said 'Mum' which delighted her, but then he pulled her head towards him and pressed his front teeth against her forehead. My mother reacted with "Ouch" and he was amused by this. His unhappy moods were distressing as he tried to cry but had difficulty letting out emotions. He often gazed upwards as though he saw something we could not. His eyes filled with tears as he pinched the bridge of his nose. I recall one particularly distressing visit when Carl was extremely upset and he ran into the male lavatory. He would not come out and we heard him screaming. My father tried to get him to come out, but eventually the male nurses arrived and took Carl back to his villa. My father cried as we journeyed home explaining how he tried to encourage Carl to come out and when he held one of his arms it felt like immovable iron. My father was an extremely strong man but he felt so helpless.

I also recall an emotional visit where my mother said she wished Carl was at home with her so that she could care for him, describing the soap and powder she would use so that he would smell nice. The realisation of us missing so much of his life made me quite emotional as it was an awful, unresolvable situation. My mother sang kingdom songs to him and my father prayed with him on each visit asking Jehovah to watch over him while they were apart.

A group of Jehovah's Witnesses from our congregation arranged to visit New York for a three week vacation to attend a five-day convention at the Yankee Stadium in the summer of 1973. My father was eager to join them, but my mother was afraid of travelling to another country, particularly by plane. They had a disagreement over it and my father insisted that he was going, therefore my mother had no choice but to accompany him. She told him she would need a strong mix of tranquillisers to help her through the ordeal, but this did not change his mind. They had not planned to take Waverley and I with them and asked Claire, my maternal grandmother, if we could stay with her. Claire enjoyed our visits, however having us there for three weeks would be a completely different matter. My parents also asked Kevin and Linsey, but they replied that children should accompany their parents on vacation.

James, a member of our congregation, had also planned to visit New York. My mother first heard about him when she worked with his first wife in a local paper mill. She was the 'ringleader' of a group of female workers and when my mother told them about her religion, she was ridiculed. The women apparently sang hymns and marched around the factory clashing dustbin lids together. James' wife told my mother that her husband knew his Bible 'inside out' and would 'tie them in knots' debating with them. Shortly after his wife passed away, my parents called at James' home and their religion interested him so he requested a bible study. In a short time he was recruited. James had an artificial leg, explaining that his real leg was 'shot off' during the war. He was a lovely man, one wouldn't call him handsome. He had an old fashioned 'comb-over' where one piece of long hair is combed over the top of the head in an attempt to hide the baldness. He did however have vivid blue eyes that were sincere and striking. When he spoke to ladies and little girls he called them 'blossom'. He became a close friend of our family helping out whenever he could. One afternoon he took Waverley and I to a beach for the day and we felt comfortable with him as he was a real gentleman. I approached James about the trip to New York, explaining that my father had agreed to take Waverley and I, but I was concerned he may have difficulty with finances. James spoke to my father and offered help as I hoped he would.

We were so excited about this trip, but there was a lot of organisation with passports and flight arrangements. My mother packed our clothes for a three-week vacation. We all travelled in a coach to the airport with other members of our congregation. We formed a group with James, an elder by the name of Aran, his wife Ria, and their daughter Yvette who was a little younger than Waverley. Aran and Ria were strict parents and Yvette was the 'perfect little bible student' who seemed to do no wrong. She was often invited to stand on the Kingdom Hall platform at our religious meetings and talk about her spiritual progress as an example for all children. She regularly pioneered since childhood and her behaviour was impeccable. Yvette was often mentioned by our parents as they wanted us to follow her example, but we would sigh and roll our eyes heavenwards when her name was mentioned. I had constant difficulty connecting with the 'truth' (as they called it) in the way that Yvette had. It was hard for me to cultivate a friendship with a God that I could not see as I did not believe he had helped to protect me from some of life's harrowing experiences. Spending three weeks in New York with Yvette and her family turned out to be an interesting experience!

Groups of Jehovah's Witnesses from other congregations also gathered at the airport. We wore identity badges displaying the words 'Jehovah's

Witnesses', the location of our congregations and our personal names. These were similar to badges we wore for district and international conventions enabling us to recognize brothers and sisters that we did not know personally.

We were guided along a small corridor to board the Pan Am Jumbo Jet, a huge plane with three sections of seats. I sat with my mother in the centre and grew nervous about the plane taking off. I assumed it would be like the episodes I had seen in the Thunderbirds series. My mother reassured me and this helped to distract from her own anxiety. She told us to suck boiled candy as it helped to release the pressure in the ears when the plane took off and landed. I admired the air hostesses in their light blue uniforms and hats as they were attractive ladies who worked hard on these flights. I wore a light blue dress that had an all-in-one 1970s style of a skirt, waistcoat and blouse. The sleeves and collar of the blouse were white with huge pink spots on them.

When we had been in flight for a while, one of the hostesses announced that we could remove our seat belts and walk around the plane. There was a cocktail bar on the upper floor, so Waverley and I were excited to explore it. We walked to the centre of the plane and climbed a small spiral staircase that led to the cocktail bar. An air hostess served the passengers with drinks and asked me if I would like a 'seven-up on the rocks'. I had not heard of this, so she explained it was lemonade poured over ice cubes. I consumed many of them when this drink became available in the United Kingdom. I carried my drink to a window seat and gazed with fascination at the 'carpet of clouds' below us. My father arrived to check Waverley and I were safe, and after getting a drink, he joined me. We looked out of the window discussing the clouds below the aeroplane. Waverley charmed one of the air hostesses with her blue eyes, cheeky smile and talkative nature. They discovered they shared the same Christian names and the air hostess invited Waverley to the cockpit to meet the pilots. My father wanted to join them, however the hostess explained they had strict security rules. He was jealous when she entered the cockpit as he would have loved to experience this.

The plane journey was seven and a half hours long as we travelled overnight on the twenty-fifth of June 1973. We arrived in New York in the early hours of the morning. We emerged from the plane and into a coach feeling tired and exhausted. When we arrived at the airport, there was a large sea of smiling faces belonging to American Jehovah's Witnesses who had gathered to welcome us. They were so organised, separating us into groups and guiding us to coaches that transported us to various Kingdom Halls. I noticed how large and elaborate their meeting halls were compared to ours. They were reminiscent of theatres with rich red velvet curtains used as a backdrop to the platform. A group of brothers and sisters had arranged for my family, Aran's family and James to stay in a large Brooklyn apartment on Union Street. The family who lived there were on vacation in Florida. Wilma, a gentle black sister with a quiet voice, volunteered to transport my family, while Aran, Ria, Yvette and James were in another vehicle. We arrived at the apartment block but the person with the keys was late arriving, so we had to wait for them outside. Waverley, Yvette and I stood on the front steps and a young brother who appeared to be in his twenties approached us. I remember his wavy blonde hair, blonde moustache and piercing blue eyes. I was unsure if he arrived with our group or was on his own when he began to converse with us. He called us beautiful English girls and asked our names. He then moved closer to see the colour of our eyes, commenting on how lovely they were. Although he seemed quite charming, there was something about his energy that made me a little uncomfortable. An older woman abruptly called him to her, telling him to get into her car. It was a relief when the person with the keys arrived as we were so tired.

Wilma escorted us to the front door of the apartment and demonstrated how to undo three robust locks on the door. We entered and then she demonstrated how to close it and replace a large iron bar. One end was placed into a metal indentation on the floor and the other end connected to the door, preventing it from being forced open. Aran and Ria were a nervous couple anyway, so the sight of these locks and a bar on the front door increased their anxiety, especially when Wilma warned us that we were in a rough neighbourhood with a high crime rate. The apartment was huge, with plenty of room for James, Aran, Ria, Yvette and my family to stay there comfortably. There were two double bedrooms for my parents, Aran and Ria. Another bedroom contained bunk beds and we were amazed to see three beds stacked together! Waverley, Yvette and I were excited to sleep on those and thought James would have the double sofa-bed in the lounge. He then expressed his concern about removing his leg at night, as he thought it may distress us if we walked past his bed to go to the bathroom. My parents agreed that he needed his privacy, so James was transferred to the room with bunk beds and Waverley, Yvette and I slept upon the double sofa bed.

At night we could hear the neighbourhood children playing in the street until four in the morning and I wondered how they coped with their schoolwork after only a few hours of sleep. On one occasion when we came out of the apartment, the children approached us asking where we were from. When we replied, they commented on how much they loved our English accent.

The week that followed was exciting for us. We travelled on a ferry along the East River, passing under the Brooklyn bridge and out to Manhattan Island to see the Statue of Liberty. I had seen its image on television many times and was fascinated at how gigantic this statue was. We entered the base where elevators took us to the feet of the statue. From there, we climbed one hundred and sixty-two steps on a steep narrow spiral staircase to the crown. It was an incredible experience to look out of the windows that make up her crown with the realisation we were three hundred feet from the ground. My father asked a guide if he could climb the ladder that led to the torch, but this had been closed to the public as there had been reports of suicides. My father was adventurous and used to climbing tall cranes that were also very high, so being out on the torch would not have bothered him.

We also visited the Empire State building and there were elevators that took us all the way to the top. It was extremely windy up there and we spent some time looking at the city while trying to keep our dresses from blowing upwards. We did not stay for long as my mother found it difficult to breath surrounded by strong winds.

The Jewish Museum reminded me of the British one and although many artefacts did not interest me, I remember the fascinating replica of the Ark of the Covenant surrounded by huge Hanukkah Menorah candle holders. The Ark had always fascinated me when I read its description in the Bible and along with the 'other-wordly' visions of Ezekiel. After leaving the Museum we visited Central Park accompanied by Wilma who introduced us to Dana, her daughter and baby granddaughter. I loved the way black children dressed. Dana's baby wore a beautiful white lace dress and matching shoes with red satin bows. Her afro hair was braided into small sections and tied with tiny red ribbons that covered her head. I noticed that her ears were pierced as she wore tiny sparkling ear studs. Dana explained that when a baby's ears are pierced, they heal quickly as they do not touch them. She looked just like a little doll and I carried her around the park while the adults conversed. I watched other children playing and their games were intriguing, particularly when they used two skipping ropes, jumping over them with ease which needs a good sense of timing to do it successfully.

Wilma invited us back to her home for refreshments and before we arrived, she explained about her son Paris who was fourteen years of age. He had a brain tumour that had caused a bruise around his eye as though he had been in a fight. We were pre warned not to comment on it. Paris' life expectancy was short, but Wilma said he was a strong Witness who loved Jehovah and preached to everyone he could. Paris was a lovely boy, so polite, relaxed and easy to talk to. He occasionally visited us at the apartment.

The time had arrived for us to attend a five-day Jehovah's Witness convention. We left the apartment early each morning to travel on subway trains to the Yankee stadium. The journey was reminiscent of an American television crime movie at times. I recall two men running through the train carriages, hotly pursued by two policemen with their guns out of their holsters ready to shoot if needed. All the policemen were armed there unlike our police force in England. The passengers on the train did not react to it and continued reading their magazines or newspapers as though it was a regular occurrence. The train seats were not upholstered, so we sat upon hard metal frames and the journey was a fast, rough ride that my mother described as a 'Devil's train ride'. She also commented that we had bruises on each nodule of our spines.

The conventions were crowded at the Yankee Stadium. I was surprised to see so many black people gathered in one place because there were very few at our England conventions. The local Jehovah's Witnesses behaved differently as they did not queue at refreshment stalls, crowding around them and grabbing their refreshments. The 'pushy' individuals were first to get served and as we waited patiently and were used to queuing, it was some time before we were noticed! My family listened to the various talks that day and one subject that disturbed my mother was about the use of drugs. She had regularly taken prescribed tranquillisers from her doctor to help with anxiety. She had tried homoeopathy, but I was unsure for how long my parents could continue regular trips to London and the expense of the medication. During the next talk, an intoxicated man ran across the field of the stadium and headed towards the platform. He stepped onto the stage and interfered with the speaker's microphone. A group of brothers immediately appeared to escort him off the stage as the audience applauded. This made the talk a little more interesting for Waverley and I. Their biblical dramas were spectacular performances, as Americans know how to act and put on a good show, with flamboyant robes and superb acting skills. They were more impressive than the performances in England.

After three days of the convention, we were accustomed to travelling on the underground trains. We stayed near the sliding doors before our destination, to pass through quickly as they would quickly and suddenly close. On one occasion my mother was the last person to leave the train and the doors closed in front of her. The train began to move away as my father tried to tear the doors open with his hands. I screamed out when I saw my mother crying at the door and we were worried about the train carrying her off. A passenger on the train noticed this and pulled the emergency cord to bring it to a halt. The doors opened and my mother emerged, however my father was then questioned about the incident by staff who had to fill in a report as to why the train had stopped. This meant that we were late for the convention that day.

Although visiting the city of New York was exciting, in reality it was dusty and dirty which disappointed my mother as she expected to find it clean and glamorous as portrayed in old Hollywood musicals. Waverley and I skipped ahead of my parents and Yvette joined us momentarily until her parents called her back instructing her to stay close to them. Waverley and I began to sing '*Yankee Doodle Dandy*' which was not intentional but we were told by our parents to stop immediately as it could offend American people. I did not understand why at the time, but I obeyed them. I was also unaware that it was the fourth of July which Americans consider an important date. Each day we returned to the apartment, it took a while for my father to unlock the door. He would then hit the floor a few times with the iron rod that secured the door to scare any cockroaches that may be around. My mother feared seeing them after hearing there were many in America. Waverley, Yvette, and I amused ourselves by listening to the radio, and dancing to music. We naturally copied the way our mother danced when her 'free spirit' emerged. Yvette joined us and tried to dance in the same way until Aran called her to him and explained quietly she must not dance that way because it offends Jehovah. He wiggled his own hips to demonstrate the offending action while speaking to her. Waverley and

I opened the biscuit container in the kitchen to take one and offered one to Yvette. Aran saw Yvette eating a biscuit and immediately took her to their bedroom and spanked her for not asking permission. We were startled by this. When Aran emerged from the room, he cried as he hated chastising his child. Waverley and I asked my mother why our father did not cry when we were spanked and this amused her.

At night, the temperature in our apartment was so hot, Waverley, Yvette and I wore only panties to bed and laid upon a sheet with no blankets covering us. The noise of children playing outside kept us awake at times along with the constant sound of police and ambulance sirens. My mother felt ill and at first my father thought it may be anxiety, or a vomiting virus caused by the heat, different food or atmosphere. My mother found the aggressive rudeness of American people difficult to cope with. She commented on how they did not say 'please' or 'thank you' in retail outlets and it sounded like a demand, for example 'give me a burger' or 'give me a drink'. We visited a food bar in the city one lunchtime shaped like a horseshoe with tall bar stools. We sat there to eat our lunch and a woman next to my mother lit a cigarette. She asked the woman politely if she would mind not smoking while she was eating and the woman aggressively replied she did mind and blew her exhaled smoke into my mother's face. I saw her turn away from the woman while she finished her lunch.

I sent a postcard of the Statue of Liberty to my teacher as this was the outing I enjoyed most. I described the places we visited and he put it on the class noticeboard. The teacher and children in my class were impressed by it. We also visited Macy's, the largest store in New York. My father had given each of us spending money of five British pounds that were exchanged for many dollars in 1973. I purchased a small doll named '*Pippa*' with a fabulous wardrobe of shiny ball gowns and accessories. I purchased a gift for my father as he had given us such a wonderful adventure. I found a pair of gold plated cufflinks in a scroll design with faceted green stones and he was delighted with them. He was also touched that I had purchased something for him with my spending money. He wore these cufflinks for many years and when they eventually became too worn and tarnished, he explained to me that he could no longer wear them but he kept them in a box. Wilma invited us to her home for a meal. Her children Dana, Tess and Paris were there. I had a 'crush' on Paris and became shy about conversing with him, so when the children separated from the adults by congregating in the kitchen, I stayed in the lounge. During the adult conversations, I noticed James and Wilma got on well together and they exchanged addresses promising to correspond after our return to England.

Our three week stay passed quickly, and we returned to the United Kingdom on the fifteenth of July. It disappointed me to travel home on a Pan Am 747 jet, as it was smaller than the Jumbo and the journey was not as smooth. I fell asleep during most of the journey and awoke to laughter from other passengers who were viewing a comedy movie on a large projector screen. A hostess served us breakfast of fillet steak and scrambled egg. I ate the egg, but did not find a medium-rare steak appetising in the morning. When we arrived home, my parents wanted to sleep for a while but Waverley and I were excited to tell our neighbours and friends about our adventures. It was a fabulous vacation and an experience that I will always remember so clearly. I am so grateful to my father for taking us on such an adventure..

A few days after our return, my mother visited the doctor about her sickness and discovered she was pregnant. We were delighted, but throughout the pregnancy she constantly worried the baby may not survive. My mother would not store any baby clothes, toys or other items. Just before it was due, all she had in her possession were two tiny vests, two pairs of booties and a few nappies laid out in a carrycot in her bedroom.

I had been taught the skill of crochet by Jean, my friend and neighbour. I taught this to my mother who put it to good use. From that moment on and for the rest of her life, she created blankets for many babies in her congregation, shawls for ladies and large colourful bedspreads. This skill gave her a deep sense of accomplishment and was therapeutic for her. I am so pleased I gave her a positive interest in life that had helped her in many ways.

My mother began to crochet a blanket for her baby and throughout the process, she constantly wondered if it would survive to use it. We were all anxious throughout this pregnancy as at forty-one years of age, my mother had a higher risk of complications. Despite our concerns the pregnancy went smoothly as the doctor and midwife closely monitored her all the way.

When the baby's due date arrived, I awoke that morning to discover her labour had begun in the early hours. It was a long day for us all, particularly my mother. I left for school and returned home for lunch to discover that her labour was still in process. I returned to school after lunch and arrived home by late afternoon to find her still in labour. I passed the bedroom and saw her breathing in gas and air through an oxygen mask. My father had arranged for us to visit our neighbours for dinner, but I did not leave the house immediately and sat in the lounge for a while. I then heard her scream and decided to leave. After having dinner with our neighbour, Waverley and I played in the garden and saw my father washing his hands at the kitchen sink. He announced that the baby's head was about to emerge and my youngest brother Albert arrived at quarter past six that evening weighing nine pounds! We were all relieved that Albert was alive and healthy. When this news reached the brothers and sisters from our congregation, they arrived with baby clothes and furniture they stored while waiting for a positive outcome. My mother stayed in her bed for ten days and I assisted her with caring for Albert. It was fascinating to witness the beginning of a human life. We awaited his first urination and bowel movement to ensure all his intestines were working as they should. My parents were delighted Albert had survived, but from that day on, he was a spoiled child. I assisted with his care until the age of two and after that I distanced myself as I found some aspects of his behaviour disturbing. As Albert got older, he ruled the family home and my parents allowed him to do so all their lives. He also listened to all the adult gossip and learnt how to use this information to his advantage and spread it to others. Witnessing my mother's personal experiences of childbirth frightened me to the extent that I did not want to have children of my own.

Flora, a widow from a nearby bungalow, visited my parents frequently. She was a jolly lady who had no teeth, blue framed spectacles, a headscarf and a green raincoat that she kept on when sitting in our kitchen/diner. I noticed a strange musty smell about her and it was obvious she did not wear a brassiere as her large breasts rested upon her generous abdomen. Flora had the appearance of a Romani woman and my mother enjoyed her visits. Her husband had recently passed away and she offered us his upright piano as she had no use for it. I loved music and my parents noticed I learnt tunes by listening and played them on toy whistles, school recorders, xylophones, and guitars. They thought I would enjoy playing a piano, so my father arranged to collect it from her. He decided to put it in the bedroom I shared with Waverley, so my father and Carmel's husband Basil pushed the heavy iron frame piano up the stairs. This took some time and I remember their deep red faces dripping in perspiration! After an hour or so, they successfully positioned it in the bedroom.

Vivien, who recruited my parents into the Jehovah's Witnesses, taught her daughter Rosie to play the piano extremely well. My parents asked her if she would teach me. They had helped Vivien in many ways, so she agreed to do so, suggesting that they purchase the *Smallwood's Piano Tutor* books. Vivien lived in a large Victorian period property and was a divorcee. Her former husband was once a Jehovah's Witness, who charmed women in the congregation and eventually left Vivien for one of them. He was then disfellowshipped from the organisation. Her eldest daughter Joan was married with two children and she had stayed in contact with her father, but Rosie cut him out of her life, angry and disgusted at what he had done. Vivien and Rosie had two lodgers that lived in the upper and basement rooms of the property to help out financially. They hosted our religious 'group meetings' on Tuesday evenings where we studied books that were recommended by the organisation.

When I began my piano lessons, Vivien taught me regular exercises from the tutor books to strengthen my hands and fingers. She told me to balance a two-pence coin on the back of each hand while playing, to ensure my wrists and hands were in the correct position which meant my fingers did all the work. I noticed that Vivien's hands shook when she slowly demonstrated the exercises as she had a condition known as multiple sclerosis. She wore beige 'peep toe' shoes that I often studied as her bunions pushed the shoes out of shape and her big toes bent almost sideways. I wondered how she could feel comfortable in them. Her illness had reached the stage where she needed walking sticks with arm supports prescribed from the hospital. Vivien was a strict teacher, and when she fixed her intense dark brown eyes upon me, I took her instructions seriously. On reflection, I wonder whether my parents thought that having a piano in my room would distract me from questioning their religion or having interests in the outside world. I enjoyed learning the instrument and worked hard on exercises and pieces that I was given to learn. It was not however enough to distract me from other matters. My mother later commented that I had questioned their beliefs more since playing the piano and threatened to give it away as it may have 'demons' within it influencing me. Flora had told my mother that in the past her husband once 'dabbled' in the occult, so this may have played on her mind.

Members of our congregation were all different. Some were fanatical, doing everything 'by the book', while others had a more laid back approach to it. Troy and Pamela Lovell were the latter. They had two daughters. Hattie was a few months older than me, and Honour was a similar age to Waverley. Their life was freer than ours. I recall the first words I spoke to Hattie after one of our religious meetings. I asked her age and discovered that we were both four years old and I asked her when she would be five and discovered she was four months older.

The Lovell family were well-spoken, and Troy worked with television companies, creating and directing commercials. They were associated with celebrities and their trendy attire was in complete contrast to other Jehovah's Witnesses. My mother described them as 'bohemian' and they fascinated her with what she referred to as their 'show-biz' lives. The Lovells were living the type of life she craved, however there were other members of the congregation that disapproved of this. Waverley and I enjoyed visiting their wonderful open-plan home with large ornate mirrors on the walls, polished floorboards, copper covered kitchen surfaces, modern furniture and the majestic presence of a mahogany grand piano in the lounge. They were a musical family as Troy was a pianist and drummer who loved jazz.

I remember an occasion when they hosted a party for the children in our congregation. Troy played the piano and we danced, while Pamela organised games including musical chairs, pass-the-parcel and musical statues. One of the games surprised me. We were all asked to leave the room and each child in turn was blindfolded and guided into the lounge. Pamela narrated the story of Nelson who sailed the seas and it included specific detail of how his arm had been amputated. Hattie laid upon the couch groaning while playing the character of Nelson and she held a layer of orange peel across her shoulder. Pamela took the hand of a blindfolded child and placed it upon the orange peel informing them they would feel a huge scab that covered the socket of the amputated arm. A bowl of water nearby contained pieces of floating orange peel and the child's hand was placed into the bowl suggesting they could feel some of the blood that came from the arm. Pamela then described how Nelson lost an eye and guided the child's finger into the centre of a peeled orange. The character of Nelson screamed as this happened and then the blindfolded child screamed in reaction. The children waiting in the other room could hear this, not knowing what would happen when they entered the room. After removing the blindfold the child was shown all the items used, but it felt completely different while hearing the story and using their imagination! I only got as far as the scab on the arm and the bowl of water and orange peel, then ripped off the blindfold as my imagination was far too vivid. My mother was horrified when she heard about this game on our return. I am sure there were other parents who had a similar reaction as the 'old school' Jehovah's Witnesses disapproved of the Lovells, but we loved being with them.

Whenever we were travelling in my father's car, he took the opportunity to assist people who had broken down and there were times when he towed their car all the way to their homes. While doing this, they sat in our car and he conversed with them announcing that he was a Jehovah's Witness. He wanted them to know that people in our religion were happy and helpful to others as it could result in their recruitment in the future. Waverley and I felt sorry for the drivers as they had no choice, particularly if he was towing their car, but to listen to his preaching until they reached their destination!

Our neighbours were fully aware of our religious beliefs as my parents called on their homes when we preached in the street where we lived. When we left home to attend meetings early in the evening, our neighbour's children were sitting on the garden wall in their bathrobes, chatting together before their bedtime. Whenever we returned from our religious meetings around Sunday lunchtime or late in the afternoon, Mrs McCallen appeared at her front door with a scrubbing brush and a bowl of water to scrub her front doorstep. My mother assumed this was done purposely to hint she should be caring for her family and home instead of going to meetings at all hours.

As the Christmas season approached, I saw and felt the excitement of local children and the 'magic' of their belief in Father Christmas. I would watch the sky through my bedroom window on the night of Christmas Eve, thinking about this. I concluded that Father Christmas did not exist, as I knew deep in my heart that if he did, he would not have excluded Waverley and I from the gifts he gave to all the children. I often thought about how wonderful it would be if he had been real.

On New Year's Eve, our neighbours invited others from our street to their party, they knew however there would be no point in inviting our family. Waverley and I watched them gather in the street at midnight joining hands and singing *Auld Lang Syne*. Their loud, lively music continued until the early hours of the next morning so we had little sleep that night. I noticed that our neighbours cared for their children well, as they were the main priority in their lives. In our lives, we knew that the Jehovah's Witness religion was my parents' main priority.

Writing about the party games at the Lovell's, reminded me of a party my parents attended hosted by Vivien. My mother told me that Vivien and her husband organised a party game entitled *Kissing the Blarney Stone*. The brothers and sisters who attended were sent out of the lounge and each person in turn was blindfolded and guided into the room by Vivien. They were instructed to kneel and she would roll up her sleeve, placing her bent arm in front of their face. They were instructed to kiss the crease where her upper and lower arm met just above the elbow. When the blindfold was removed, they saw Vivien's husband pulling up his trousers giving the impression they kissed the crevice of his bottom! Most of them saw the humorous side of this, but one sister took offence and abruptly left their home. I do not know whether the woman reported this to the elders, but if she had, Vivien's husband would have been 'reproved' as he was an elder. My mother also told me that she won a competition for the most glamorous ankles and her picture appeared in the local newspaper. An elderly brother my mother was fond of, ignored her for months. His reaction upset her as she did not think she had done anything wrong.

Each year near the Easter holidays we attended the Memorial. This is considered one of the most important meetings of the year. Anointed members of Jehovah's Witnesses were the only ones to partake of the bread and wine. It is a celebration of the ransom sacrifice of Jesus to free us from sin. I asked my mother how the anointed members were certain of this. She explained they had a strong desire to live in heaven and not on the earth. I observed with interest as the unleavened bread was passed around to all members of the congregation. Only one or two would partake of the bread and red wine and children were only allowed to touch the plate and wine glass as they passed, as the adults were concerned they would either spill the contents or be tempted to consume them. An elderly lady known as 'Dainty' because of her size, was a devout spiritual woman. She was a spinster and at each of our meetings she sat in her wheelchair at the front row of the Kingdom Hall and gave full attention to all the talks. When partaking of the bread and wine she closed her eyes and consumed the bread so slowly, it was still in her mouth by the time she received the wine.

After the memorial, a sister who baked the bread would offer it to the children and although it was tasteless, we ate it because it had been part of the ceremony. The adults would take home the remaining wine to consume later. I remember how the crystal wine glass felt as it passed and even now as I pour red wine and hold the crystal glass it evokes these memories. We were encouraged to converse with Dainty after each meeting as my mother described her as a wise, spiritual woman. She was unable to walk, so brothers and sisters would take time to approach her and converse. Dainty wore circular gold-rimmed spectacles and a beige woollen coat with a sparkling brooch at her neck between her collar. She wore a matching hat secured with a pearl hat pin that covered her short fair curly hair. I asked if she was well, and she would look up at me with her sky-blue eyes and smile. We missed her after she passed away as she rarely missed a meeting and I often wondered whether she was in heaven looking down at us.

When my father and I were out on the preaching work, we called at the home of a local family who invited us in. Tom, a very handsome man who loved reading his bible, was a member of a local spiritualist church. My father arranged to visit him again, however my mother refused to accompany him as she was afraid of 'demons' in their home. I offered to accompany him as I had enjoyed visiting Tom and his family. You could immediately tell that they were warm, genuine, welcoming people. They all had a keen interest in music and when they heard about my piano lessons, they encouraged me to play their organ in the lounge. Tom agreed to a regular bible study and Amy, his wife, listened, while I kept Mary and Philip, who were their children, amused with games and we listened to music. I grew to love the Shelden family and as they lived only a few streets away, I visited them regularly and enjoyed musical afternoons there. Tom and Amy were wonderful, caring parents and totally devoted to their children. I received unconditional love from them throughout my life. They loved celebrating Christmas and

Tom would play the role of Father Christmas to visit our local school giving gifts to all the children. Mary and Philip had no idea that Father Christmas was their father for a long time, until Philip noticed the scar on Tom's forehead. I asked my father when he would tell them that Jehovah's Witnesses did not celebrate Christmas. He replied that he planned to delay this information, as if they found out too soon, they would stop their bible study. My father said that if they grew to love the religion first, it would not matter when they eventually discovered this.

A few weeks later, Tom mentioned to one of his work colleagues he was having a bible study and they told him Jehovah's Witnesses did not celebrate Christmas. Tom then asked my father and he had no choice but to confirm this was true. Tom gave the matter some thought and discussed it with Amy before they decided to end their bible studies. My father was disappointed and he no longer visited them on a regular basis. I continued to visit them as I enjoyed their company. Tom stayed in contact with my family and he had occasional religious discussions with my father. They told me they liked him but Amy told me there were times during their bible studies, my father would become frustrated when they debated his beliefs and on one occasion, he thumped his fist on their table when stating the religion's point of view. After a while, Tom stopped attending the spiritualist church, as he was concerned they were working with demonic forces. We had discussions about his beliefs and then Tom began attending a Pentecostal church. Amy enjoyed their music and entertainment and they continued frequenting this church for many years.

Paul attended the religious meetings with his mother and was two months younger than me. He was well-spoken and although he wore spectacles they did not hide his good looks and classic features. Paul and

I had been 'childhood sweethearts' for years and I regularly conversed with him after our meetings. His mother was a strict German widow who was possessive with him, insisting that he remained at her side as she had the role of both parents. No one seemed to have a problem with us liking one another when we were children, but this changed in the years to follow.

As you can see by reading the story so far dear reader, I had strange childhood experiences within the Jehovah's Witnesses. I was however unaware that entering my adolescence would make life more complicated.

CHAPTER 4

ADOLESCENCE

I did not expect to reach the age of thirteen, as we were constantly told Armageddon would have destroyed the 'old system' by then. We were taught that only strong Jehovah's Witnesses would survive. As I found it difficult to connect with this religion or behave in the way they wanted, I would be considered one of the weaker members so I did not expect God to spare me.

On reflection it was like living with a terminal illness where one expects to die the following day. Puberty began for me at ten, so by the age of thirteen I had small breasts that would fill a small brassiere. The girls who attended my school were wearing them, but when I asked my mother about it, she refused to purchase one telling me I did not need them. Jean, my neighbour gave me two of hers that she had grown out of and I wore them without my mother's knowledge. I did however make the mistake of confiding in Linsey's sisters who were of similar age and they repeated this information to Kevin, who, to my embarrassment, informed our parents in my presence. My mother did not take them away and after a while she gave in and purchased new ones for me. I began to menstruate between the age of thirteen and fourteen and although I was educated about this process at school, it was still a shock when it actually happened. My mother gave me an old fashioned sanitary method that I found uncomfortable and hideous, so I immediately visited the shops to purchase a modern alternative. She warned me that I could become pregnant, but this did not worry me as I had no plans for relationships at this time. On occasions my mother would became angry and accuse me of wanting sexual relations with boys. She had explained the 'facts of life' to Waverley and I by using a silver handled knife. She held it in one hand describing it as the male genitalia and poked the blade through a circular shape she had made with the fingers on her other hand. My mother explained that virgin girls had a hymen that bled on their wedding night during intercourse. She described how women laid upon a special sheet so the blood would be shown as proof of virginity. I had such a vivid imagination the description caused me to feel faint and sick. That was enough to put anyone off! I left Waverley and my mother to lie on the settee in the lounge, but it did not seem to bother Waverley, who continued to listen. My mother emphasised that Jehovah forbade sex before marriage, and we had to remain virgins until our wedding day.

My mother's behaviour was erratic and made little sense. She applied cosmetics to my face from the age of eleven which upset my father. She styled my hair in a way that was far too 'adult' for my age. I noticed a change in men's behaviour towards me when I walked to Vivien's home for my piano lesson. Men stared at me while driving their cars and there were times I cried because I was aware that they may have had lecherous thoughts. I had witnessed the way men behaved towards my mother who seemed to enjoy it. She would dress provocatively before the council workmen visited our home to do maintenance work. Later that day she told my father how their hands trembled whenever she stood near them. My mother also visited working men's cafes and I felt uncomfortable with the way they behaved towards her. Even now I prefer to avoid these establishments as they trigger these memories and the energy at these places has not changed.

Most of the students at my school wore the 1970s fashion of platform shoes, bell-bottom trousers and shirts. I had to wear what my mother provided; tight pencil skirts, blouses and high heel shoes. Members of my class thought I considered myself a higher class to them as I behaved differently. They referred to me as 'Madam Muck' and 'Scrubber' which on reflection was hardly surprising with the type of clothes my mother provided. She did not want me following the 'worldly' fashions, as the Jehovah's Witnesses instructed us to look and behave differently. I sat at the front row in each of my classes and worked hard, which placed me in top achievement classes throughout my education.

Waverley was in the year below me and she saw how my preaching to others (as instructed by my parents) resulted in me being disliked and a target of verbal bullying. Waverley then decided not to preach at school as she wanted to be liked and had a better time at school than I.

I remember the time her school friends wore fancy dress for Halloween and called at our home while 'trick or treating' to show Waverley their costumes. My mother opened the door, screamed and ran away, as she saw them as 'demonic costumes'. There was however an energy about the autumn season and Halloween that stirred my curiosity. I felt more 'alive' at this time of year, but I kept those thoughts to myself.

I had a school girl 'crush' on a few of my male teachers. Being raised in a male dominated religion, I felt attracted to those with an air of authority about them. A few of the girls in my class tried to befriend me and arranged to meet me after school. When they visited my home, my parents took out their bibles and publications, preaching to my friends who did not return again. One year, my English teacher Mrs Douglas organised a pantomime for our school entitled *The Sultan's Treasure*. She noticed my acting skills and offered me the lead role of Queen Sultana. I enthusiastically accepted the role. At this time I met Julie, a new girl who arrived at our school as she had moved in with local foster parents. I noticed she was an unfortunate victim of the thalidomide drug as her left arm was deformed. Some pupils made cruel remarks about it, but I befriended her as I too, was ridiculed for being different. Julie was a good dancer and performer, so we choreographed a dance together to perform during the interval of the pantomime.

On the evening of our performance, my mother provided me with a costume and arrived at the school to apply cosmetics to my face. She secured a string of pearls on my head as a head-dress. The performance was a huge success, and Mrs Douglas conversed with my mother telling her I was good enough to attend a drama school. She added that I 'walked away' with the performance that evening. My mother replied that our religion would not allow me to pursue a career in the arts.

The dance Julie and I performed was also successful. Mr Smallson was there that evening. He was my maths teacher and I had struggled with mathematics. At times I avoided his classes as he would become frustrated and angry when I could not understand his explanations. Mr Smallson also taught English and drama and that evening I asked him for feedback. I was pleased to hear that I had impressed him for a change.

Julie and I developed a good friendship during the two years she attended our school, but she then moved away to new foster parents in another area and we lost contact. Mrs Douglas organised two more pantomimes over the next two years, the first was entitled *Oliver* and she offered me the role of Nancy, but my parents would not allow me to perform as the character of Nancy was a prostitute. The second was *Wizard of Oz* and I was offered the role of Dorothy, but they would not allow me to play that role either as it was a story about a wizard, witches and fairies. This was hard for me to understand as my parents often watched this movie on television around Christmas time. Mrs Douglas then lost interest in my abilities, concentrating on other promising pupils and it was difficult for me to watch their rehearsals when I could not be part of them.

Waverley and I travelled on trains and buses into town during our teenage years and we often visited the Lovells to spend time with Hattie and Honour. We were relaxed in their company, watching television, or listening to music. Troy wore a short dressing gown most of the time at home and they explained to us he preferred to walk around naked at home when there were no visitors. We were shocked about this, as our father would not allow us anywhere near the bathroom at home while he bathed. We were instructed to stay on the ground floor of our home until he had dressed. My mother described him as an 'ultra' modest man. When Honour saw our shocked expression, she added: "Well we don't *stare* at it"!

One of our visits to their home was particularly exciting as Pamela arranged for us to visit the Graveton cinema with Hattie and Honour to see *Jaws,* the latest movie. It was rather disturbing for children aged twelve and thirteen as there were scenes of shark attacks. I hid my face behind Hattie's arm when she warned me about the gory scenes, as they had seen the movie before. Pamela had prepared barbecue spare ribs for our dinner on our return from the cinema and listened intently as we told her what we thought of the movie. Hattie had braids in her hair the previous night and when she unfastened them, they produced a wealth of long brown wavy hair. Pamela gazed admiringly at Hattie. My mother enjoyed us brushing her long dark brown hair in the evenings, so Waverley and I decided to braid her hair like Hattie's. The following day her hair was wild with tight waves and although he loved it, my father laughed. I remember when my mother wore a tight pair of ski pants knowing that my father did not approve of women wearing trousers. He laughed at her so much she felt self-conscious and did not wear them again. Women were not permitted to wear trousers to our religious meetings or out on the preaching work but it was their personal choice to wear them at home. The first time I tried a pair of jeans, the shop assistant zipped up the 'fly' my mother saw my expression and said: "That's put her off them!" She was right as I associated those with boys. A few years later I noticed most girls wore them, so this changed my view of them. Waverley being a 'tomboy' loved her jeans and did not want to remove them. She occasionally attended our religious meetings with them rolled up beneath her skirt!

We spent an afternoon at Hattie and Honour's home and later Pamela transported Waverley and I to Graveton train station. We entered a single carriage and although we were warned by our parents not to use them, we were alone and our destination was two short stops away. The first stop was at Northfield station. A man who appeared to be in his thirties entered our carriage. He had dark wavy hair, was smartly dressed with a coat draped over his arm. Waverley sat on the long seat opposite me and as the man sat beside her, she began to converse him. Waverley was a friendly child and would talk to most people she met. He found it odd when he saw me eating a lemon as I enjoyed the sour taste. The man said he was travelling to London Bridge station and he complimented Waverley on her fur coat asking if it was real and where she got it from. Waverley replied she did not know, and he picked up the end of her fur belt to feel the texture. He then moved to sit beside me and asked whether my trench coat was real leather. He instructed me to stand up so that he could get a better look at the coat and although I felt uncomfortable, I did so. The man asked what the lining looked like and he began to undo the belt and buttons of my coat. This upset me and I moved away from him, telling him to stop. As I sat down, he reached over and put his hand inside the top of my coat. As he felt the lining inside, the back of his hand brushed against my breast and I once again moved away. He loomed over me as the train slowed to stop at our station. I indignantly told him: "This is where we get off!!" and to my relief he did not stop us. As we were walking along the platform, the carriage we left passed us and the man had his face pressed up against the window watching us. I was very upset about the incident and told my parents about it on our return home. My father immediately contacted the local police by telephone explaining what had occurred, giving them a description of the man who was apparently travelling to London Bridge station. After investigation, they contacted us and said that no man of his description was seen leaving the train at London Bridge station. It sickened me that this man had put his hand inside my coat and I refused to wear it or the t-shirt beneath it again. I cried and told my mother I would never get over this, but she assured me I would as time passed.

When I attended the religious meetings, I did not agree with some aspects of their teaching, particularly those that caused division within the congregation. The elders stressed how important it was to become a strong member of Jehovah's Witnesses. One could only remain strong in it by limiting association with weaker members of the congregation. There was already an obvious division between middle and working class families and certain members of the congregation who considered themselves strong in the 'truth' were no doubt thinking of those they would avoid. After all, how can weaker members receive the encouragement to strengthen their faith if they are excluded by the stronger ones?

Our congregation had split into two as apparently the numbers had grown. The Lovells were in the Graveton congregation and we were in Northfield. We did not see them as often in two different congregations. I developed closer friendships with Selena, Sandra and Trudi, who like me, found it difficult to connect with the religion and were considered weaker members. I had known Selena for many years as her mother provided child care for Waverley and I while my mother worked part time in a local factory.. Selena had two younger brothers and the youngest one who was six years of age, crossed a busy road with his father one afternoon, when he lost one of his shoes. He ran into the road to retrieve it and was killed when a car struck him. This incident haunts Selena to this day. She visited a psychic woman who told her that her little brother retrieved his shoe because their parents had a recent disagreement over purchasing a new pair of shoes for the older brother. I heard that there were many disagreements between their parents over financial issues. We were devastated about this tragedy and it severely affected Selena's family.

Sandra had a large family of seven siblings and was the only daughter. Trudi often attended religious meetings with her grandmother as her parents were not Jehovah's Witnesses. She lived with her father and step-mother.

Waverley was at this time, a 'tomboy' and befriended boys her age at the religious meetings. One afternoon she and Harry were playing in the small Kingdom Hall library on the upper floor, after a meeting. They knew that they were not supposed to be in there and heard someone approaching, so they hid behind two padded chairs. Three elders entered the room with my father and Waverley said they were reprimanding him over our behaviour as men in the congregation are supposed to have complete control over their families. Aware that hiding in the library would be worse for my father, they hid in silence. Harry was an asthmatic and breathed heavily, so Waverley, worried they may hear him, told him to breathe quietly and fortunately they were not discovered.

I attended my first teenage party at the age of thirteen. A teenage girl from our congregation hosted one at her home and as her mother was not a strict Jehovah's Witness, we knew the party would be fun and looked forward to it. My mother purchased a long cream dress for me printed with tiny blue flowers. It had cream puffed sleeves, a high collar and pearl buttons from neckline to waist. I enjoyed singing and dancing to the music which impressed Paul, my childhood sweetheart. When I rested, we sat together on the couch holding hands and he kissed my cheek. We had a wonderful time. Ella was two years older than I, a friend of Tracy's and from a middle-class family, approached me the next day after our Sunday afternoon meeting. She whispered that she would not reveal my 'disgusting behaviour' at the party to my parents! I assumed that she spoke in jest about Paul and I holding hands on the couch. My mother asked me what Ella had said, but I did not explain, knowing she would suspect there was more to it. As we grew older, Paul wanted to be with me more at the meetings, until the time his mother angrily approached us, pulled Paul away from me and instructed me to leave him alone as we were both too young. Shocked by her reaction, I stayed away from him from then on, as his possessive mother was not the type of woman I would want for a future mother in law!

One evening at the Kingdom Hall, Selena and I were conversing about life at school. We exchanged a couple of risqué jokes that the school-children were circulating, but did not realise an older sister in the congregation had been eavesdropping. She immediately reported our conversation to the elders, who told our fathers. Selena and I had to individually attend a judicial committee meeting with three elders and our parents to receive a reprove. My parents were upset and I was shocked that this matter was taken so seriously. They told us it would be a public reprove announced at our next religious meeting. The reason for it is not divulged to the congregation, however a talk on the subject is given at a meeting the following week. The elders advised my parents to leave me in the car for the first part of the meeting so I was not present for the announcement made during the interval. I then entered the Kingdom Hall for the second half of the meeting, where some congregation members were civil towards me, while others ignored me. The following week, a talk on risqué conversations and jokes was given by Aran. Selena sat with her parents and we briefly glanced at one another blushing with embarrassment. This was my first experience of how brothers and sisters could quickly change towards a congregation member who has made a mistake and received a public reprove.

I regularly conversed with Sister Kelsey an elderly woman at our meetings. She wore autumn brown and gold clothes with coordinating hats. I admired her gold dress rings with huge faceted stones that she wore on each finger of each hand. Sister Kelsy promised me that when she passed away, she would leave me one of her rings. I excitedly told my mother who replied she would not allow me to have one as Sister Kelsy and her husband once 'dabbled' in the occult. Apparently it had caused her husband mental health issues that my mother described as 'madness'. This disappointed me, but my parents feared anything associated with occult practices. When we left the Kingdom Hall each evening, we passed the nearby spiritualist church in a beautiful Victorian house at the time its members were leaving. My mother described them as 'evil people'. Opposite the church was a dark war memorial park with a tall statue of an angel on a pillar that stood in the centre behind iron gates. I often dreamt about this church and the dark park opposite, which intrigued me. My parents told me they once accepted an eiderdown from someone previously involved in spiritualism and the quilt felt extremely heavy on their bed when they laid beneath it. Waverley was a toddler at the time and on the nights she slept in their bed, she apparently shook and perspired in her sleep. My parents discarded the quilt and these strange occurrences apparently ceased. Any activities such as Yoga were forbidden within our religion as the postures and movements were apparently associated with a 'snake god'. The practice of meditation was considered dangerous as silencing the mind could allow demons to enter.

I continued my piano lessons with Vivien each Thursday after school in her magnificent large Victorian house. On entering the gate, I passed a huge lavender bush and would pick one of the stems, inhaling the aroma of the flower on my way to the front door. Vivien had taught her daughter Rosie to be a wonderful pianist and she tried to teach me how to read music. Frustratingly for her, when I had learnt a tune, I no longer needed the music, as I had memorised where the correct piano keys were. Vivien constantly reminded me to look at the music and not the piano keys. This made reading music a slow process for me and it took longer to learn a complete tune. I could however hear tunes and find the correct notes to play them on the piano. Rosie relied completely on music sheets and could not play by listening. This enabled her to immediately play any tune when the music was in front of her. Rosie was a carer for her mother all her life and she was a little older than Kevin. She seemed to have no interest in finding a husband stating that she was too fussy. Rosie told me she once dated a Brother who was very handsome but it did not last as he was conceited and selfish. She was a strong Jehovah's Witness and a regular pioneer going out on the preaching work for ninety hours per month. My parents encouraged me to follow Rosie's example and she was like an older sister as she helped me style my hair and I copied her style of dress.

We had fun holidays in Cornwall when Vivien and Rosie shared a large static caravan with us. On the long journeys, Rosie sang songs from various musicals and taught us the words. At night in the caravan, Vivien would giggle to herself. My father thought it was Waverley and I, so he scolded us, saying that if he heard us again, he would spank us. We protested, saying that we were not laughing but he did not believe us. Hearing this caused Vivien to laugh and my father rushed out of the bedroom to spank us. In the darkness he kicked over a bucket that we had used before going to bed. He then had to clean urine off the floor and Vivien laughed until she cried! This was one of many hilarious incidents that occurred on our vacations with them!

Rosie surprised us all when she announced that she was introduced to a Brother at a religious convention. He was twelve years her senior and she told us that he was the only male she felt attracted to and planned to see him again. We did not meet Brett until the next convention and he certainly knew how to 'charm' the ladies. He would visit Rosie on a Thursday evening during my piano lessons and we then travelled to the Kingdom Hall together. Olivia arrived to collect us in her orange Volkswagen Camper van. She was a large lady who lived with her husband Bob and at times she could be quite stern. Brett was extremely charming, he joked and teased me constantly, so I soon developed a 'crush'. I looked forward to his arrival during my piano lessons and while Vivien left the room to prepare herself for the meeting I continued my practice. Brett would enter the room to tease me and Vivien scolded him for distracting me from practice. I recall my parents discussing their relationship and my father was concerned about Brett's interest in Rosie. He mentioned that Vivien's home was worth a considerable amount of money and he hoped Brett was not dating Rosie because of her inheritance.

One summer afternoon, Vivien and Rosie hosted a farewell party for Donald, a Nigerian Brother in our congregation as he was moving to Barbados. Donald was a kind, jovial, spiritual man that many members of the congregation admired. Vivien hosted the party in her large garden. I watched Rosie and Brett set up a record player and attach it to large speakers positioned at the open window for background music. They played a song entitled *Barbados* by *Typically Tropical* and Donald laughed as it bellowed from the speakers. I danced to the wonderful rhythm and Brett looked at me smiling as he raised his eyebrows. I was terribly jealous of Brett and Rosie's relationship and I stood near them as they sat together on the staircase in the hallway. Brett teased Rosie about me having a 'crush' on him. She smiled at me and linked her arm through Brett's asking me why he would want me when he had someone like her! This comment was hurtful and stayed with me for years. I thought Rosie was naïve to trust a 'charmer' as it was obvious he loved the admiration of other women and I doubted he would be a faithful husband. At the young age of thirteen I had already decided that most men could not be trusted. My father however, had more than proved his love for my mother.

The time arrived for Brett and Rosie's wedding. I usually loved weddings, but was not excited about this one and wore a long black evening dress for the occasion. The preparations had been stressful for Rosie, and she was already petite, but lost more weight in the months leading up to the wedding. My mother was concerned she may disappear altogether. Rosie chose not to wear a veil and had white silk flowers decorated with pearls in her hair. Her dress was white lace with a long chiffon train extending from her waist, edged with a large frill. Rosie looked stunning that day. All members of our congregation were delighted to witness their union as she had taken her time in finding a partner. A rectangular wooden stool for two people was regularly used for wedding ceremonies at the Kingdom Hall. It had a white quilted cover and was positioned in front of the celebrant just below the platform. Many of the young sisters thought the day would come when they would be seated upon it with their future husbands. Jehovah's Witness ceremonies were often humble affairs without the glitz and glamour of church weddings. They included the usual marriage vows and a talk would be given about including God in the marriage along with biblical advice on how couples should conduct themselves. It was mainly another opportunity to preach to any guests who were not Jehovah's Witnesses. The party after Brett and Rosie's ceremony was held at the Graveton British Legion Hall with a Ceilidh, also known as a barn dance for entertainment. While the band were preparing, they played background music and I danced with my father, who taught me the waltz, foxtrot, quickstep, and jive. He would jokingly say: "Do you come here often?" and I laughed. When the barn dance began, I danced with Perrin, a teenage Brother who was rather quiet. There was something about him that reminded me of the singer *Bryan Ferry*. One of the elders approached me and commented that he noticed who I had been dancing with, before giving me an approving wink. It seemed members of the congregation were constantly trying to 'matchmake' younger brothers and sisters.

On the subject of weddings, I recall attending a meeting a while after Tracey was married. My family was not invited as it was mainly for their family and middle-class congregation members. I heard it was a lavish affair with a horse drawn carriage and all the trimmings of a 'worldly' wedding. A Watchtower publication was released with an article on expensive weddings and the 'showy display of one's means of life'. They stated Jehovah's Witness weddings would not have God's approval if they were celebrated in this way. Tracey's mother Brenda was in the back room reading the article and drew her son Clarke's attention to it. I could tell they were not happy, as they knew that members of the congregation would immediately think of Tracey's wedding when they read it.

I mentioned before that Brothers and Sisters were keen to 'matchmake' those who were single and were happy when they found a mate at conventions or the Kingdom Hall. Members of the congregation however, had a completely different view when Uncle Vernon dated Beverley, a sister twenty years his senior. Vernon had spent many years as a single man and was my mother's youngest sibling. My grandmother did not want him to leave her, so she interfered in his past relationships. After her death, he still acted as though she were there and put little effort into finding a new relationship. Beverley was recruited into the Jehovah's Witnesses by my parents when her former husband was in prison, and she often spoke about him with love, despite him treating her badly. He eventually passed away at a young age and she had a teenage son who was often in trouble with the police. Vernon and Beverley got on well together and when their courtship began, Waverley and I were amused about it. We giggled when they kissed one another goodnight in our hallway. Beverley stayed overnight at our home one weekend and her loud snoring terrified Albert who thought it was a monster. I remember all members of our family along with Vernon who was sleeping on the couch, congregating at the top of the staircase discussing what to do about her snoring. None of us could sleep and Beverley, oblivious to this conversation continued, but she laughed about it the following day. Vernon was viewed as a weak member of the congregation and Beverley's single middle-aged friends advised her to end the relationship as he could weaken her spirituality. After dating a while, they voluntarily attended a judicial committee meeting with the elders on two occasions after confessing they had sinned and felt guilty. Vernon blamed himself for their mistakes and eventually their relationship ended. One reason was generational differences, but the main one was the influence from Beverley's friends. She told my mother that Vernon became too controlling and interfered in her life, not wanting her to go out on the preaching work. She told my mother that his kisses were 'out of this world'! Uncle Vernon still reminisces about their time together and a few years after their courtship Beverley passed away. Uncle Vernon still remains a single man.

It surprised me to reach thirteen years of age, as I thought Armageddon would have destroyed me before then. My parents arranged a family holiday in Cornwall and invited Claire, my maternal grandmother, uncle Vernon, cousin Carmel, her husband Basil and small daughter Della. All the adults jointly paid for a large guest house in Fowey. It was apparently Claire's first vacation and at seventy-three years of age, she intended to enjoy it! She was concerned about leaving her elderly cat but my aunts recommended a cattery and assured Claire that she would be well cared for. Our grandmother was extremely entertaining as she shared a bedroom with Waverley and I. She recited risqué rhymes and one night she danced the 'Can-Can', kicking her legs so high her feet were level with her head! My father thumped on the door instructing us to go to sleep as our laughter and talking were keeping them awake. Uncle Vernon and I had a close uncle–niece relationship, as he was one of two men in my life that I trusted. During this holiday he spoiled me with gifts and I gave him plenty of hugs in return. My father warned me not to get too affectionate as Vernon wanted a wife of his own and I could arouse other feelings within him. I did not believe Vernon would do this, but I understood why my father would be concerned. When Albert was a little older, my father commented that he would not leave Albert alone with Vernon. I wondered if this meant he was unsure of Vernon's sexual preferences and I thought my father judged him unfairly. I did not mention this to Vernon as I knew he would be hurt. Claire loved her holiday and enjoyed reading risqué cartoon postcards in the gift shops. My father told her not to look at them, but she chuckled and ignored him. On one occasion at the beach, Claire walked into the public lavatories and laughed as she emerged, realising she entered the male one by mistake. We attended the local religious meetings and introduced Claire and Vernon to members of the Cornwall congregation. Enid and Elsie invited us to their home for tea and our usual fun evening of card games. Claire had occasionally visited our local Kingdom Hall, but did not take the religion seriously. My mother described her as 'too sentimental' because she loved celebrating Christmas and birthdays, but she managed to recruit uncle Vernon who attended meetings regularly. Our vacation was going well until Claire asked about the welfare of her cat. My father contacted my aunts by telephone for an update and was in the public call box for quite a while. He then emerged to have a whispered conversation with Vernon who immediately entered the nearby Inn to purchase a small bottle of brandy. We discovered Claire's elderly cat had passed away and discussed whether to tell her and spoil her holiday, or delay the news until she returned home. My father and uncle Vernon decided to let her enjoy the rest of her time in Cornwall, but during our long journey home, all Claire could talk about was seeing her cat again. When we eventually arrived at Claire's home, my father carried her suitcases into the house and she told us that my father was the best son in law she had. This surprised us, as she had not approved of him since the day my parents first met.

Claire was devastated when she heard of her cat's passing. Two weeks after her holiday, she awoke one morning, completed her chores and sat upon the couch to rest. Vernon awoke a while later and when he spoke to Claire, she did not answer. It appeared she was sleeping but Vernon was concerned about her grey complexion. He contacted my father who left work immediately and when he arrived, could tell that Claire had passed away. Our family was devastated and although my mother was upset, I remember that she did not cry. Vernon was with us and then my aunts arrived. All three of them hugged and cried, but my mother did not react as she placed cups and saucers on the dining table. Their mother-daughter relationship had not been close, as my mother described to me some of the traumatic memories of her past. She told me that Claire was a violent, angry woman. Uncle Vernon was in his thirties and he did not want to live alone. He moved in with Carmel and Basil until they had a second child and then he moved into a council apartment.

Life became more difficult for me during adolescence. I was naturally attracted to boys as many girls of my age were, but my mother accused me of wanting sexual relations. This was untrue and disturbing as the thought of taking this step scared me after her horrific stories. On reflection these were probably told with the intention of scaring me. My mother occasionally struck me in temper, pulled my hair and threatened to take me to a doctor for a virginity test. I replied that I would be confident to do so and on one occasion I put on my coat and told her to take me there. She smiled to herself and did nothing. I now wonder if the accusations were a projection of her own life and whether she lost her own virginity at my age, convinced that I would do the same. Aunt Muriel, my mother's eldest sibling, regularly visited Graveton Sea School and dated the sea cadets. My mother told me she was fourteen when she accompanied her. She dated some of the sea cadets and said she felt ill when she kissed one who smoked cigarettes. Aunt Muriel never married, but had two children. The first child was Carmel, who was raised by my grandmother and the second female child was given to a childless couple. Muriel had rented a room at the Inn where she worked and was told by the landlord that there was no room there for her to raise a child. My mother was raised within a promiscuous household and she also accused me of this behaviour, but said that Waverley was her 'sweet pure virgin'. Waverley was a 'tomboy' who did not seem interested in boys her age unless she joined their football games. My parents believed this to be innocent fun.

For two years I told my parents I wanted to take the step of baptism within the Jehovah's Witness religion. My friend Josie was baptised at twelve which impressed the Brothers and Sisters. I continued to ask them and they eventually agreed when I reached the age of fourteen. I approached the elders about it and one visited my home each week to study their book for baptism candidates. They asked various questions to test my knowledge and were then satisfied I met their requirements. I was baptised in the month of November of 1976 at a district convention. I sat apart from my family in the second row with eleven other baptism candidates from various congregations in the district. We listened to the talk and towards the end, we were asked to stand and answer two questions: *Have you repented of your sins and dedicated yourself to Jehovah and accepted his way of salvation through Jesus Christ? Do you understand that your baptism identifies you as one of Jehovah's Witnesses in association with Jehovah's organisation?* Replying 'yes' to these answers is a public declaration the candidate has faith in the ransom sacrifice and unreservedly dedicates themselves to Jehovah.

I genuinely thought it was what I wanted to do with my life at the time, however there were still some unanswered questions that continued to bother me. The candidates were guided to a backstage room while brothers and sisters sang a Kingdom song. I changed into my swimming attire and draped a large towel around my shoulders as we were instructed to keep ourselves covered until we entered the pool. All candidates stood in line upon the stage awaiting their turn and I glanced around the hall, noticing a row of handsome young men sitting up on the balcony. Apparently the young men looked forward to the baptisms at conventions to see the sisters in their swimsuits! I could not swim at the time and was apprehensive of water. My mother was also unable to swim and told me she cried out of nervousness. When I entered the pool, my father, who was a volunteer attendant, walked down the side aisle towards the pool. Two Brothers stood either side of me, instructing me to hold my nose with one hand and place the other arm across my chest. I hardly had time to draw breath as they placed one hand on my back and the other on the arm in front of my chest and lowered me hastily into the water. It was over in a few seconds, but as I was not prepared, I swallowed some water and could not stop coughing as I emerged from the pool. My father later commented that all other candidates emerged from the pool with huge smiles and I was the only one coughing. It felt good to be congratulated by the brothers and sisters and I felt a change within but was also aware that more would be expected of me from that moment on. I hoped that taking this step would stop the accusations from my mother about things I had no intention of doing. A few handsome young Brothers from other congregations began to notice me. One of them, Ian, regularly pinched the buttocks of young Sisters as he passed by. He wore spectacles and his face was covered in freckles. Although he was a good looking young man, he was not as handsome as his older brother. I wrote to his older brother on one occasion, he did not respond, but had shown the letter to his cousins Tracy and Clark. I heard from Selene that Clark told her they all read it and 'had a good laugh' about it. I was embarrassed on hearing this and regretted sending it.

My parents hosted a few parties for Jehovah's Witness teenagers at our home. Waverley and I attended a few hosted by the parents of Selena and Sandra. Clark was an extremely handsome young man and many sisters from our congregation including me were attracted to him. Tracey and Clark attended dance classes with other middle-class teenagers who could afford to. They learnt the dance routines featured in the movie *Saturday Night Fever*. They all stood in line performing the moves at our parties and the rest of us watched them, but I was distracted by Clark. Tracey was dating Kyle an elder's son and they often sat together at the Kingdom Hall. Tracey was a good looking curvy young woman, and at school she spent her breaks and lunch hour in the company of male prefects who were a year older than her. One of them was particularly handsome and it was obvious she liked him. I sat in Tracey's classroom while students from both our classes attended a Christmas carol practice. I saw a heart drawn on her desk containing her initials and the initials of this prefect. She saw me looking at it and told me it was not her initials and she had not drawn it. I attended the summer school fete and I noticed Tracey walking to the far end of our school field with this male prefect. About ten minutes later, Kyle unexpectedly arrived and asked me if I knew where Tracey was. I pointed to the far end of the field and replied I saw her heading in that direction. It seemed he arrived to surprise her and had no knowledge of her association with the prefect. I did not intend to cover up for her, as I had not forgotten the time she went out of her way to tell my parents I had *Happy Birthday* sung to me in junior school. I did not feel responsible or guilty if Kyle caught her out. I heard their relationship ended soon after this.

Tracey was admitted to hospital for a tonsillectomy and seemed to recover well from it. When she attended her first religious meeting after returning from hospital, I saw her rinsing her mouth in the ladies bathroom. She told her mother her throat was haemorrhaging which meant she had to return to the hospital. Brenda was told by doctors that Tracey had lost a huge amount of blood and needed a transfusion, but her parents refused on religious grounds. Jehovah's Witnesses believe that the bible tells them to abstain from blood. Scriptures cited for this are: *Genesis 9:4, Leviticus 17:10, Deuteronomy 12:23, Acts 15:28.29.* They also cite the scripture *Leviticus 17:14* as saying God views blood as representing life. The medical staff tried to persuade Tracey when they could not get through to her parents and although she felt herself dying, she still refused. The medical staff administered a blood expander. Tracey's health improved and when she returned home, I accompanied my parents when they visited her. It took some time for her to regain strength but fortunately she survived this ordeal. I recall Brenda telling my mother that she fought her natural instincts when she knew her child was dying. She was tempted to agree to the blood transfusion, but knew that she would be disfellowshipped for doing so.

I stayed with Selena occasionally on weekends. Her parents were not as strict as mine, so I enjoyed being there. They allowed us to stay up late viewing old horror movies on television and I remember watching *The Day of the Triffids* when Selena's father, a comical man, crept behind the couch with a houseplant and rested it upon my shoulder. Selena offered me her single bed when we slept in her room and she had a camping bed set up beside it. Natural experimental courtships with teenage boys were forbidden and Selena suggested we practised on one another. I remember the roughness of her hands as she suffered with a skin condition in her younger years. I understand many teenagers experiment together in this way and although there was no harm in it, we were aware the elders would not agree. The situation with Selena was completely different to experiences with the abusive family member who was eleven years older than I.

Selena seemed obsessed with teenage boys and one afternoon we visited the local swimming pool. She wore a small yellow bikini and this received a lot of attention. Two teenage boys spoke to her in the pool while a friend of theirs sat in the spectators room above watching them. He had seen Selena and told his friends to speak to her. They were waiting outside as we left the swimming pool and she arranged to meet one of them that evening. I accompanied her when she met up with him but felt like a 'gooseberry'! At night we laid in bed discussing boys, emotions and quietly sang popular songs. I did not tell my parents anything that occurred while I stayed there, as they would have stopped my visits. Selena's mother thought my parents were far too strict, and I remember them having a disagreement over it. Her mother warned my parents that if they did not 'bend' one day they would 'break' and I would leave them. Selena began to write letters to Anthony, a teenage boy she met at one of the conventions from another congregation. Sandra was also writing to Anthony's friend and they informed me that Frank, another friend of theirs, would be interested in writing to me. This seemed to amuse them, so I suspected that Frank was not as handsome as the other two.

Selena, Sandra and I arranged to meet up at the next district convention at Twickenham football stadium in London. Selena pointed out a teenage boy sitting in the stands and said he was Frank. It surprised me to see he was handsome after all. I met him later that day while I was doing volunteer work taking a refreshment vending tray around the stadium. When the tray was empty I took it back to the department and walked with him for a while. I had volunteered at other conventions, preparing hundreds of pizzas by topping pastry bases with meat and vegetables in readiness for baking. It was more fun than sitting on hard stadium seats all day listening to the talks, plus I had time away from my parents watching my every move. Frank seemed to like me and I enjoyed his company. He offered to buy me an ice-cream but I declined, as my mother advised me not to accept anything from boys, as they would expect repayment in other ways. We eventually met Selena and Sandra who spoke to him and to my surprise called him Anthony! I then realised that when Selena pointed to Frank, I saw the wrong person, however they assumed I had intentionally gone for Anthony and they ignored me for quite a while. I eventually had an opportunity to explain, however in one way their plan of matchmaking me with a boy they considered 'ugly' had backfired. It was a few months before Selena let go of the grudge and believed my explanation. Anthony told me his family visited a local park in Maidstown on Sunday afternoons with other Jehovah's Witnesses in the area. I persuaded my father to take us there and although I enjoyed it, I decided not to pursue a relationship with him and lose two friends, despite the incidents that occurred. It took a few years for me to realise they were not.

Start here Cass

Linsey's sister Sarah invited us to her wedding. I thought Sarah the most attractive girl within their family, as she was reminiscent of the actress *Lindsay Wagner*. Sarah married a tall man whom I did not consider handsome, but she seemed happy with him. I began to choose clothes that I wanted to wear, and for the wedding reception I wore a red t-shirt with a 'key-hole' neckline and a long brown pencil skirt with brown stiletto shoes. My hair was bright blonde and collar length as my mother kept Waverley and I as blonde as possible. Since our childhood she would creep up behind us with left-over peroxide that she had applied to aunt Verity's hair with an old toothbrush. We protested when she ran the brush over our hair as the mixture smelt awful! Sarah's brothers liked Waverley because she was a happy, smiley child, but they were unkind to me. A few years had passed and at the wedding, they behaved differently towards me. One was serving drinks and when I approached the table, he said "What do you want to drink gorgeous?" There were many Jehovah's Witnesses in attendance that evening and other teenagers from Sarah's congregation. I assumed the event would be boring until a disc jockey arrived with his disco equipment and set up musical entertainment for the evening. One of the young men asked me to dance, so I accepted. Slow dances were often done at a respectful distance, where young men placed their hands on a girl's waist holding her at arm's length and the girl placed her hands upon his shoulders. The young man made polite conversation as we danced and introduced me to his friends who were dancing nearby. It was the first time my father had seen a young man ask me to dance and when I returned to the table, he would not look at me or speak for a while. At previous weddings I had danced only with him. On reflection I understand how difficult it must be for fathers when young men are attracted to their daughters, as they realise they will no longer be the only male in their daughter's lives.

On our return from the wedding, I put my red t-shirt in the laundry for washing and a few days later, I could not find it. I asked my mother about it and she replied she had discarded the t-shirt as she believed 'demons' were attached to it. I was so disappointed as it was my favourite item of clothing but said nothing. On reflection, my mother may have done this because of the male attention I received at the wedding. There were times that she brushed her hair standing in front of a mirror and reacted angrily, if she caught sight of me in the reflection telling me to keep my reflection out of the mirror when she used it My mother was terrified of growing old, but as children she assured us we would never grow old or die in the present system, as Armageddon would arrive long before then. As my mother aged her anger grew more frequent. She told me that when she was a young girl and her mother began to age, she had derogatory thoughts about her appearance. My mother assumed I would have the same thoughts about her, but this was untrue as I admired her. Yet again this was another case of projection.

There were a few young brothers interested in dating me and two of them were ten years older and friends of Kevin. Fred visited our home often and my mother wanted me to date him. He was not what I considered handsome despite her comments about his 'soulful eyes'.

Fred's laugh was embarrassing and reminiscent of the sound of a machine gun. I conversed with him hoping that his personality may outweigh the rest and he gifted me a newly purchased *Saturday Night Fever* album. Waverley and I loved it, but when I eventually decided to tell him I would not date him, he took his album back. Waverley was most upset, suggesting I should have dated him so that we could keep it! I purchased the album for her forty years later and she found this hilarious.

James had corresponded with Wilma by letter for three years after our exciting adventure in New York. Wilma's son Paris sadly passed away two years after our visit at the age of sixteen. We heard how he preached to hospital staff in his final days.

James surprised us all when he revealed that he proposed marriage to Wilma by letter and awaited a reply. He visited us a few days later with her letter of acceptance, telling us that Wilma planned to travel to England for their wedding and live here with him. We were all excited about the wedding and pleased for James.

A week before the event, Wilma arrived accompanied by Eleanor, her friend and her daughter Dana. We conversed about Paris and being an impulsive teenager I told her I would not marry and wait for the 'new system' to meet Paris again. Her expression conveyed she doubted this and rightly so, as I thought Armageddon was so close I would not have to wait for long. My parents invited Dana and Eleanor to stay at our home and they both slept in my double bed while I slept upon a couch in the lounge. Waverley and I took it in turn to sleep there as she enjoyed the adventure. Having two black American women in our home meant it was far from peaceful, as their laughter and loud voices seemed to carry for miles. I am sure our neighbours heard them. Dana and Eleanor were fascinated about us having a milkman who delivered milk in glass bottles from his three-wheel van. They awaited his arrival early one morning and stood outside the front door with their hair in curlers, fluffy slippers and brightly coloured dressing gowns. Eleanor and Dana captured photographic images of the van and posed with bottles of fresh milk on the front doorstep. They commented how clean England was compared to America.

Dana and Eleanor were glamorous women in brightly coloured clothes, shoes, hats and accessories that my mother admired. The night before James and Wilma's wedding I sat at the dining room table watching Dana manicure her nails. They were strong, long, natural nails, but unfortunately one broke, and she used a strong glue to reattach it, commenting she did not want a short nail on her ring finger for the wedding. Dana explained that women in America visit a beauty salon for weekly manicures. The beauty industry was popular out there, so I contemplated a career in beauty therapy that could be a lucrative career for the future, as most trends, fashions and interests in America appear in the U.K. We conversed about Paris and Dana told me that he liked me a lot and spoke about me for some time after we left. His family missed him, and I learnt more about this lovely young man that left us too soon.

The day of the wedding arrived and I asked Clark to collect me in his car. My parent's car was full as they were transporting Dana and Eleanor to the Kingdom Hall. I excitedly awaited Clark's arrival and wore a beautiful off-the-shoulder beige dress decorated with autumn leaves. Clark arrived in his convertible car with the top down as it was a warm sunny day. I enjoyed this journey sitting beside a very handsome young man in his expensive car. I often walked past his family's greengrocer shop around closing time and helped him clear the outside stall by carrying boxes of fruit inside. I tried to get to know him better, but he was a quiet person. I did not realise there was something he kept to himself that was not revealed for some time. The wedding was a wonderful occasion and it surprised me when James and Wilma stood upon the platform facing the audience to recite their vows. The bride and groom usually sat on a stool below the platform with their backs to the congregation. I assumed this was the American way weddings were conducted. A musical band formed by a few young brothers was booked for the evening entertainment at the reception. They got a little carried away and the older brothers and sisters thought the music too loud and 'worldly' so there were a few complaints. I tried to persuade Brett to dance, but he declined and replied he would rather watch me.

I copied the dancer's moves I had seen on television since the age of two and my ambition was to be a professional dancer. My mother had a friend who was in a well known chorus line and travelled overseas to perform. She had shown me photographs of her in the chorus line.

At the wedding my way of dancing was frowned upon. I remember one of Kevin's friends commented that I must have 'ball bearings' in my hips that allowed them to glide smoothly! The wedding was a success and it was an emotional day when Dana and Eleanor returned to America. It was however more emotional for them as Wilma stayed behind to begin her new life with James.

I enjoyed Saturday evenings at home when we socialised with relatives. Uncle Vernon, cousin Carmel and her family would visit us. My Aunts Mary and Jade occasionally joined us and my father set up his narrow decorating table for games of table tennis. Our aim needed to be accurate for the ball to land on this table and taught us to be skilled players. There were either card games, or the men played darts as there was a board permanently fixed to the wall of our kitchen/diner. I played vinyl records at our music centre and my mother and I sang songs and danced to music. Uncle Vernon and I walked to the local off-licence at the Inn to purchase bags of potato crisps and bottles of lemonade for our family. On a few occasions Vernon invited me to accompany him for a drink in the lounge bar before returning home. I sat there with my lemonade and conversed with him for a while. We were able to discuss many things without my parents eavesdropping, particularly on Vernon's thoughts and doubts about the religion. We were gone for a while one evening and my father arrived to see us emerging from the lounge bar. He was extremely angry and had a heated argument with Vernon as we walked home. My father accused him of encouraging me to visit public houses. Vernon replied that there was no harm in it, but we were forbidden to visit the off-licence shop again.

On our way home from the Kingdom Hall, we regularly passed an Inn in Graveton town and while waiting at the traffic lights we heard loud dance music and saw flashing 'disco' lights through the windows. It looked like a fun place to be, but my mother reminded me that they were evil places of drunkenness and debauchery.

As older children, Waverley and I were accustomed to preaching in the streets alone, as we had done so since the age of eight. I remember a man who was highly amused when he raised the subject of evolution, and I had a 'debate' well prepared on the subject. One Saturday afternoon we were preaching in our home town at a small block of apartments. Waverley volunteered to call at two apartments on the first floor while I visited two on the ground floor. I rang a doorbell and stood in position with Watchtower magazines in hand. The door slowly opened and I was shocked to see a man wearing a blue lace dress with bright blonde hair piled high on his head that was obviously a wig. He wore thick facial cosmetics and had painted nails. I also saw his painted toenails as his legs and feet were bare. This was the first time I had met a transvestite and I took two small steps backwards in surprise. I hastily offered him the magazines, he declined and I hurried away! I told Waverley about this and when we returned to the apartments, I sent her to call there. He opened the door wearing a women's long blue quilted dressing gown and declined the magazines again. We knew that my father hated the thought of any man wearing women's clothes or having homosexual tendencies as he told me it would make him physically sick. I wondered how he would have reacted if he had called on this person and doubted he could have coped if they wanted a bible study! The intriguing part of the preaching work was the unpredictability, as we never knew who we would meet or how people would react to us.

In the first week of June 1977, my father arranged a week's vacation in the Isle of Wight. I preferred Cornwall and was not excited about visiting this place. We had Bed and Breakfast accommodation in Ryde and arrived on a Saturday accompanied by Vivien while Brett and Rosie visited Bournemouth for their wedding anniversary. My parents discovered from the owner of the guest house that Ryde Kingdom Hall was near our accommodation and there was a meeting on Sunday morning. I asked my father if I could stay at the accommodation while they attended the meeting as I had no desire to get up early, but he insisted we were all attending as a family. The hall was quite small compared to ours and we had arrived late, but there was an empty row of seats near the front. Curious about local members of the congregation, I discreetly looked around me and in the back row, I noticed Roland, an extremely handsome young man who smiled at me. When the meeting ended and we socialised, Roland approached me to introduce himself. I explained that we were on a week's vacation, and he replied he was also visiting, staying with his friend Mark. Roland also mentioned that a group of brothers and sisters had arranged a barbecue on the beach that evening and invited me along. I replied that I would need to ask my father, so I offered to introduce them. As I tried to get my father's attention, I heard Roland commenting to Mark he was 'meeting 'the Dad''! My father wanted to attend the barbecue as a family and explained to Roland our accommodation was nearby. He volunteered to call on us later that afternoon and travel with us in our car to direct us to the beach. He seemed quite intense and I felt a little nervous, as he was seventeen, three years older than me.

There were 'butterflies' in my abdomen all afternoon and I tried not to think about it. Waverley kept watch at the window and alerted me when she saw him walking towards the house. Our landlady knocked on the door of our room with a huge smile, to tell me someone was asking for me. I descended the stairs and stopped half way when I saw Roland in the hallway. He wore a v-necked t-shirt, blue jeans and a black leather jacket that was in complete contrast to the suit he wore at the hall. I also noticed what he described as a silver shark's tooth hung from a black cord around his neck. I discovered years later that it is not a tooth, but a lucky horn protection charm! Our religious teachings would not approve of such things and I was surprised he got away with it. Roland had short, thick, black, wavy hair and a swarthy, mixed race complexion. He gazed up at me as I paused on the stairs and said "Wow!" I had not dressed to impress in a pink and white t-shirt, salmon pink flared trousers, and a pair of trainers, but I did have a beautiful figure and my clothes fitted well. I invited him up to our room as he continued to act 'in awe' of me. He entered our bedroom and spoke to Waverley as I continued to brush my hair. Roland then asked if he could borrow my hairbrush and as I passed it to him, he assured me that he had no fleas and added there may however be a few pink ones with yellow spots! He may have sensed my apprehension and tried to relax the atmosphere by adding a little humour. My parents were in the next room and when they were ready, we left the accommodation and walked to my father's car. He owned an impressive looking Zephyr with a long seat in the front to accommodate a third person. It was a stylish car for its time that I was pleased about when we transported Roland. He sat next to me in the back seat and I remained quiet as I could not think of anything to say, so we listened to the car radio. A tune entitled *Telephone Line* by the *Electric Light Orchestra* played and he asked me if I liked it and I replied with a nod. I felt shy and awkward as I had never been pursued so intensely by a young man.

We arrived at the beach where a large group of Jehovah's Witnesses had gathered. Roland knew many of them and introduced me to a group of attractive teenage girls that were around his age. They wore the latest fashions, heavy facial cosmetics and had long manicured nails. He revealed that one of them was a former girlfriend and I studied them as they sat in line upon a high wall. One of them spoke to me in a condescending tone: "So you are a 'schoolgirl'"! She asked questions about where I lived and commented to Roland he would need to do a lot of travelling. After he conversed with them for a while, one of the girls asked Roland to help her off the wall, claiming it was too high for her to jump down. He obliged, placing his hands on her waist, lifting her off the wall with ease. The other girls asked for help and as it seemed this would take a while, I left them to it and walked along the beach.

I wondered why he was attracted to me when the other girls he knew were stunning in appearance and nearer his age. I noticed however their conceited personalities required more beautifying than their appearances! Within a few minutes Roland caught up with me apologising for their behaviour and we sat on the beach for a while. He laid back on the sand and I laid on my front beside him supporting myself on my arms while sifting through the sand while he gazed up at me. My father had been searching for me and I heard him call my name. He instructed me to return to the group. I was surprised to meet Connie there who was an attractive girl from Kevin's congregation. I conversed with her and introduced her to Roland. My family then decided to leave as Vivien was feeling tired, but before we did so, my father invited Roland to spend the next day with us, as he would be returning home on Tuesday.

The day that I spent with Roland was warm, sunny and wonderful. He said he was eating his breakfast that morning and the song we heard together was on the radio. Roland said he stopped eating, put down his spoon and listened, thinking about me. Although I was unsure of him at first, my feelings changed after I succumbed to his charm. He removed a steel ring with a leaf pattern from his finger and gave it to me. In the evening my father transported Roland to Mark's family home. My parents conversed with Mark's parents in the dining room, while Roland and I sat together on the couch in the lounge and kissed for the first time. Other members of Mark's family were watching the movie

Born Free on television. I did not want to leave Roland as we had a wonderful day together and I knew it would be some time before I saw him again. He promised to write to me. I tried to distract myself from thinking about him for the rest of the week and one evening my father suggested we visit Shanklin Pier. We entered the entertainment hall and there was an organist on stage playing tunes. Some of the audience were on the dance floor and my father and I joined them. I volunteered to sing a song on the stage and asked my father to sing with me. He was not too keen but I persuaded him to join me while the organist played the tune. My parents would sing a duet to a song entitled *Sentimental Journey* and harmonised together. I had learnt to sing it this way. so my father and I performed the song together that evening. The organist presented me with ice-cream chocolates as a 'thank you' gift for singing. As we travelled home at the end of the week, I thought the vacation in the Isle of Wight had turned out to be more eventful than I expected!

A few days after our return, we visited Kevin who had heard all about Roland from Connie at one of their meetings. She apparently asked Kevin to warn me that Roland was a huge 'flirt'. I had no knowledge of what occurred after we left the beach barbecue and I wondered whether Connie saw him with the group of girls he knew, or he may have flirted with her. Roland lived in Southampton, and we regularly conversed by letter. He sent me photographs of himself and I took them to school to show my classmates. I had shown them to Selene and Sandra who apparently discussed us with others in the congregation as I heard that they were jealous and thought Roland was too good for me. At one time I hoped they were genuine friends, but as years passed I discovered how untrustworthy they were.

I checked the post regularly for letters from Roland and any letters sent or received were read by my parents. All teenagers in the religion were required to do the same. Roland wrote to me regularly for a while and then I heard nothing for a few weeks. I wrote again asking if something was wrong. One afternoon I returned from school feeling rather down and my mother asked me what was wrong. I replied it didn't matter and as I glanced at her sitting in the armchair, she was fanning herself with a letter from Roland. It amused her when my mood suddenly improved as I thought his feelings for me had changed, but he apologised for not writing and promised he would not do this again.

I arranged to meet Roland at the international convention held at Twickenham football stadium and wore a new dress for the occasion. I waited for him at the large iron gates between two formidable looking lion statues, but there was no sign of him. I was upset when he did not appear that day and I waited at the gates again the following day. Contrary to my doubts, he eventually arrived explaining the car had broken down during their journey so they did not arrive until late in the evening. We wandered around the stadium together and met Roland's former girlfriend and her friends. I was surprised to see her in tight jeans at a convention as women wearing trousers was not permitted at these events. She conversed with Roland while tossing an apple in her hand and I noticed her manicured long, scarlet fingernails. She invited us to accompany them on their walk and he asked me if I wanted to join them, but I shook my head. After observing their conversation, I wondered whether she and Roland had a sexual relationship while courting as it was obvious that she did not adhere to other religious rules. I felt too innocent and young to associate with their group especially after the last encounter. I discovered that Roland was ambitious and planned to have a career in the fire service but he also said he wanted to get married. He stated that he would like a daughter that he could bounce upon his knee. We both sat in the stands with my family to listen to the morning talks and in the lunch break, we walked to a nearby river and sat on the grass. That day was my fifteenth birthday and he asked if he could give me a birthday kiss. A sudden strong breeze then blew my skirt upwards and exposed my underwear. As I hastily pulled it down, Roland pointed to my underwear saying: "That's what I want!" He attempted to unbutton my blouse and when he saw that I was uncomfortable, he stopped. I thought he would realise I behaved differently to the other girls he knew, after all they were eighteen and I was fifteen, but maybe it was my innocence that attracted him.

The final day of the convention came to a close and Roland walked with me to the car park. We sat upon the grass beside my father's car until they arrived. He laid me back in his arms to give me a farewell kiss, but at that moment my father arrived. He angrily scolded Roland who apologised and then left us. The rest of my family appeared and as my father drove away, he told my mother how badly we had behaved in the presence of other Jehovah's Witnesses. He described it as a 'lovers kiss' but our generation called it a 'French kiss'. All the teenagers I knew were accustomed to kissing this way as a closed mouth kiss was viewed as 'old fashioned'. When my father calmed down, he commented that I must be better looking than he thought, as Roland was an extremely handsome young man. My mother told him not to worry about it and when we visited the petrol station, she turned to speak to me and saw that Roland had left a 'love bite' on my neck. She told me to hide it from my father by buttoning up my blouse and to wear a roll-neck top until the mark had gone. I did as she instructed but I did not think I had done anything wrong. Unbeknown to them, his affections could have gone much further if Roland had his way!

My father arranged another family holiday as we loved our yearly visits to Cornwall. I asked him if we could visit Roland and his family on the way. Although it would mean diverting from his usual route to Cornwall, he reluctantly agreed. I was surprised to find that Roland's home was a modest, basic three-bedroom house. He was delighted when he opened the door, saying it was like a dream to see me there. We took the opportunity to hug and kiss as it took a while for my parents to help Vivien out of the car. Roland was an extremely fit young man. When I was in arms, I enjoyed the feel of his toned back, muscular arms and the wonderful aroma of his aftershave. He explained that his mother was not at home and brewed tea for my parents. Roland wanted to introduce me to his grandmother who lived nearby, so we left my parents in the house and walked to her home accompanied by Waverley as chaperone. His grandmother was also out that day, so I did not meet his family on this visit.

A month later, Roland stayed at our family home for a weekend. He arrived in his Hillman Imp car with a blown exhaust. My father winced when he heard it. Roland charmed my mother who was convinced that he was attracted to her. He sat on my bed listening to my piano practice while Waverley turned cartwheels and displayed her gymnastic moves to receive some of his attention. She began training as a gymnast soon after she came out of her callipers and also won award badges for her abilities. Waverley appeared on the front page of the local newspaper because our Headmaster was impressed with her progress and thought it would make a good story. She was inspired by Olga Corbett and talked about becoming a famous gymnast.

Although Roland and I were physically affectionate we did not have a sexual relationship, although I suspected he had with former girlfriends. My mother had warned me that when a girl lets a young man go 'all the way' he will lose respect for her and will not marry her. She also said that, 'what a man wants today, he may not want tomorrow'.

We wrote to one another for a period of six months and my mother was surprised to receive a letter from his mother. It was an informal letter where she described her home as 'Clapham Junction' with so many youngsters coming and going to visit Roland and his brother. She then described my relationship with Roland as more of a friendship and we wondered why she had written this. On reflection, he may have wanted to end the relationship and his mother was 'paving the way'. Roland told me their district religious convention was on the first weekend of December 1977. It was the same venue we used in Surrey where I was baptised the previous year. I asked my father if we could attend on Sunday to surprise him, so we travelled by train and arrived for the afternoon session. I visited the ladies' bathroom to freshen up before entering the hall and a few minutes later, my mother joined me. She explained that they entered the main hall and immediately saw Roland standing at the back, as he was one of the attendants. He was apparently shocked to see them and my mother said he did not smile. A young woman stood beside him (I later discovered they were holding hands) and he whispered something to her before she walked away. I followed my mother into the hall and stood beside them quietly. Roland guided us to a row of empty seats, and we listened to the afternoon talks but my mind was elsewhere. When the afternoon sessions were over, we socialised and I met Roland's mother and I discovered his parents were no longer in a relationship. Roland boasted his father had won the Mr South Africa muscle-man competition and also competed for Mr Universe. I assumed from this information that his father was not a Jehovah's Witness. We walked out of the hall together and stood in the rear car park behind the building. Roland spoke to me between gulps of milk from a bottle that he had no good news for me. The only news he did have was that he had been accepted into the fire service and no longer wanted to get married. He assured me he was not dating anyone else, but his words were cold, matter-of-fact and difficult to hear. Roland promised me that if he changed his mind about marriage, he would contact me again. We returned to the front of the hall and joined his friends. At that moment a fire engine sped past with flashing lights, wailing sirens and they all cheered. I looked at the flashing lights that were blurred from the tears in my eyes. I cried most of the way home on the train and my mother asked me to stop as it was upsetting my father who sat there looking at the floor. I sat beside him and clung to his arm for comfort. This was the first time I had experienced heartbreak.

My opinion of young men within the Jehovah's Witnesses changed after the experience with Roland. These young men were not as clean, wholesome and trustworthy as my mother described them. It also affected the way I felt about this religion. At my baptism a year ago I thought that being a member of the Jehovah's Witnesses was what I wanted and tried to put aside past experiences, but Roland's behaviour had caused me to reconsider. It took a long time for me to get over it as I believed I loved him. I stayed in contact with his friend Mark from the Isle of Wight and confided in him about the situation and he sympathised. Mark visited our home and stayed at weekends. My mother liked him, but although I did not find him physically attractive, his friendship made me feel that I had a connection to Roland.

The relationship with my mother became more difficult, as my rebellious attitude increased after losing Roland. She had on occasions used foul language calling me awful names, but still she would repeatedly quote the scripture from Ephesians 4:29 "Let not a rotten word come out of your mouth but only what is good for building up as the need may be…" I remember my mother using the word "foul" in place of "rotten". My mother said that my grandmother often cursed in the past and she was raised hearing it, but apparently hated it. I rarely cursed in my childhood, adolescence and adulthood. At times my mother suddenly attacked me in anger by hitting me, pulling my hair and venting her frustration. She threatened to have me committed to a mental hospital and related stories of how 'mad women' would menstruate on the floor and masturbate in front of you with hairbrush handles. The thought of this terrified me and I pleaded with her not to send me there. I contemplated running away from home but had nowhere to go and no one to talk to. My relatives had believed for years that I was a liar. On reflection, any of my family members could do exactly what they wanted, as they had ensured that no one would believe me.

Younger members of the congregation were advised to discuss their problems with mature brothers and sisters as they would receive wise advice. Stania, a German sister in our congregation, was kind, approachable and easy to talk to. I confided in her about my upsetting experience with Roland and she advised me to have many boyfriends, then if the relationship ended with one, I would still have others. This made sense, so I decided to take her advice.

I attended a party hosted by someone in our congregation where a band of brothers played lively music. I kicked off my shoes to dance. A young blonde brother arrived who Selena and I both found attractive. He conversed with me for a while and said he was going outside for a while as it was a warm summer evening. I decided to join him and after finding my shoes, placed each foot in turn on a chair to fasten them. Kevin saw me and demanded to know where I was going. I replied that I was going outside and walked away. He came out to check on me a while later and found me in an embrace with this young man which angered him. I ignored him as he was the last person I would take advice from about my behaviour!

The following summer, I attended the International Jehovah's Witness convention at Twickenham football stadium. I decided to wear clothes that were more like the girls Roland associated with. I hoped that if I met him again, he may change his mind about dating me. As I walked around the stadium, I met a few young men that I knew from other congregations. I conversed and walked around with them for a while. I met Roland's younger brother Derren who had ended his relationship with his girlfriend. He looked like his brother, so I decided to spend time with him. We walked around the stadium together and sat in the stalls listening to some of the talks. During the lunch break we visited the river where Roland took me the previous year. Derren was quick to become physically affectionate and as we kissed, he put his hand inside my blouse. I did not stop him at first, but then became emotional and explained I could not continue because of my feelings for Roland. Derren understood and promised he would speak to him about it.

I did not meet Roland until the next day. I called out to him as I ran to him to greet him with a hug. He said that he loved this welcome when he visited my home, but on this occasion he was embarrassed. I asked if he had seen Mark or his brother Derren who both promised to speak to him, but he had not. Roland said he had a new girlfriend, so I removed the ring he gave me and returned it suggesting he gave it to her. He replied that he could do better than that and had plans to purchase an expensive engagement ring for her. Roland then asked if I was dating Mark as he had seen us together. He did not believe me when I denied it as he saw us embracing while he consoled me. He described Mark as ugly and asked why I would be interested in him. I replied that a young man's personality was more important than his looks, as I had recently learnt that some good looking men can have hideous personalities. He had no answer for this and I walked away from him as my tears fell. Mark was on attendant duty nearby, so I went to find him. The weekend was an eventful one but also heartbreaking.

Soon after the convention, the committee of elders from our congregation sent my father a letter. He read it out to us. They stated that they disapproved of my attire, make-up, and flirtatious spirit at the last convention. My father was summoned to the Kingdom Hall library over this, describing it as being 'dragged over the coals' again. I explained to my parents that I spoke to many young men at the convention after taking the advice of Stania, an older person in the congregation. My father was upset about this as he had longed to become an elder for years, but to qualify, he had to have his wife and children under total control. We were a strong-willed family, so this was unlikely to happen.

My father was obsessed with how he appeared to others and he once advised us to stay in the religion even if we did not believe in it as it would make our family look good.

Mark and I stayed in contact and although he was attracted to me, it was not reciprocated. My parents approved of him and after my traumatic experience with Roland, I decided that looks may not be important and agreed to date him. I tried to concentrate on his good points, he had beautiful hands, dressed well and was liked by many because of his outgoing personality. Mark was eager for physical affection on his visits and when he discovered Waverley accepted bribery, he offered her money to leave us on our own. I did not stop some of his advances that crossed boundaries as I had with other boyfriends, but later regretted this as I still found him unattractive. I arranged for us to go out more to avoid us being alone.

We visited an elderly couple who were having bible studies with my parents. They were lovely, particularly the elderly man who wanted us to call him 'grandad'. It felt good to be with kind, loveable people. They were heavy smokers and the woman rolled a cigarette in our presence. Watching this process fascinated me and I asked her what they were like to smoke. She offered me a 'puff' when Mark was outside with the elderly man, so I tried and quickly returned the cigarette to her before they returned. Mark noticed a piece of tobacco on my lip and reached over to remove it. I knew he was upset and on our return home, Mark read passages of the bible to me and I cried. He instructed me to tell my parents when they returned, stating that he would tell them if I did not. I had no choice but to confess and they were not pleased. My mother suggested that Mark put me over his knee and spank me to keep me under control. He seized the opportunity and pulled me over his knee and she laughed. From that moment on I no longer wanted to date him and waited until he returned home before I broke the news on our next phone conversation. On reflection, he had been more than willing to engage in sexual activity and kept this from my parents, but made such a huge fuss over a puff of a cigarette! Mark did not take the news well, replying that he refused to accept it. He called our neighbours telephone on many occasions asking to speak to me, but I let my mother take his calls. I also heard from some of the local children who played outside the nearby telephone kiosk that Mark would call asking for me, but after many unsuccessful attempts he ceased trying.

Some of the girls from school who were my age, visited Graveton town in the evenings. Anthea, the school caretaker's daughter, invited me to join them and the only way I could do this was when Anthea asked my parents if she could have a bible study with me. They were delighted and allowed me to visit her one evening a week. I left home with my religious books and Anthea waited at the end of the road. I hid my books behind a wall knowing it unlikely anyone would take them, and we boarded a bus into Graveton town. I thoroughly enjoyed walking through empty streets in the town at night singing the songs of *Abba* with my friend at the top of our voices. We met a few other girls in town and walked along dimly lit roads near the docks until we reached Graveton sea school. I thought about the times my aunts and my mother walked these streets at my age. My friends waited for the sea cadets to come out for the evening and we accompanied a few of them around the town. They were handsome in their uniforms and they knew it! I could see why local girls were attracted to them. Max, one of the cadets had the nickname of *Fonzie,* a television character that was a charmer and popular with girls. I met him again in town one Saturday afternoon while shopping and we had a long conversation. He took one look at me and made a correct estimation of my chest measurement. Anthea had met one of the cadets regularly who was tall and a little overweight but she liked his personality. I arranged to meet Max alone in the town and on one occasion I slipped out of a religious meeting to meet him, but tried to persuade him to return with me. He walked with me to the Kingdom Hall and I asked him to wait outside while fetching my father to introduce them. When we returned Max had disappeared and hidden behind the building. My father searched for him there, but he emerged from the other side and told Waverley he could not go through with it before running away. On reflection I do not blame him as although I was used to our religion, I did not at the time realise how frightening it could appear to those on the outside!

Anthea and the other girls attended discotheques organised by the sea school where local girls were invited to join them. I knew that I could not stay out long enough to attend these and Anthea hinted that Max was very popular with the girls on these evenings. I managed to get out one evening with Anthea and her friends when they visited the town. Max did not expect me and I decided to surprise him. On our way to the sea school, we met Max walking with a group of cadets and a few girls. I asked if he wanted to leave them and join us, noticing that he held an umbrella that belonged to another girl he arranged to meet that evening. He stood there not knowing what to do and I walked away. My friends called him unrepeatable names and I decided not to meet him again. Max asked my friends to pass on his apology. I was pleased that I still had boundaries where physical affection was concerned and did not let him use me. The interactions I had with young men seemed to have a repeating cycle and I concluded young men within the religion behaved no differently to those outside of it!

I left school at the age of fifteen being one of the youngest in my school year. I worked hard throughout my education and was placed in high achievement classes throughout my schooling. By the tenth year, I discovered my parents would not agree to me attending a' higher achievement school' let alone college or university. I lost any enthusiasm for schoolwork and paid less attention during my lessons and associated more with disruptive classmates. I no longer preached to them and developed better friendships as a result. The teachers eventually moved me to the back row of the class and I did minimal revision for examinations. I passed them but did not achieve top grades. I remember the day I walked out of the school gates never to return, tossing my pencil case in the air and my school friends were also delighted to leave. It felt odd from that day on when I saw children walking to and from school, as I thought I should still be there after all those years of attending.

CHAPTER 5

WORLD OF EMPLOYMENT

It was time for me to enter the world of employment. I signed on with the unemployment agency and had the expected conversation with my parents who encouraged me to find part-time work and be a pioneer within the Jehovah's Witnesses. To be a pioneer, a person is required to preach for ninety hours a month (at least three hours a day)! Rosie was constantly praised by the brothers and sister for pioneering full time throughout her teenage years and continued after her marriage. I did not enjoy the preaching work, so the thought of doing three hours each day did not enthral me! The conversation with my parents included other aspects of their religion, and I once again asked questions with no satisfactory answers.

One afternoon I accompanied Rosie on the preaching work. We called on a lady in my home town who claimed she was put off our religion years ago because a woman called at her home every day. The woman apparently repeated that the world could end at any moment and she would die if she did not join her religion. She described the woman having long dark hair, wearing bright yellow tights and red shoes. I explained that the person she described could have been my mother who had mental health problems. I added that she was on medication that affected her behaviour.

My parents decided they could no longer cope with my bible studies and questions, so they arranged for Brett and Rosie to conduct a weekly one with me. I did not mind, as it meant I spent more time with Brett. On the evenings I visited his home, he would tease and 'play fight' with me. Rosie would scold him over this. She provided an evening meal before the bible study and while she prepared it, I laid on the carpet watching television. I enjoyed the television series *Man from Atlantis* and while I was deeply involved in an episode, I felt a sudden hard smack on my posterior and turned to see Brett standing over me. On another occasion while we were 'play-fighting' he teased me and I attempted to hit him with a rolled newspaper. Brett took it from me and pulled me towards him, pressing my body to his. He asked me what I was going to do as I could not get away, but he released me before Rosie caught him. Brett's 'nick-name' for me was 'trouble'. I was quite an 'ugly duckling' at thirteen and he took no notice of me, but at fifteen I 'blossomed' and Brett paid me more attention. I appreciated looking prettier and one evening before our bible study, Brett and Rosie moved me from the couch to an armchair. Apparently, Rosie saw me glancing into the opposite mirror too often and brought it to Brett's attention. I mentioned this to my parents and Brett explained they had moved me to another seat as I was more concerned with my looks than the bible study. The bible study ceased shortly after that and I cannot remember why they stopped and whether it was their choice or mine.

The elders were concerned about the change in my appearance. As my body changed, my blouses were tighter around the chest area and at times the buttons popped out. One of the elders asked me not to stand so close to him when we conversed, as his wife had noticed this and brought it to his attention. I was unaware of this.

In the summer of 1978, Anthea asked if Waverley and I wanted to earn some pocket money helping out Trent, a friend of hers. He delivered soft drinks in the neighbourhood. Waverley was eager about this as she usually ran errands for elderly neighbours. She returned their empty drinks bottles to shops and they gave her the money. Waverley saved many coins that she stored in a large jar. Each day she tipped the contents onto the dining room table and counted it. My parents described her as an industrious and hard working daughter.

I recently researched information on family dynamics and discovered some parents will observe all their children. It is often the one who is hardworking and good at earning money who is given the family role of the 'golden child'. This child would most likely care and provide for them in the future when they are elderly. When the child reaches adulthood, it is then 'pay-back time'. The parents expect to be cared for in return for the golden child having this favoured position within the family. I acknowledge this does not apply to all families but in my experience there is a lot of truth in this.

Waverley, Anthea and I awaited the arrival of Trent's truck. Jocelyn, his wife, joined us with their baby seated in a buggy. When Trent arrived, Anthea climbed into the front seat beside him and as we joined her, she introduced us. He leant out of his open window to converse with Jocelyn and talk to his baby before we set off. The deliveries were fun. Trent and the young man he worked with joked together about the attractive housewives they called on to collect their bottles. It was a sunny afternoon and while we were on the drinks round, Trent flirted with me. He was twenty four, eight years older than I. I reminded him he was married and Trent replied that he and Jocelyn were separated and planning a divorce. I asked Anthea if this was true and she confirmed it was. I liked Trent, so we arranged to meet when he finished his rounds in other areas. My parents were unaware of this assuming that I was out looking for work. My father detested people who were unemployed and would not let any of us sleep in late except for our mother. He would enter my room and pull the blankets off me to wake me if he was home. I awoke early each morning and if he thought I had not done sufficient housework, he would refer to me as 'bone-idle'. I helped with some of the chores at home but did not make a huge effort, as Waverley was considered the most industrious one in their eyes.

Our local dentist Mr Ahellen advertised for a Dental Nurse at his practice. I had appointments at the surgery for as long as I can remember and although some of my childhood experiences were horrific, I was fascinated by dentistry and applied for the position. My interview was successful and I began working there the following week. It did not take long for me to learn the procedures and I discovered how hard a dental nurse's work is. Betina the receptionist explained what it was like to work within the surgery. She said I would need to be one step ahead of the surgeon at all times. All tools had to be sterilised, surfaces cleaned, appointment cards for the day laid out and details of all treatments ready in advance. All impressions taken for new dentures were bagged, labelled and taken to the dental technician upstairs and completed dentures collected. Betina also advised me that I would need to adapt to the surgeon's moods, as he may be abrupt when in a foul mood, but not to take it personally.

Each morning I had a thirty minute walk from home to the surgery and for the rest of the day I was either standing or moving around at speed. My first three days went well and I worked extremely hard, but on Thursday we worked a half-day. When we prepared for our last patient before lunch, I leant over the desk to write in the appointment book. Mr Ahellen tapped my posterior with a patient's card commenting we had one more patient and we were finished for the day. When the last patient left, Mr Ahellen left the room to visit the dental technician and I cleaned all surfaces and placed used tools in the steriliser. Betina finished clearing her reception desk and said goodbye before leaving. The dental surgeon on the first floor did not work on Thursday, and when the technician left I had an uncomfortable feeling that we were both alone in the building. Mr Ahellen entered the surgery and asked if Betina had gone home and when I replied she had, he commented that we were alone. He approached me and touched me inappropriately asking whether a Jehovah's Witness would object to this. He then repeated this on another area of my body. I objected and told him we would not tolerate this behaviour, he stood behind me and momentarily rubbed his body against mine. He stepped away and apologised, assuring me in an off-hand manner he would not repeat it. Mr Ahellen commented that I would learn this behaviour is part of life within the workplace. He mentioned the *Carry-On* movies, saying that those scenarios are reality! I left the surgery stunned, that a man who I received treatments from since the age of six would act this way towards me.

When I arrived home, Rosie was visiting my mother and I tearfully told them that Mr Ahellen was attracted to me. They were amused by this as they assumed they knew him well and commented I was reading too much into the situation. When Rosie left, I told my mother exactly what happened and it shocked her. When I returned to work the next day, there was a distinct atmosphere and I found myself backing away from him whenever he came near me.

At lunchtime, Trent was waiting outside in his truck. I joined him and explained what had occurred the day before and he angrily punched the dashboard when he saw him leave the surgery. After the uncomfortable atmosphere that morning, I decided not to return. My mother visited the surgery two days later to collect my wages and informed him I would not be returning. She commented on his behaviour and suggested that he employed a nurse who was not so attractive. Mr Ahellen did not deny it, but attempted to divert her attention by telling her he saw me get into a truck with a man. An older sister of one of my classmates revealed she once worked for Mr Ahellen and he behaved the same way towards her but she did not take it seriously. I could not understand how women were expected to tolerate this behaviour and I was relieved to be out of the situation.

I wanted to find another work placement quickly so that I could spend less time at home. The atmosphere was fraught with disagreements and aggressive frustration directed at me from my mother. I enjoyed spending time with Trent and confided in him about the situation at home. We arranged to meet one afternoon and I sat at the junction of a main road leading out of our small town, awaiting his arrival. I had a few carrier bags with me containing some of my clothes as I decided not to return home as I could take no more. I wrote a letter to my father explaining it would be better for him if I left home, as the elders were constantly harassing him about me. I thought if I was no longer there, they would have no reason to do so. I did not feel wanted at home, nor did I expect my parents to search for me as I was viewed as the 'black sheep' as I was strong-willed and outspoken. I asked Waverley to give the letter to my parents around nine that evening which gave me time to get away. As I waited at the junction for Trent, Olivia passed me in her Volkswagen camper van and stopped to offer me transport which I declined. It was two hours before he eventually arrived in his green Cortina and I explained that I did not want to return home. I could tell from his expression he was concerned about this and thoughtful as he slowly placed my bags into his car. He transported me to his local town where he arranged to meet a friend at an Inn. Trent informed him I had left home and his friend replied that my father would be after him, but I told them he would not search for me. Trent inquired about a vacant apartment and his friend then decided that he too would move in with us. This concerned me as I did not know him. We were shown an apartment by a man who owned an Indian restaurant and although it was grubby, the price was reasonable. We then visited a couple who lived in a terraced house with a small child as they were friends of his. Trent explained the situation and they invited us to stay with them that night, offering us their lounge floor to sleep on. I was extremely stressed and although he tried to be affectionate with me, I was too tense for any amorous activity. The floor was hard to sleep on but I was far too worried to sleep.

Trent had his deliveries to do the next day and after picking up his truck, I accompanied him on his rounds. He collected his assistant and when we travelled along a main road to the next town, I saw two police cars following us and speaking on their radios. They followed for a while, but did not stop the truck. Trent finished work early that evening and left me at his friend's house while he returned his truck to the depot. He was about to get into his car and discovered all his tyres were flat. My father stood by it and they conversed for a while until Trent's boss arrived angrily instructing my father to re-inflate the car tyres. Trent returned to the house looking pale and told me my parents were on their way. I panicked, terrified of their reaction and they soon appeared at the door looking pale and drained. Trent told me I had to return home and as I got into the car he approached the rear window and held my hand. My mother ordered me to let go of his hand saying that he was not my boyfriend. On the way home, they told me he still lived with his wife and they were not separated after all. I had confided in Anthea telling her where Trent and I were and my parents questioned her. She did not immediately reveal the information to them until they warned her if anything happened to me, she would be responsible. Anthea went away to think about it and returned to tell them my whereabouts. Jocelyn had also visited my parents and gave them negative information about Trent. They explained that she told them he would get me pregnant, not care about it and then leave me. On my return home, I went straight to my bedroom and cried myself to sleep from exhaustion.

The following day, Jocelyn visited my parents again. She was a tiny woman with a hard facial expression, extremely bushy eyebrows and rotting teeth. Jocelyn thought I returned voluntarily. She asked me if I had finally 'seen sense' when I walked into the room. My mother replied that I had not as they found me and brought me home. Jocelyn said she had apparently been to prison for grievous bodily harm and threatened me by telling me to stay away from Trent or she would put me in hospital. I was relieved to be home, as I felt less secure about living with Trent and I had no desire to see him again.

My parents were summoned by the body of elders to bring me to the Kingdom Hall for a judicial committee meeting. They interrogated me about leaving home, but rather than ask about the reason I left, they were more interested in what happened during my overnight stay with Trent. I explained that I was stressed and even if there had been an attempt at sexual intercourse it would not have been successful. The elders debated that if a man tried, penetration would be inevitable and I replied this was not true. My father was extremely uncomfortable hearing this conversation about his daughter. One of the elders looked straight into my eyes and asked if I was still a virgin. I returned his stare and replied that I was. They seemed to accept my answer and went on to discuss the letter I wrote to my parents. In the letter I explained how bad I felt for my father when they constantly criticised the behaviour of my family and held him responsible. I thought if I were no longer there it would be one less reason for them to pick on him. As I was the 'black sheep' in their eyes, I thought no one would care if I disappeared. My mother and I were sent out of the room, and I watched through the glass partition between the main hall and smaller room as they once again 'raked him across the coals'. I guessed that I would receive another 'public reprove' announced to the congregation, but there would be no difference in the congregation's behaviour towards me, as they were still distant since I had the last reprove three years ago.

The next day, I awoke confused about what to do next and how it would all turn out. My mother ignored me in the morning, however by late afternoon when we were alone, I sat quietly in the lounge deep in thought. I heard a sudden scream as my mother launched herself at me. She punched me, grabbed two handfuls of my hair and shook me by it. I broke free and ran out of the house towards the corner shop and saw Trent emerging from his truck. He saw that I was upset and walked towards me. I ran into his arms sobbing as he was the only one who understood. Trent suggested I sat in his truck for a while and noticed clumps of hair falling into my lap. I explained to him what had happened. A friend of Anthea's family, who was a well-known gossip, walked past the truck and saw me with him. She immediately reported this to Anthea's family and said I was still seeing him. I stayed with Trent for a while until I calmed down and returned home where my mother continued to ignore me. As my father was at work and Waverley was rarely home, they did not witness all of my mother's rages or her treatment of me. The next day I stayed in my room practising on the piano and it shocked me when Jocelyn walked in. Her voice trembled with anger as she said she heard I had seen Trent again. Jocelyn placed her shaking fist under my chin and threatened to put me in hospital if I saw him again. I tried to explain it was not how it appeared and I had not planned to see him that day but was unsure whether she believed me. Jocelyn visited my home weekly and on one occasion she arrived in a maternity smock, informing us she was pregnant again. She was too big in the abdomen for someone who had just discovered this, as she wore her tight jeans the week before. Two weeks later she returned to her usual clothes saying she had miscarried. Jocelyn said that Trent disliked me and referred to me as 'cow-face' which I did not believe. As she continued, I 'zoned out' as I was no longer interested in their lives.

My parents welcomed her visits knowing she had threatened me, but on reflection, if my own mother could act violently towards me, then why would it have bothered her! My parents preached to her hoping she would stop visiting but that did not stop her. The visits continued for a year until the day she arrived and discovered I had married and no longer lived there. After hearing this, they did not see her again.

The unemployment agency provided work experience schemes where a young person could work with a company for six months for a minimum wage of twenty-five pounds per week. It provided employees with experience and an advantage when seeking a permanent position in the future. My first work experience placement was with a laundry company on the outskirts of Graveton. I worked in the accounts office on the upper floor and received tuition on how to add up price tickets using an adding machine. I then wrote the total on a large accounts sheet. There were six adults in the office, all over forty years of age who 'chain smoked'. When I returned home each day, my clothes and hair stank of cigarettes and my mother commented on this. She provided a packed lunch for me each day and on one occasion when I took out the lunch box, written on the lid in a pink felt-tip pen, were the words 'Mummy loves you. Xxx'. My co-workers noticed this and thought it was sweet, as they assumed I had a devoted and loving mother. I explained to my colleagues I could not participate in their Christmas celebrations and felt awkward when I heard them discussing a celebration dinner, and cards were exchanged amongst them. I occasionally helped out on the reception desk switchboard where a large jolly lady taught me how to operate it. I enjoyed being with her. She warned me to be extra careful when the Directors were engaged in telephone conversations as it was easy to deactivate the wrong switch and cut them off. She had done it herself and they were not impressed! I enjoyed my time in reception more than the office, as I was out of the smoky atmosphere and met different people delivering and collecting laundry. The women in the office there were not a happy group, they seemed quite depressed most of the time and discussed their problems. I worked there for two months until they informed me just before Christmas that there were mistakes on the accounts and they assumed they were mine. I was a little upset about being asked to leave, but also relieved I was no longer working in a smoky, grim office.

My second work experience placement was as a sales assistant for a toy shop in the town of Graveton. Joyce the owner was a middle aged woman who interviewed me and thought I would fit in well. She instructed me to arrive at the shop on Monday morning and wait outside for Suzanna, the assistant manager who would unlock the doors. I arrived at nine that morning and waited outside watching shop owners unlock their doors and prepare their stock. A wonderful aroma came from the baker's shop opposite as they baked bread and cakes to sell that day. I then heard loud music coming from a green Ford Cortina that sped along the road and stopped beside me. Suzanna kissed Glen, her fiance and emerged from the passenger seat. She was a slim, pretty girl, of nineteen years of age, with bright blue eyes and long, wavy, honey-blonde hair. Suzanna was very friendly, chatting away as she guided me around the shop explaining the morning routine. There was a baby section on the upper floor selling perambulators and pushchairs delivered in huge boxes for us to assemble. On the ground floor there were many *Matchbox* toy cars on shelves that collected dust quickly and required regular cleaning. The cash till was not difficult to operate, so I found this work a better experience than my last placement. Gail the manager arrived and Suzanna introduced us. She was a small, friendly woman with short brown hair who told me she was getting married in a few weeks time and invited me to her wedding reception.

On my return home, I told my parents about my first day and mentioned the wedding invite. My father replied that I could not go, as it would be full of 'worldly' people and this disappointed me. My Uncle Vernon visited us at the weekend and asked me about my new job. I replied that I got on well with the staff and mentioned the invite to Gail's wedding that I would not be attending. Vernon asked why and I did not reply, but my father had been eavesdropping, so he suddenly appeared telling Vernon he would not allow it. The conversation escalated and they had a disagreement as Vernon did not feel this was right.

I met many customers while working in the toy shop and a young man asked me to show him the baby toys on the upper floor as he wanted to buy a present for his niece. I did so, and after a while, he admitted he used this as an excuse to speak to me and ask me out on a date. I declined the offer. I then met Leonard, an outrageously dressed punk-rocker who worked in a hairdressing salon next to the shop. He introduced himself and invited me back to his home for lunch. Leonard lived with his mother in a large period property that had a circular turret room where he stored his drum kit and practised with his band. He introduced me to his mother and I immediately noticed her piercing but friendly blue eyes that were rather bloodshot. I sensed a different energy from her and within the house. I commented on this and Leonard told me his mother was clairvoyant, and the house was haunted. He related an experience he had when visiting their kitchen during the night when he saw a spirit apparition that hastily disappeared. This did not frighten me as I was rather intrigued. Leonard was outspoken and asked if I would have sex with him. I replied that I wanted to wait until I was married, surprised that he would ask me so soon after we met. I did not feel comfortable with him after this and did not visit his home again.

On reflection however, I wished I had spent time conversing with his mother as I could have asked her many questions.

Another young man entered the shop one afternoon to speak to me. He pointed to the small cafe opposite and told me his Indian friend Matt liked me and wanted to know if I would go on a date with him. He seemed nice and I went out in his car a few times with him and his friends when I visited Graveton on my days off. It was fun to travel to different places with them like other teenagers. One afternoon, Matt entered the shop to inform me in the presence of the staff, that his parents had arranged a marriage for him. He had known about this for some time and his betrothed was due to arrive in the U.K. for the wedding ceremony. Matt explained he could not see me for a while but would let me know when he wanted me again. I should have expected this as I knew about Indian culture and arranged marriages. I thought it rather arrogant of him, as did my colleagues, to think that I would still be waiting, let alone continue to see him after his marriage!

Brett was a sales assistant for a furniture and carpet shop just around the corner from the toy shop. He offered to transport me home at the end of each working day to save me money on train fares. I accepted his offer and during our journeys home, Brett made sexual advances as I had transformed into what he described as a 'very attractive young lady'. Brett boasted about his former life dating 'bunny girls' and women who were very beautiful. The 'crush' I had on him from the age of twelve had not completely disappeared and as he 'turned on the charm' I did not object. As we spent more time together on our journeys home, his conversation became more explicit, describing in detail his fantasy of a sexual relationship between us. He openly spoke about his marital relations with Rosie, describing her as a passionate lover, adding that he thought I would have the 'edge' on her. Brett would leave the passenger door of his car unlocked, suggesting that I walked there alone after work so no one saw us together. I sat in the car waiting until he arrived. This was a regular occurrence but on one occasion, Rosie travelled to Graveton by bus to surprise him and they arrived at the car together. I was shocked to see her and she smiled at me, but it was obvious she was puzzled. I got out of the car and offered her the front passenger seat and I moved to the back seat. There was silence on the way home until Rosie asked me if I lost my train ticket. I did not know how to reply, as I then realised she did not know he transported me home each day. Brett uttered an uncomfortable "no" and there was another awkward silence. I offered Rosie one of my *Polo* mints to change the atmosphere and she replied with an abrupt "No thank you".

Brett later suggested I returned to travelling on the train, but one afternoon Brett and Rosie passed the toy shop as we were closing. She opened the door and said "If you would like a lift home today, you can have one as *I'm* with him!" My colleagues were aghast at the way she spoke, as it was far from friendly but I accepted the offer anyway. Brett and Rosie later planned a vacation for the first two weeks of June to include their wedding anniversary. I occasionally visited the shop where Brett worked on my lunch break, and he said he would miss seeing me during his two week vacation. I knew I would miss him too, however something occurred within those two weeks that changed my life.

The toy shop I worked in had a glass front that enabled me to observe people who passed by. I saw Marl walk past the shop each day who was a good-looking young man of mixed race, half British and half Filipino. He dressed like the television character *Fonzie* in the American series *Happy Days* and strode confidently arm in arm with his extremely attractive girlfriend. I sensed he could be a troublesome type.

On Monday, the fourth day of June, the toy shop was quiet. I noticed Marl sitting at the back of a small café on the opposite side of the road. He conversed with another young man who had a swarthy complexion that I later discovered was Kirk, Marl's older brother. A young white male named Dan wearing a leather jacket sat with them. There was something about his body language that I liked and when he glanced my way I winked at him. He returned the wink, while conversing and laughing with his friends. Marl and Dan left the cafe and entered the toy shop to speak to me. Dan thought that I would be interested in Marl as he was better looking and many girls liked him. I replied that he didn't interest me, which shocked Marl and amused Dan. I discovered Dan had the day off work to attend a dental appointment. A week before this meeting, Waverley and I attended the Woodvale Halls discotheque with friends, telling our parents we were visiting the cinema. It was the first discotheque I had attended, and although I enjoyed it, I was initially afraid to dance there as my mother said I would be raped if I danced in front of strange men. I asked Dan if he attended this event and he replied he had. I said that I would be there on Wednesday evening and as he left the toy shop, he said: "Right!".

Wilma's daughter Tess travelled from New York to visit her. Tess was a little older than me and one afternoon we arranged to visit Graveton together. I asked Tess what it was like to be a Jehovah's Witness in America compared to the U.K. and she told me the elders held their committee meetings in nightclubs and drank alcohol and this surprised me. From what I heard, life seemed completely different there and the restrictions seemed more relaxed. We also discussed forbidden sexual activities within the religion including those for married couples. This led to a conversation about oral copulation, as there seemed to be immense pressure on women to do this for men. Tess revealed she had done this and I commented that I would never engage in such an activity. She laughed and replied: "That's what I said" and hinted I would eventually change my mind. Tess told me that if I visited her Kingdom Hall in America, it would not be long before I had a ring on my finger as many brothers would want to date me. Tess seemed 'free and easy' about our religion, so I invited her to accompany Waverley and I to a discotheque in Graveton. She agreed to go along with the 'story' I told my parents and told Wilma we were visiting the cinema.

On Wednesday evening, we called at the home of Wilma and James to collect Tess. She wore bright coloured clothes and glass high-heel shoes that fascinated me. We travelled on a train to Graveton station, a short walk from the venue. On arrival at Woodvale Halls, we entered the lounge bar to purchase a drink while Waverley stayed outside the bar as she was still fourteen. Leonard was there, sitting with a group of friends and when I told him I was meeting Dan, he asked if he had got further with me than he had! His question disgusted me and I walked away. A few minutes later, Dan arrived with Marl and his girlfriend. We purchased a drink, then entered the large hall. Tess began to dance to music and Dan sat on the edge of the stage. He told me he had bad experiences in relationships that put him off wanting another one. I accepted this and continued to be friendly with him. After a while, he told me he had changed his mind. We danced together, he kissed me and as we got on well, I arranged to see him again. I introduced him to Tess and when he discovered she lived in New York he said "I bet you really 'freak out' on the dance floor" and we laughed. Tess enjoyed herself, but compared to nightlife in New York I am sure it would have been a rather tame evening for her.

When Tess returned home, Wilma interrogated her about where we were, as the clothes and shoes she wore were not the correct attire for a cinema. Tess replied that we visited a discotheque, but she had agreed to go along with our story as our parents did not know. Wilma predictably passed this information to them and before we were interrogated about it, Waverley insisted we told them she did not go to the venue, as she was there to accompany me. Waverley told my parents she wandered around the town and met us when we came out of the discotheque. My parents were then angry with me believing that I left Waverley to wander around the town alone which could put her in danger. Although this was not true, I took the blame, as Waverley threatened she would not accompany me again and I knew my parents would not let me go out without her.

At the end of each working day, Dan, who was an apprentice goldsmith, left his place of work early and met me at the toy shop. He accompanied me on the train journey home and walked with me from the station before parting company near my home. I was not allowed out long enough to see him in the evenings, but we occasionally met if I walked to the nearby telephone kiosk to contact him. Dan drove his small moped from Graveton to my home town that took him about fifteen minutes, but our time together was brief. Two weeks after I met Dan, my father had arranged a two week vacation in Cornwall. I was not as eager to go this time, as it meant I would not see Dan for fourteen days. Dan told me that he did not mind me speaking to other young men while away, as he would be talking to other girls. I later discovered that he thought if he gave me permission to do so, it would have the reverse effect. At this time I did not view it as a serious relationship and did not take him seriously. I guessed that whenever Dan was with Marl, many girls would flock around them. Brett and Rosie arrived home from their vacation on the day we left for ours, which meant I would not see Brett for four weeks. I had not thought about him much because Dan had entered my life.

The vacation in Cornwall was an eventful one. We attended meetings at the Cornish Kingdom Hall, where the brothers and sisters were pleased to see us again. I was excited to see Gavin each year but on this occasion, my feelings changed a little as Dan was on my mind. Gavin assumed we would resume our usual two-week romance as his sister Lynette told me he had taken a two-week break from his relationship with his girlfriend. His girlfriend heard about me and asked Lynette for more information. I made no arrangements to see Gavin, particularly after the previous year when his parents invited us to their home in a stunning village with a beautiful harbour. Lynette, Gavin, Waverley and I had walked around the harbour that evening and he pulled me into an empty garage to kiss me, making a clumsy attempt to put his hand in my blouse that I blocked. Gavin seemed accustomed to behaving this way with girls and confident I would let him, so I did not intend to put myself in the same position again.

While browsing retail outlets in the small Cornish town, we visited a clothes shop that surprisingly belonged to Rosella. She was the Spanish lady who owned the guest house we stayed in on our first vacation eleven years ago. It had been a long time since we last saw her and she told us her husband had passed away. Her two sons were now in their late teens. A handsome young man stood beside her, and she introduced us to Rydon, her eldest son. We both conversed and I explained to him that we last met when he was eight years of age while we stayed in their apartment. They had sold the guest house and moved to a larger house further up the hill with a wonderful view of the harbour. My parents hired a static caravan on a site next to a beach about two miles from the small Cornish town. Rydon visited us on a few occasions and we walked together along the beach. He was a college student and explained that someone had introduced him to transcendental meditation. This practice concerned me as I was taught about the dangers of meditating and emptying one's mind, but he assured me it was safe. We laid upon the sand gazing up at the blue sky and he instructed me to concentrate on one word, thinking of nothing else. I had to repeat the word as a mantra over and over. I tried this as I watched clouds slowly float across the blue sky but it was unsuccessful as my concerns about it prevented me from relaxing. Rydon told me that it takes discipline and practice to accomplish it successfully. I have studied and researched how religious cults often recruit college students and on reflection, it was possible this had happened to Rydon. He invited me to his home for dinner one evening and we sat at a long polished dining table adorned with a silver candelabra. Rydon lit the candles and turned off the lights while Rosella served us a fabulous meal. He later transported me back to the caravan, but stopped on the way for some physical affection but he was far more respectful than Gavin. We eventually returned to the caravan where I was surprised to find Gavin with my parents. My mother told him I had been invited out to dinner by a handsome young man. Rydon and Gavin conversed as they attended the same school, but there was an awkward atmosphere. I visited Rydon's home frequently and when he left me alone in the kitchen, I bent down to adjust my shoe and heard a voice shout "Corrr get them off!" I turned to see an elderly parrot in its cage and Rydon explained it once belonged to an old seaman. It swore atrociously if anyone mentioned the bible and I commented it was a pity the parrot had not met my parents. I would have enjoyed its reaction! We walked around the Cornish town together and although I knew the location well, Rydon knew the short-cuts through various alleyways behind the buildings. By late afternoon we returned to his home where his younger brother Carso was covering his boat in the driveway. Rydon and I sat in his room conversing and playing music, but his mother seemed uncomfortable about this, asking him why we could not sit in the lounge with her as she felt excluded. It was Rydon's decision after all where we were, but I could tell he felt torn between wanting to be alone with me and pleasing his mother. On the day we left Cornwall, Rydon arrived to say farewell and waved as my father drove away. We conversed by letter for a few weeks and then the communication ceased after he returned to college. I wonder if this had anything to do with the new meditation group he had joined.

I looked forward to returning home and seeing Dan again. On my lunch break at work, I visited Brett at his shop so we could update one another on our vacations. He expressed how much he had missed me and when he reached out to touch me, I moved away. At the end of the working day, Dan arrived to accompany me home on the train. As we walked towards the station, Brett appeared behind us on his way to the car park. He asked if I wanted transport home and when I refused, he asked to speak to me alone. Brett said it was not a good idea to travel home on the train with a young man who was not a Jehovah's

Witness. This annoyed me and I replied it was also not a good idea to travel home with a married man. He had no answer for this and walked away. Dan was puzzled, so I explained the situation with Brett and the rules of my parents' religion. I told him Brett was an elder and I was watched constantly.

Dan walked me home one Thursday evening and this was the time my parents visited the supermarket. I invited Dan into the house for a beverage as no one was home. We were there a short time when my parents unexpectedly returned as I saw their car arrive, so Dan and I made a hasty retreat out of the back door, through the garden, past the rear garages and out to the road. I thought we had escaped in time without being seen and as it was a lovely sunny day, we walked to the entrance of the local woodland. A beautiful cornfield was on our left before entering the woodland, so we decided to sit within the corn, enjoying the warm sunshine. We conversed about many things and although Dan and I were affectionate, I still kept personal boundaries and he respected that. I discovered young men within our religion were eager to indulge and instigate sexual behaviour the minute we were alone. 'Worldly' young men however, seemed to be more patient. My mother had said all the young brothers were clean and wholesome, while 'worldly' young men were sexually perverted, but in my experience this was untrue.

Little did we know that while we were in the cornfield my parents had seen us leave the house through the front window and were out searching for us. They met uncle Brandon on his daily walk and he told them he saw a girl who looked like me, walking toward the woodland with a young man. My parents panicked assuming I had gone to the woods to engage in sexual activity and ran past the cornfield into the woodland to find me. I had an early evening appointment at the hair salon, so Dan and I arranged to meet in the park later on and I walked alone to the High Street.

As I reached the salon, my parents stopped beside me in their car. Aunt Mary was in the back seat and I cheerfully greeted them, explaining I was about to visit the hair salon. My mother stared coldly at me and shouted "Get in this car, you slut!" I then realised they saw Dan and I leave the house and quietly got into the car. We returned home in silence and Aunt Mary stared straight ahead of her not looking at me. My mother accused me of visiting the woodland for sexual activity and I denied this, but as I had laid on my back in the cornfield, it had left a green stain on the back of my t-shirt which did not look good! Dan waited a while at the park and when I did not return, he guessed something had happened and returned home.

I had a close relationship with Aunt Mary throughout my childhood and would visit her home on her days off from work. She taught me how to iron shirts correctly and press creases into trousers as she once worked at a laundry with my mother. I had plenty of practice on my uncle's clothes as he was a smartly dressed man. On one occasion, Mary asked me to stand in front of a mirror beside her, telling me to look at the colours in my eyes and hers because they were the same. I hoped for a long time that she was my mother as there were many skeletons in the family closet. I asked her if our eyes being the same colour meant she was really my mother and she looked down at the floor and sadly shook her head. I still held hope that she was and family members were concealing the truth. Now that I am older I can see a lot of my mother's features and some of my father's.

After the incident with Dan, it appeared Mary believed all my mother had said about me and she distanced herself, as my other relatives had. Uncle Vernon was the only one who did not react this way and I hoped he could see the reality of the situation.

When we returned home from the hair salon, Aunt Mary left and my father sat me down for a discussion. I explained that I did not visit the woods nor did anything immoral and he replied that he did not want me dating a 'worldly' young man. My father also mentioned that he recently visited Brett who helped him with car maintenance. Apparently Brett said: "I feel sorry for you because you have a huge problem with Lucia!" Hearing this angered me and I replied that Brett had no right to judge me after the way he had behaved while transporting me home. My father then wanted an explanation and I told him what had occurred. He immediately transported me to Brett's home and Rosie happily welcomed us. We sat in Vivien's lounge while Rosie went upstairs to her part of the house and made us a beverage. My father asked Brett if they could converse in another room and when they returned, Brett's face was pale. I was surprised he had not denied it. Rosie appeared with a tray of tea cups and Brett asked if he could speak to her in private. Rosie was crying when they returned and Brett repeatedly said that 'it was all so silly'. My mother cried too because Rosie was so upset, but I felt nothing but anger at this time.

Rosie asked Brett how he could consider being intimate with a young girl who had dated 'worldly' young men. She also mentioned Trent, the man I ran away with as they did not believe that no immoral activity occurred the night I stayed away. I asked Rosie why she married Brett who was far from innocent and she replied by asking me if this was about his first wife. Hearing this surprised me, as I did not know he had been married before. I told her that I referred to his past liaisons with 'bunny girls' and Rosie had not heard about that. I also reminded her of the incident three years ago when she asked me why Brett would want someone like me when he had her. I told her that she was wrong to trust any man.

Rosie and Vivien were angry with Brett as he had behaved in a similar way to Rosie's father. Brett was summoned to a meeting with the committee of elders who removed his position as elder but did not disfellowship him because he was repentant. My mother asked me for details of Brett's sexual conversations and passed the information to Vivien who was disgusted. Rosie decided to stay with Brett as no adultery had been committed, but while I waited for a bus to work one morning, I saw Rosie transporting Brett to work as she no longer trusted him to travel alone. Years later I heard that my mother spoke of this incident to my second husband and apparently said: 'That 'poor man' lost his eldership because of our daughter!'

After the elders dealt with Brett, I was summoned to meet with them at a judicial committee meeting. This was the third disciplinary meeting I attended in three years. Before the meeting, I thought about my future life and what I would say. The elders visited our home instead of the Kingdom Hall and my parents left me alone with them in the lounge and closed the door. The elders asked all the usual questions, whether any sexual activity occurred and it seemed the version I gave them was the same as Brett's as they did not pursue it. I told them I had given the situation a huge amount of thought and decided I no longer wished to be a Jehovah's Witness. I explained that no matter how much effort I made within their religion it was never enough. The elders replied that if I wanted to be disfellowshipped, it meant I was unrepentant about what occurred with Brett. I replied this was untrue and repeated my reasons for leaving had nothing to do with this. They attempted to talk me out of it but were unsuccessful. I was aware that I would be shunned by all Jehovah's Witnesses who I had known throughout my life, but leaving the religion meant I could make my own life choices. I could also continue seeing Dan as I could not then marry within their religion. My parents treated me as the family 'black sheep' and 'scapegoat' for most of my life, particularly my mother. I had been on the 'outer circle' of the family for years, Waverley knew all the family business and she once said to me: "No one would tell *you* anything!" This would have been since my disclosure and would not change. Family members labelling me the bad person suited the guilty family member as it was a welcome distraction from what he had done. The elders concluded the meeting and sent me out of the room while they prayed, as they would not do so in the presence of disfellowshipped individuals. My parents had eavesdropped from the kitchen/diner and were shocked at my decision. The elders said farewell to them and ignored me.

The moment they left, my parents moved me out of the bedroom I shared with Waverley, stating they would not want me influencing her. Albert moved into Waverly's room and I remained in the small bedroom for the rest of my time at home.

My six month period of work at the toy shop came to an end and I had to find another work placement. I stayed in contact with Suzanna as she had become a good friend and that continued throughout our lives. When my family attended their meetings, I visited Dan's home and met his mother Jenny. She was reading a magazine when Dan stood in the doorway of the lounge and introduced me. Jenny looked up at me smiling as her spectacles magnified her beautiful large blue eyes. She was a friendly, loveable woman, reminiscent in some ways of the actress *Bette Davis*. I met Dan's older twin brothers, Clive was a university student and lived with them and Ben lived with his wife who was twenty years his senior. They were all heavy smokers, which meant the house was filled with cigarette smoke when they were all in the lounge together. Dan's parents were divorced and his father worked and lived in another country. He arranged to meet his sons when he visited once a year and saw them for only a few hours which had a profound effect on Dan. Jenny was still in love with him and frequently drowned her sorrows with copious amounts of alcohol. I discovered that Dan had lived overseas in China with his parents until the age of twelve and when they divorced, Jenny returned to the United Kingdom with her children. She told me that she gave Dan the biggest bedroom in her detached chalet bungalow to compensate for the divorce and took only a small amount of money from his wages to help with housekeeping. I then thought about my parents who took half my wages after I put aside my fares for travelling.

Dan frequently went out with friends on their motorcycles in the evenings and told me that he would stay out all night to watch the sun rise. I couldn't imagine what it was like to have that freedom. The first time I entered Dan's bedroom I noticed pornographic images he had attached to the walls that he had removed from magazines. Being raised in a religion where it was wrong to have a poster of a fully clothed popular singer on one's wall, this was rather disturbing! The majority of books and other items in his room revolved around the same subject. Jenny had Catholic beliefs and Dan had a figure of Jesus on a crucifix on the wall above his bed. The figure was surrounded by indentations as though it had been repeatedly struck with something. Jenny thought it healthy for a young man to be interested in pornography, however I was taught the opposite. Dan enjoyed television programmes where women danced provocatively and popular quiz shows where scantily clad female models posed with prizes. He watched all movies containing nudity and sexual activity. Having done research on the subject I now realise that this was an addiction. My parents' religion had instructed not to look at such things, so I was not used to seeing them. I discussed this with Dan and his friends, who told me all young men pleasure themselves while viewing pornographic images and the women who posed in this way 'asked for it'. I found this difficult to accept.

The atmosphere at home was extremely uncomfortable. My parents were permitted to speak to me for necessary family communication, but did not converse on spiritual subjects. Penny was a member of their congregation who my parents recruited some years ago. I remember when she wore mini skirts when my parents visited her. This upset my mother who was convinced Penny deliberately crossed her long legs under my father's nose and swung them during the bible study to distract him. Penny was a very attractive woman who resembled the actress *Anne Bancroft*. She was also a heavy smoker and she would need to give this up before her recruitment. Penny managed to do so, but her husband refused and did not join the religion with her. She was never a spiritually strong member of the congregation. After my disfellowshipping was announced to the congregation, Penny visited our home and she immediately hugged me. I cried when I received the unexpected show of affection, and my parents reminded her she was not meant to do this. Penny replied she had known me from a small child and she could not bring herself to ignore me. My parents then spoke about the incident involving Brett and I. Penny was shocked, as although she was aware that we both received a public reprimand, she did not realise both announcements were connected. My parents instructed me to go to my room while their conversation continued.

My key to the house had been taken from me after the incident with Dan, as my parents said I could no longer be trusted. There were occasions however that they were out, so my mother left the downstairs window on the latch so I could climb through it, or I left my bedroom window open and climbed up the side of the porch. The porch was high and climbing it was a dangerous task. In the evenings, I was instructed to be home by half past ten, while Waverley could stay out until midnight because they thought she could be trusted. Whenever I joined Dan and his friends on their nights out, they transported me home before continuing their evening. I wished that I had the freedom to stay out longer.

The Employment Centre arranged another six-month work experience placement. It was for a trainee dental nurse at a surgery in Dartfleet. I told Dan I had an interview and he was upset that I would be working again and would have less time to see him.

My interview was successful, and I began work the following week. Mr McConnell was a tall overweight Irish dental surgeon who introduced me to another nurse named Janet. I understood his accent because I had worked with Mr Ahellen who was also Irish. Janet was a nurse for another surgeon at the practice named Mr Morren. She took me through the daily routine and the use of equipment, mixing of various substances that were needed daily for dental work. Janet was an attractive lady with long dark hair, heavily applied facial cosmetics, but was a hard worker and an excellent nurse. I quickly learnt the daily routine and how to work in unison with the surgeons, technician and receptionist. Mrs McConnell arrived unexpectedly and she introduced herself. She was a well-dressed woman in expensive attire and regularly helped herself to money from the cash box in the surgery before venturing on shopping trips.

Each day I had a thirty minute walk from home to the bus stop on the main road for my journey to work. A group of pensioners would board the bus each morning and I was surprised to hear their risqué conversations. Pensioners usually scowled when teenagers spoke on these subjects, but here they were doing the same and enjoying it! It was on these bus journeys I first met Reginald the bus conductor, who joked with the elderly passengers. I enjoyed watching him, as his charm and charisma fascinated me. He gave me a slow wink while taking my fare and although we were unable to converse at this busy time of day, I looked forward to seeing him.

One morning as I walked to the bus stop, Dan unexpectedly stepped out of an alleyway and stood in front of me. He had been lying in wait for me and instructed me to open my coat so he could see what I was wearing. He then remarked on my smart appearance, asking if I was searching for another boyfriend. I denied this and told Dan that I had to leave or I would miss my bus. At the dental surgery, Janet decided it was time for the staff to have new dental overalls. Our navy-blue ones were old and worn so we needed something smarter. She tried to persuade Mr McConnell in the past with no success, but there was a new nurse and receptionist to support her suggestion and he reluctantly agreed. Janet ordered stylish ice-blue overalls with a mandarin neckline and a long zip fastener at the front. Mine fitted me perfectly and I loved it. At the end of our working day, Dan arrived at the surgery and saw my new overall. He insisted I kept the zip fastened all the way up to my collar. Some days he arrived unexpectedly while I was working to check I wore it as he instructed but I refused to do so, as it was far too hot in the surgery and it felt uncomfortable.

Being raised within a strict religion, I failed to see the warning signs of his obsessive dominance as I had experienced it from men all my life. Dan gave me a list of tasks to complete, purchasing certain items, keeping a diary, noting down special dates, etc. He set a time limit for these to be completed and at the deadline, he went through the list one by one to check I had done them all. If one task was not carried out for some reason, he lost his temper. On reflection, Dan knew about my upbringing and used this method of control to assess how far he could take it. On one occasion, he passed me a box of matches telling me to take out a match so that he could light his cigarette. As I opened it, a huge house spider jumped out of the box onto my hand which shocked me and he found it amusing. He told me that a wasp once crawled inside his jacket and stung his chest as he rode his motorcycle to work. He caught the wasp, put it in a matchbox and took it with him to work so he could torture it. I heard about other acts of animal cruelty he had carried out during his childhood and these were extremely disturbing. Jenny warned me her son had a bad temper and told me of the times he threw his dinner across the room and had been violent towards her.

Dan and I visited the discotheque one evening where our courting began. I thought it would bring back good memories, but something occurred that upset him that evening. He instructed me to dance beside him and after a few minutes, ordered me to stand still. He did this repeatedly and I followed his instructions. Dan had learnt the art of regurgitation from a childhood friend at school. He used this method to have days off school pretending to be ill. At the discotheque he vomited into my hat so that I could no longer wear it and then we left the venue. We walked through the town to the bus stop so I could return home and Dan hit me in the presence of a queue of people who said nothing. At that moment, Reginald arrived on his bus as he had then transitioned from conductor to driver when buses changed to a 'one man' service. He saw what happened, stopped the bus and told me to board it. He did not ask me for a fare as he wanted to take me away from Dan and transport me home. I continued the relationship with Dan making allowances for his behaviour because of his difficult childhood and the separation from his father.

Working at the dental surgery progressed well, although I found general anaesthetic day difficult. Mr McConnell's practices were far from ethical. The worst example of this occurred when the last female patient entered the surgery that day. She was nervous about dental treatment and the local doctor administered a Valium injection. They explained to me it would sedate the patient so that they are calm and relaxed during their treatment and will not care about what they experience. When her treatment was complete, I guided her to the waiting room instructing her to rest until the effect wore off. She then warned me to watch out for Mr McConnell as he apparently touched her inappropriately during the treatment. She added that if her husband found out, the dental surgeon would need his teeth fixed! I did not reply and wondered whether the drug may have clouded her perception of events and thought no more of it. A month later on our next general anaesthetic day, a male patient arrived who was terrified of visiting the dentist. At only thirty one years of age, he asked for all his teeth to be removed so that he would no longer need to visit. I found it disturbing that unconscious patients struggled and cried out while their teeth were extracted. I had to cross their wrists and hold them down with one hand using my body weight. I then placed one knee across their legs to stop them kicking out and held a metal kidney bowl in the other hand to contain the extracted teeth. The frightened patient put up an almighty struggle and as his leg escaped from under my knee, it kicked the kidney bowl filled with blood and teeth out of my hand. The blood soaked the front of his shirt and splashed onto my overall. We could not take him out to the waiting room, as the sight of him would disturb the other patients, so we made him comfortable in the empty surgery until he recovered. Our Valium patient at the end of the general anaesthetic session was an attractive woman of twenty. I remembered an exchange of smiles between the doctor and Mr McConnell after she was anaesthetised. It brought to mind the conversation I had with the female patient a month ago. I tried to dismiss these thoughts and continued my work. As I mixed a substance needed for the treatment, I heard Mr McConnell saying the patient's name. I turned to check all was well and saw his hand beneath the plastic cover on her chest and he was touching her inappropriately. I walked out of the surgery in shock and spoke to Candice the receptionist about what I had seen. She and Janet were both twenty one and got on well together. Janet heard me speaking to Candice in reception and joined us, instructing me to keep quiet as patients in the waiting room may hear me. I explained what had happened to Janet and they both replied that Mr McConnell was a happily married man. I then realised that they did not want to know, let alone risk losing their jobs. The young woman came out of the surgery after her treatment and a friend who accompanied her sat with her in the waiting room for a while. I heard them whispering and giggling together. Out of curiosity, I asked the patient how much of her treatment she remembered while under anaesthetic. She replied that she remembered plenty! The patient then approached reception to pay for her treatment still laughing and Mr McConnell came out of the surgery and laughed with them. I angrily left them and walked into the surgery to clean the instruments. Mr McConnell followed, still chuckling to himself. I stared at him and angrily stated that I did not find it funny! His smile disappeared and I walked out of the room.

Dan arrived just as I finished for the day and he noticed I was upset. I explained to him what had happened that day. Mr McConnell called me into the surgery. He had promised me in my interview that I had learnt how to fill in the National Health Service forms. When I could complete them he would give me a rise in wages. I accomplished this quicker than he expected and reminded him of his promise many times but there was no response. After this incident, Mr McConnell told me he would raise my wages by one British pound a week! I no longer felt comfortable with him but I continued to work there. A heavily pregnant female patient who was administered Valium for treatment attended her appointment the following month and Mr McConnell touched her openly in my presence during her treatment. I could tell by her expression that she was upset about it, but she said nothing. No one was willing to support me when I spoke out, so I felt I had no choice but to ignore it.

My mind was racing as I left the dental surgery on Thursday evening. I was aware the television program *Top of the Pops* would air that evening. Dan looked forward to it each week, as he enjoyed watching the group of attractive female dancers. He once confessed to me he watched these dancers while pleasuring himself and this ruined my enjoyment of the program. Whenever female dancers appeared on television my mother would comment that all boyfriends would be enjoying them. This was obviously an attempt to feed any insecurities I already had as I was aware she did not want Dan and I to continue our relationship. I hastily left the surgery to cross a busy five-way junction and saw my bus approaching. When I thought the road was clear, I stepped out and felt something hit me and I fell backwards onto the pavement. An older woman ran over to assist me, then two more people joined us. I felt pain in my leg, so they helped me to the nearby doctor's surgery. All I could think of at this time was missing my bus and being late for Dan. The doctor telephoned for an ambulance to take me to hospital, but I was upset, insisting I had to leave and catch the next bus. The doctor told me I had to stay with them and threatened to sedate me if I didn't calm down. The ambulance men arrived and flirted with me thinking it would cheer me up. That was short-lived when I arrived at the hospital and a nurse administered a tetanus injection into my thigh muscle that caused extreme cramp.

Dan contacted the dental surgery by telephone when I did not arrive and Mr Morren explained there had been an accident and he saw me boarding an ambulance. Dan contacted my parents who arrived at the hospital before he did and I immediately asked for Dan which upset them. The car had hit my wrist that had swelled because of a hairline fracture. The car bumper had also removed a chunk of flesh from my shin. The hospital had heavily bandaged my wrist, and provided me with an arm sling. They told me I would be off work for two weeks. After receiving treatment at the hospital, my father immediately transported me to the police station to make a statement about the accident. He was concerned I could be prosecuted for 'jaywalking' if I did not explain what happened. I was exhausted but managed to give the police officer a statement. The next day a middle aged woman who had assisted me after the accident visited our home to see me. She then admitted she was driving the car that hit me and explained it was dark and she did not see me, which was understandable as I wore a black leather jacket and jeans. The woman promised she would visit every day to check on my progress and left her contact details. After a discussion, my parents insisted that I contact her by telephone asking her for financial compensation for the time I was unable to work. They said that her visit proved that she was at fault. I did as they asked and the woman told me she was unable to help me out financially. After this telephone call we did not hear from her again.

I loved my new black leather jacket. It was a smaller version of Dan's, however the purchase of it had caused problems. I admired Dan's leather jacket and wanted to purchase one for myself. My parents refused to let me until they had consulted the elders and I had to wait. I did not see why it mattered as I was disfellowshipped from the religion anyway. Although I did not hear the elder's response, they either refused to get involved, or saw no problem with it and my parents then relented.

My relationship with Dan continued to be problematic and after a huge disagreement, he announced we would take a break from seeing one another for a week. He wanted to punish me by having no contact with me. I found the first few days difficult, but after that, I grew accustomed to his absence and felt happier within myself. One afternoon, I covered reception duties and Dan unexpectedly phoned the surgery. I answered the telephone cheerfully which angered him and I received a long lecture on how this time apart was intended to punish me. He cried and went on to say how torturous it was for him and I should be miserable too. On another occasion when Dan escorted me home after another disagreement, he suggested we end our relationship, so I agreed and walked away. I entered the family home where my father was waiting for me, so we sat at the dining room table and discussed it for a while.

The following morning, Jenny phoned me at the surgery to let me know Dan had an accident on his motorcycle after leaving my home. He was in hospital and Jenny added she was aware we had ended our relationship, but thought I should know. On reflection I should have stayed away, but I was concerned about him and visited the hospital. Dan said he purposely drove his motorcycle into the back of a parked lorry because he wanted to die. He had a broken arm and shattered both knee-caps. I felt guilty about this and resumed our relationship. I walked a mile to the hospital each evening to visit him after work. It took months for Dan to recover from the accident.

The first time I became intoxicated with alcohol was on Christmas Eve of 1979. I worked half a day at the surgery, then at lunchtime, Mr McConnell brought out two bottles of white wine and filled our mugs for a Christmas toast. Jackie, Candice and I had no lunch, so the wine affected us quickly and we left the surgery giggling and swaying. Dan knew I could not return home in this state, so he walked me around Dartfleet town. We entered an Inn but the landlord asked us to leave as he could see that I was young and intoxicated. We then visited a café where Dan bought me a plate of egg and chips that I did not find appetising in the least. At first, I was happily drunk but after a while my mood changed and I became emotional and quite ill. This was something I vowed never to do again, however I was young and my social life out in the world was just beginning!

My relationship with Dan was a mix of fleeting happy moments and volatile arguments. There were times he could be loving. He wanted to make my first Christmas a special one by purchasing many gifts for me. I had a wonderful time at Jenny's home and it snowed heavily adding to the magical atmosphere. Dan had not seen snow in his childhood and I remember him in the garden with his arms outstretched as he enjoyed the feel of snowflakes falling on him. Jenny loved her three sons but wished she had a daughter. We spent a lot of time together and she considered me to be the daughter she never had.

After dating Dan for a few months, I thought it was time to take the relationship further. I was disfellowshipped from the Jehovah's Witnesses and was no longer bound by their rules, so there was nothing to deter me. I regretfully gave him my virginity and from then on we spent most of our time in his bedroom. My mother sensed something had changed after my father arrived at Jenny's home unexpectedly one evening while we were in Dan's room. We hastily dressed and joined him in the lounge, however the nervousness and guilt on Dan's face was obvious as he conversed with my father. He may have told my mother about this as she suspected Dan and I were committing fornication and said she would not tolerate this behaviour. My mother instructed me to purchase a suitcase in Dartfleet town, so that she could pack my clothes so that I could move out.

The following day I purchased a suitcase during my lunch-break. On the homeward bus journey, I met Reginald who was riding the bus as a passenger and he walked me home carrying the large cardboard box containing my new suitcase. Waverley came out of the corner shop and as we conversed with her, my father suddenly appeared in his car. He saw Reginald kiss me before handing me the large box and as he jogged along the road, my father chased him in his car. I returned home and gave the suitcase to my mother. My father arrived demanding to know who Reginald was and I explained how I met him. He commented he was much older than me and wondered what Dan would think about it if he told him!

My mother said no more about me leaving home for a few days, but when the subject arose again, she asked if I would live with Dan if she evicted me. I replied that I would as I had nowhere else to go and she said we would have to marry rather than 'live in sin'. My father often told me he would not allow me to leave home unless I was married. If I did try to leave as a single woman, he said he would make my life as difficult as possible. On reflection I believed he had the power to do this, as I knew of no independent single women to advise me otherwise.

Two months before this, Dan created an engagement ring for me in gold with a single red garnet. He brought it to my home and asked my father if he would agree to us getting engaged. My father refused and Dan took the ring to work and melted it down. This upset us both and we decided we would go ahead with an engagement anyway and he purchased another ring at a jewellers. It was silver with a solitaire cubit zirconia that sparkled like a diamond. It seemed odd they had refused our engagement and two months later they were talking about us getting married. I discussed it with Dan, and he was happy for us to marry as it meant I had more freedom. I was only seventeen but could no longer tolerate the atmosphere at home. We visited a registry office to arrange a date that ironically was my father's birthday and my parents signed a consent form for the marriage. During my lunch hour from work, I visited the bridal section of a large store in Dartfleet where Aunt Jade worked. I chose a bridal veil and when I took it to her for purchase, she only agreed to sell it to me on condition I had my parent's blessing. I replied that the marriage was their idea. My Auntie Mary and Jade were on vacation at the time of the wedding, so they visited us one evening and asked me to try on my veil and dress so they could see me wearing them. Aunt Mary wanted me to brush back my fringe when I wore the headdress of white silk flowers and pearls, but I was used to having a fringe. My mother had objected to me wearing white, as she assumed I was no longer a virgin. I insisted on wearing it because I was marrying the man I gave my virginity to.

I moved the last of my belongings to Dan's home and my mother accompanied me to the bus stop to assist me with the bags. One of them contained soft toys and one fell out, so my mother carefully placed it back in the bag with a sad expression. The night before my wedding, my father told me there was still time to change my mind, but life at home was difficult and I could not see it improving. The following morning my father had his weekend 'lie-in' and while my mother prepared his breakfast, I laid on the bed beside him, my hair in curlers and wearing an all-in-one pyjama suit. He stretched out an arm and I rested my head on his shoulder enjoying the familiar smell of my father's body odour. This was something I had done regularly at weekends for as long as I can remember. My father commented that I would look very pretty on my wedding day. I did not want to leave him but I had made my choices. Dan and I married in the first week of June 1980 exactly a year after we first met.

CHAPTER 6

FIRST MARRIAGE

I told Reginald that I agreed to marry Dan and he was most upset. He told me that he went out on an all day drinking session on my wedding day. Reginald lived with a woman, but explained to me he did not feel their relationship was right for him. She was using his surname and he said that she had changed it by deed poll and they were only living together. On one occasion, I tried to contact Reginald as he had spent a few days at his parent's home. His mother answered the phone and when I asked for him she told me that he was at his home with his wife. I asked her if they were married and she repeated that he was with his wife. This was a different version of what he had said and it gave me doubts about him. Reginald was a charming man who treated me in a chivalrous way like actors in the old romantic movies my mother loved. She said this was the type of behaviour I should expect from a man. I had confusing feelings about this as Reginald was the person I ran to when I was upset and needed to talk. He seemed to understand me and was prepared to listen when my parents had not. He also confronted Dan about his behaviour on more than one occasion.

My wedding went as planned and a few of our relatives and friends attended the ceremony. On Friday evening, Dan had his stag night at a local Inn with friends, but the following day he looked pale and his stomach was still rejecting all the alcohol he had consumed. My father and Tom Shelden signed our marriage certificate as witnesses.

After the short ceremony at the registry office, we had an afternoon party at Jenny's home for Dan's relatives. My parents informed Jenny there would be limited alcohol at the evening reception, so she ordered plenty for Dan's relatives that afternoon. Waverley and her best friend Kelly were bridesmaids and Dan's mischievous twin uncles kept them supplied with drinks. I remember them both lying on the bed and giggling in Clive's downstairs bedroom as he was away. Kelly encouraged Waverley to change from her 'tomboy' image as her body grew more curvy after she stopped her gymnastics. She suddenly developed a bigger bust which received a lot of attention from the boys at school. Waverley then began to wear facial cosmetics, figure hugging clothes and copied Kelly's way of styling her hair. They both looked similar, although Kelly was brunette and Waverley blonde. She said that they often sat outside the local Inns of our home town, while young men purchased alcoholic drinks for them because they were under age.

Our evening wedding reception was in a small hall at Graveton. Tom and Amy Shelden had attended the registry office ceremony and Tom was our best man. Dan agreed to this because I had a close friendship with their family and Tom agreed to transport me to the venues in his beautiful white Audi that looked like a wedding car. My parents provided what they could and my mother, who wore my old white dental coat, worked hard preparing catering for the buffet. She suggested I wear her long white petticoat under my chiffon wedding dress as it was a little transparent. When I returned it to her two days later, I remember her checking it thoroughly for stains by holding it up to the kitchen window and I hoped she was not looking for the spot of blood she said could occur when someone lost their virginity. As I left the reception, I sensed the disapproval and saw sadness in their eyes as we said goodbye. My life choices were completely different from the expectations they had.

Married life with Dan was in complete contrast to the life I knew as a Jehovah's Witness. I left my employment at the dental surgery earlier than the six month period as I could no longer tolerate the unprofessional behaviour of Mr McConnell.

On Friday and Saturday evenings, Dan and I frequented nightclubs with Marl, Kirk and Joel. This was exciting for me. We also visited the arcades of Piccadilly Circus in London arriving at midnight and staying there until the early hours to play arcade games and fruit machines. There were a few strange men staring at us and Annette, Joel's girlfriend, advised me to avoid and ignore them. Dan and his friends smoked and ingested recreational drugs. They offered some to me, but I refused to take hallucinogenic substances as the side effects were unpredictable. After hearing of the terrifying visions my mother had, I did not want to take that chance. Marl and Kirk often left us to visit small cinemas where 'hard-core' pornographic movies were shown. Joel, Annette, Dan and I stayed at the arcades until they returned. I was surprised how many people were out and about in London as it seemed almost as busy as the daylight hours. We often stopped at motorway cafes on our journey home. Marl, Kirk and Joel owned Ford Minis and they took turns transporting us all, asking Dan to contribute to their fuel. We stayed at the cafe until the sun rose before heading home. I heard that Kirk once owned a large motorcycle and Dan would ride his FS1E moped when they went out riding together, as he had not yet passed his test. Their friends found it amusing that Dan, who was six feet tall with long legs, looked too large for his small moped, while Kirk was only five feet in height with short legs and his motorcycle seemed too large for him! We often visited the home of Marl, Kirk and Joel, but on our first visit Dan walked me through back alleyways so that I did not know the exact location. He explained that on one occasion he arrived and found one of his girlfriends there and did not want it repeating. He felt inferior to his friends as he thought they were better looking and received more female attention.

Joel offered to give me a Tarot reading one evening as he had purchased a new pack of cards and needed the practice. I was a little reticent after warnings from my parents about 'dabbling in the occult', but after giving it some thought, I agreed. Joel asked me to shuffle the cards and when he laid them out, the card representing influences around me was unsurprisingly The Devil. This brought to mind the warning my parents gave me about being with people who were under the Devil's influence when I left their religion. The last card in the spread was The Tower. Joel explained that this card was warning me that if I remained in my present situation, it would affect my mental health and security. I knew that I had married into a mentally unstable family and despite the reading's accuracy, I did not act upon the warning or the advice given.

Dan stated that I would never find out any information of his past life or relationships and it was unfortunate that I did not do so until after our marriage. Joel commented that he was surprised Dan chose to date me, as the girls he had dated before were large women, or as he described it: "built like brick sh!t houses"! He told me Dan had moods and would self-harm. When a girlfriend had ended their relationship at a party, he cut his skin with broken glass and began to inhale glue. At another party when he had an argument with a girlfriend, Dan jumped off a high wall and smashed his face on the ground. He was apparently taken to hospital covered in blood. I noticed there were many deep scars on his face and when I asked Dan, he did not deny it..

Living with Dan was not easy for many reasons. Jenny was an alcoholic and Finn, her lodger, was repulsive in his health and hygiene habits, but he was also her lover. Dan said that a few lodgers had previously moved in when they were in a relationship with Jenny. They tried to take over the home and act like a father to Dan and his brothers, but this resulted in physical fights when they rejected them. Finn visited his bedroom whenever Dan and I were in ours, and I was horrified when Jenny revealed she found tape recordings he made of sounds coming from our room. One evening we were getting ready to go out and I was in my underwear. Dan left the room to fetch something and I saw the door begin to open. Finn's fingers were curled around the edge of the door and I screamed out: "NOOO!" but he continued to walk in and see me. He told Dan he was looking for something and I hated that he had seen my body. I was surrounded by men who liked hard-core pornography, and although I had experienced abuse in other ways before leaving home, it seemed I had leapt 'from the frying pan into the fire'.

When I objected to Dan's obsession with pornographic magazines, television and videos, he became violent, and eventually I could take no more. I packed my suitcase as Dan cried and contacted my parents asking them to take me home. When they arrived, I got into their car and Jenny approached my mother saying that Dan and I should have lived together before getting married. My mother was horrified Jenny would even suggest this.

On our return home, Waverley was out that evening and my father waited up for her. It went past her curfew time of midnight. He left the house to search for her in his car and found her walking home with a young man. They both returned home very upset and he told my mother he found her walking with a young man. My mother then replied I told her a while ago that Waverley liked a young 'worldly' man. On hearing this, Waverley angrily punched my arm, but I was too exhausted from fighting off Dan to retaliate and withdrew from her. My mother noticed a St Christopher pendant around Waverley's neck and demanded she remove it. My mother said it contained the Devil's influence and caused her to act this way. I returned home hoping for refuge and once again found myself within a violent situation. My parents then directed their anger over Waverley's mistake towards me and my father reminded me that if I returned to his house I would once again abide by his rules. This included returning to their religious meetings. There was nothing I could say or do, so I left them all conversing and retired to the bedroom upset, confused and wondering what to do next. The next morning Waverley appeared with a swollen bruised eye where my father's hand caught her when he struck out. Seeing this shocked him and he stated that the family were not going to attend any religious meetings until her eye had healed. My father and Waverley left the house to go to work and while my mother visited the shops, I packed my suitcase and left a note informing them I was returning to Dan. I did not feel I was in a safer place with them, or any better off as there was no understanding, help or compassion.

Waverley's ambition was a career teaching physical education at schools, as she enjoyed sports, but my parents refused to support either of us in attending college. She did not want to be a pioneer within the Jehovah's Witnesses, so after leaving school, she immediately found full time work at a local factory. This was where she met Aaron, a young man a few years older than her with a reputation of being a 'tough guy'. He had the 'gift of the gab' and seemed to talk his way out of most situations and was good at fighting. These were attributes Waverley admired, so they began dating.

My parents had warned me in the past that if I became pregnant, they would evict me from their home. Aaron, Waverley's boyfriend said that she wanted children and he mentioned she was also a smoker. Waverley warned me that Aaron lied about many things, so I doubted his words. She left home for work in the early hours each morning, telling my parents she was working extra time and visiting Aaron's apartment for a while, before they travelled to work together. After a few months Waverley became pregnant and delayed telling our parents after hearing their threats to me. She explained her appointments with the doctor were for frequent headaches. Waverley was four months into her pregnancy before the doctor insisted she had to tell her parents. Aaron called at their home asking them to come to the doctor's surgery. My parents, not knowing who he was, were concerned something serious was wrong with her after hearing about her headaches. When they arrived at the surgery, they found Waverley sitting on the steps crying as she explained the situation. Dan and I heard about this and visited my parents home as I wanted to check that Waverley was okay after their threats to me. They decided not to evict her as my father commented the tiny life inside her did not ask to be there. This hit me hard after all the threats they made to me. Although my father looked lovingly at Waverley, my mother was not pleased with her as it destroyed the illusion of Waverley being her 'sweet little virgin'. My parents said that she and Aaron would have to marry as soon as possible.

When my parents informed the elders, Waverley was summoned to meet with the committee accompanied by them. The elders interrogated her on how many times she had sexual relations as well as other intimate details. Waverley received a public reprimand for this. She married Aaron two weeks after my parents heard the news. My mother could not judge Waverley, as she was also pregnant with Kevin before their marriage. My father said to my mother Waverley had done something more serious than I ever had, as they assumed I would be the one most likely to get pregnant. I will never forget the words my mother later said to me: "It is the nice girls who are caught out and become pregnant, but the 'old slappers' know what they are doing and avoid it". I then realised no matter what I did, she would constantly twist the situation to place me in the role of the 'bad daughter' and 'scapegoat. Waverley would always be considered her good daughter no matter how she behaved.

I attended various job interviews but as a newly married woman, the interviewers asked if I planned to have children. I replied that I did not, but my interviews were still not successful as I doubted they believed me.

One afternoon when I returned to Jenny's home, two police officers were there. They had arrested Finn and held him at the station for questioning. Apparently, a little girl had been abused at the quarry where he worked and the description of her abuser matched his appearance. The officers searched his bedroom and discovered a bag of ladies' underwear. They asked me if I wanted to check if any belonged to me, so out of curiosity I looked in the bag. It was a relief to find they were extremely large in size, but disturbingly they were heavily soiled. The police officers were amused by this. They found his 'hard-core' pornographic magazines and although they discovered Finn had these perversions they eventually released him as they found nothing linked to children. I remember that Finn was also employed as a grave digger and one evening he brought home strands of long hair he found in a grave along with bones and other items. I asked Jenny why she continued a relationship with him as I could see nothing attractive about him and she replied, 'the devil you know is better than the one you do not'.

I met Dan's father Jeremy when he visited the U.K. accompanying Dan when they arranged to meet in the local Inn. He was an upper class, handsome, well dressed and well-spoken man who worked as an architect. His comments could be tactless and insulting when he spoke to people and his second wife was the same way. Dan did not like her. I remained silent, listening to them all as they conversed together. I later heard that of all his sons' partners, Jeremy preferred me. Dan remembered his father having an affair with his second wife as he saw his car outside her home on many occasions and this distressed him. He described their relationship as 'two ships passing in the night' and felt abandoned by his father. A young boy entering puberty is at a time when he would need his father the most and I wonder if his addictions helped to relieve his stress and tension.

Jenny had arranged to go out with Jeremy to discuss financial matters after he had spent time with us. She was waiting for him when he transported us back to her home and it was obvious she was intoxicated.

It affected the way she applied her facial cosmetics and she staggered towards the car. I felt so sorry for her as she looked rather pitiful. Jenny said that she still loved him, but it was obvious he did not feel the same way about her.

After eighteen months at Jenny's home, she used her powers of persuasion with a person who owned the Church Housing Association explaining that I was not happy living in the house with her lodger Finn. We were placed on the waiting list and soon offered an apartment. I was relieved about this and hoped the relationship with Dan and I would improve with our own property and a new start. Unfortunately the disagreements and fights over Dan's pornography addiction continued. He confessed that when he was single, he prayed to God, promising he would no longer use pornography and pleasure himself if he helped him to find someone. Addictions however are difficult to stop. My mother had warned me I would be punished for leaving their religion and I wondered if this abusive relationship with Dan was part of the retribution.

I stayed in contact with Reginald as he was one of few people I could confide in. We occasionally met during the day and although he was extremely charming and attracted to me, I saw him more as a 'father figure'. I was also unsure if he would be a faithful partner, knowing that he lived with a woman as a couple. My neighbour Janice and her husband from the apartment below, seemed nice at first, but soon involved themselves in our lives. She once quizzed me about Dan's friends visiting and staying until five the next morning. They were suspicious when they saw me walking home with Reginald one afternoon and threatened to tell Dan, aware he could be violent towards me. I cried in the apartment and could hear them laughing about it with the other neighbours in the car park. Janice commented on hearing regular arguments and the fights we had. I was however relieved when she did not carry out this threat. She also told me that she had seen Reginald many times on the buses flirting with women and one afternoon he leant out of the driver's window to tweak the nose of a young woman standing beside it.

Reginald arrived at my apartment unexpectedly one summer afternoon as I was hanging out clothes on a garden rotary line. He told me he had saved enough money to get me out of my present situation and suggested I pack a suitcase and leave with him immediately. Reginald said he would place me in alternative accommodation. I was unprepared for this and shocked. I did not know Reginald well and the thought of leaving with him and not knowing what the future would bring, frightened me. I sharply rejected the offer and he left. It is a choice I have regretted to this day.

I felt isolated, so I decided to return to the Jehovah's Witnesses and began attending meetings. I had to tolerate the shunning to prove my repentance. My decision to return gave the elders power over me. I received strict instructions on what I had to wear, but when one of them suggested I cut my long hair short, my mother intervened and said she would not allow this. She asked the elder if he wanted me to turn me into a 'plain and dowdy' woman like his wife and he said that was not his intention

CHAPTER 7

FIRST CHILD

Dan rented a new television set and video tape player for our apartment. Soon after this he rented pornographic videos and subjected me to abuse. I immediately became pregnant as these movies over-excited him and he chose to be careless. He was aware that I was terrified of childbirth and during our courtship in the middle of copulation he often threatened to impregnate me. Dan had purchased a new motorcycle on the day I received the results of my pregnancy test. When he heard the news Dan, his complexion turned pale. He did not seem happy about it and was more interested in going out on his motorcycle than becoming a father.

I did not want to bring a child into an abusive relationship and the thought of giving birth terrified me after witnessing my mother's experiences. The next day I visited Reginald to discuss it. I could not live with the consequences of a termination and I was also aware the child could suffer with Dan as a father.. After giving it some thought, I felt that I had no other option but to continue with the pregnancy. Reginald said that he wanted a relationship with me and he asked me if he could make love to me. I refused, as that was the last thing I wanted in this situation. With a mind full of confusion and so many other problems to think about I could not consider it. Reginald was a 'charmer' and many women liked him, so I was still not convinced he would be a secure and faithful partner. He spoke of his past life and when I heard he visited prostitutes on a few occasions, I explained to him it had put me off being intimate with him. He became emotional and wiped away tears that rolled down his face.

I had tried to get along with my neighbour Janice in the apartment beneath us, however our friendship changed when she and her husband discovered my unplanned pregnancy. Janice and another female neighbour had difficulty conceiving and they commented how ironic it was that a couple who didn't really want a child could conceive easily, while they were desperate and unsuccessful. My pregnancy was stressful and difficult. There were some ante-natal appointments I avoided when bruises on my arms and legs were visible, as the nurses would have guessed I was in a violent relationship. I continued to attend religious meetings, doing everything they asked and was reinstated after a period of six months. Brett was delighted at the announcement as he felt partly responsible. He welcomed me back but made the mistake of saying: "Now we can mess around like we used to!" Rosie stood beside him as I stared at him in disbelief. It was obvious Rosie was upset by his thoughtless comment and thought it better to walk away.

My labour began a week before the expected date. I felt distressed as there were provocative dancers on a television programme and he told me to pleasure him as he watched them. I did so because I did not want him to become angry and soon after this, it felt as though my abdomen popped like a balloon and water began to trickle out of me. I told Dan not to call an ambulance, as labour can take a long time, but he panicked, contacted my parents and also the ambulance service. My parents arrived and stayed with me while I sat on a large plastic beer bucket as the water was falling into it. I also felt tightening sensations in my thighs and my mother explained these were contractions. An ambulance soon arrived and transported me to hospital. On examination, the nurses saw the water was green in colour which meant the baby was already distressed. The staff were abrupt with me and were not happy I arrived early that evening. They told me it meant they could not go home. With the nursing staff being far from reassuring, I was unable to relax during labour. I looked forward to visiting a firework display each year and had planned for that evening. The onset of labour meant I would miss it for the first time in years.

After six hours of contractions on Guy Fawkes night with me panicking and Dan telling me to keep quiet because he was trying to sleep in the chair, the medical staff said that I would need an emergency caesarean section. I explained that I did not want a blood transfusion and they panicked, reminding me it was a major operation and I could die without it. Dan cried when he heard this, but I would not let him or the medical staff change my mind. On reflection, I was more concerned about what my parents would think if they saw me having one than saving my life. I awoke a few hours later to see my daughter Tania lying in a hospital cot beside me. She was quiet and looking around her. Dan said that we had a beautiful baby girl and at the time seemed quite besotted with her. A woman in the bed opposite me had given birth to a daughter and she was receiving a blood transfusion. The staff transferred me to a room of my own the next day and one of the nurses asked how long I had been a Jehovah's Witness. I replied that I was born into it.

The nurse then explained my blood count was extremely low, and I would need to take prescribed iron tablets for a few months to build it up to the correct level.

While in hospital I frequently thought about Dan and what he would be doing at home on his own. My neighbour Janice told me his friends Marl and Kirk called at our apartment while he was out. When she mentioned this to Dan, he asked her not to tell me as I would be upset about it. The thoughts of having them smoking, drinking, gambling and watching pornographic movies in my home would have upset me. I stayed for a week in hospital and on our return home, Dan seemed pleased that we were back. He cleaned the apartment and even put up a small welcome home sign for us to see. Dan appeared kind and thoughtful at first which pleased my parents, but this did not last long. There were times when he became angry and punched my head while I breast fed Tania, she was crying while trying to feed.

Dan and I tried marriage counselling and met with a male and female counsellor. I expressed my insecurities and how I did not like Dan looking at women in magazines and television programmes. I explained that I felt I was not good enough for him. The male counsellor replied that he looks at other women, but it had nothing to do with how he felt about his wife. The female counsellor was his colleague and they were very friendly during the session and while they were conversing she touched his leg. They were joking and Dan began to laugh with them both as he felt they were siding with him which pleased him. I felt alone in the session as if no one understood how I felt and I did not return for another.

On our first Christmas with our daughter, Dan instigated an argument and walked out on Christmas Eve. As I was still meant to be with the Jehovah's Witnesses, I was torn whether or not to celebrate it, but had bought gifts for him and Tania. He stayed with his mother Jenny for two days, where he could eat her food, drink her alcohol and do exactly what he wanted. I was alone with Tania in our apartment and did not want to go to my parents and hear them say: "I told you so" or "as you make your bed, you then must lie in it". I hardly ate anything over the Christmas holiday and when I returned to the clinic for Tania's check in the new year, the health visitor said she had not gained any weight. My milk ducts had blocked because of the stress I was under and Tania was not getting enough when she fed. From then on the health advised bottled milk so that she could gain more weight and I no longer breast fed her. Tania was a beautiful baby and people would stop me in Graveton when I was out shopping. They said she was a credit to me, as I dressed her in beautiful dresses with small ribbons in her hair of the same colour. I cared for her as well as I could.

I invited Janice to visit us often and she enjoyed cuddling and feeding Tania. I thought it would give her comfort while she was trying to conceive. One evening Janice asked if I was worried she may take my baby and I replied the thought had not entered my head. I could not understand why she had asked me this. I then discovered she visited our neighbours in the other apartments and said I had accused her of trying to steal my baby! They chose to believe her and from that moment on Dan and I were ignored by all of them.

Dan regularly invited Marl, Kirk and their girlfriends to our home for card games to win money from them. These would continue until the early hours of the morning. It did not seem to worry Marl and Kirk that we had a family to support and they often won most of Dan's money.. I sat there holding Tania while they were smoking and wanted to cry at the thought of Tania breathing in their cigarette smoke. I also knew that Dan would be angry about losing his money and would take it out on me after they left.

I decided to attend Judo classes to learn self defence, as it would be useful at home. When Dan discovered I planned to attend these classes, he decided to join me. A formidable looking woman threw me to the ground during one lesson and I severely bruised my knee. I wore a support bandage for a while and on my next visit to the Kingdom Hall, the elders wanted to see me and discuss my progression. They asked about my bandaged knee and I explained that I injured it at a Judo class. They replied that I should not participate in any form of martial art as they are connected with other religious practices and promote violence. I knew these classes are mainly about self-defence rather than attacking opponents, but I did not debate with them on the subject as I knew it would be pointless. I then stopped my classes. The elders also commented on the clothes I wore, as apparently my long skirts were too 'figure hugging'. I replied that Rosie wore the same type of skirt and I did not see anything wrong with them. Dan occasionally attended meetings with me and sat beside me when I met with the elders but he said nothing although he did not agree with their counsel.

Dan and I moved to a two-bedroom maisonette when Tania was a year old. It was six apartments away from our former residence. I was told by doctors after my surgery that I should not lift anything heavy, but I had struggled with a heavy carrycot up and down two flights of stairs since returning home. Jenny spoke to the woman in charge of the housing association and they moved us to the ground floor property. The maisonette was in a beautiful Victorian property with large rooms and high ceilings. The lounge and kitchen were on the ground floor, and the bathroom and bedrooms were in the basement. My father occasionally visited me on his own as I lived only two miles from them. Uncle Vernon also visited regularly as he was shunned by the Jehovah's Witnesses for disassociating himself. He intensely studied the bible and asked many questions about their interpretations. My mother told him not to visit as he constantly debated their faith and caused her severe headaches. She thought these were a symptom of dealing with the Devil's influence. He cried many times about being shunned by her as the separation from his sister was difficult for him to deal with.

We visited a nightclub on New Years Eve with Marl, Kirk, Joel and Annette to celebrate the coming year. I was surprised to see three Jehovah's Witnesses there that evening. I had known them since childhood, particularly Callum who instigated games during out childhood after the religious meetings. His favourite one was known as 'He', where he would creep up behind me and push my shoulder saying 'He'. I would need to chase him and touch him to pass it back. This game frequently caused trouble for Waverley and I, as we were instructed not to run around the Kingdom Hall. The temptation to get Callum back was impossible to ignore and he rarely received the blame for it. Callum, his girlfriend and two other teenagers knew we had noticed them at the nightclub, but they continued to dance albeit awkwardly, in an attempt to enjoy themselves. They disappeared before midnight as everyone celebrated the new year.

On our next visit to my parents, Dan immediately told them he saw Callum and the other young members of their congregation at the New Years Eve nightclub party. My parents passed this information to the elders who confronted them about it. Unfortunately I discovered years later that Callum had depression and he told his girlfriend he had suicidal thoughts. She did not take this seriously and the elders were of no help as they were not qualified to deal correctly with mental health problems. They did not approve of members seeking help from 'worldly' counsellors as the extent of mind control used within this religion would become apparent during the counselling sessions. Callum's depression was ignored, as Jehovah's Witnesses are supposed to be 'happy people'. They would not want outsiders knowing that some of them had depression. I remember an elder scolding me for crying at a funeral, as he said we had to show everyone that death does not make us sad because we have the hope of the resurrection. At twenty one years of age, Callum drove his car to a local woodland, fixed a hose to the exhaust pipe to feed the emission of fumes into it and took his own life. He was the only child of an elder and his wife. At this time they believed anyone who commits suicide does not receive a resurrection. He was not allowed a Jehovah's Witness funeral service either, but despite all this, his parents remained within the religion.

Dan had another motorcycle accident in 1985 where he broke both wrists and some of his fingers after crashing into the side of a Porsche. The driver had turned into his driveway without indicating as Dan was travelling in the opposite direction. The smallest digit on his left hand bent to a ninety degree angle as it healed and interfered with his work. Surgery to straighten it was unsuccessful so he was readmitted to hospital to have the top half of his finger amputated. Whilst Dan was in hospital, Marl and Joel visited me. I opened the door and as they walked in I paused waiting for Kirk to follow. On a previous visit he had climbed the scaffolding to look at the building work in process on the top floor and I thought he may be up there again. I realised he was not with them and when I joined the others, they told me Kirk was in a fatal car accident on their return from Wales. He had just purchased a new Ford Mini and was travelling back in it with his father. They stopped on the hard shoulder of the motorway, waiting for Marl to catch up, when a driver suddenly swerved and crashed into the back of their stationary car. The last time Kirk visited I remember him sitting Tania on his knee and straightening out her dress. He commented that she needed a little friend and soon after that we discovered Sadie his girlfriend was pregnant. He was excited about becoming a father and for him to pass away so tragically at only twenty six years of age with Sadie in the eighth month of her pregnancy was too terrible for words. His death has affected me, his family and friends to this day. Marl and Joel did not know Dan was in hospital when they broke the news, so I told him when he returned home the following day. We attended Kirk's funeral about a week later. I did not believe in the spirit world as some of my religious teachings still remained with me. I sensed however there was something after this life but did not know for sure. Annette explained that Kirk's body was merely a shell and his spirit had moved on but I found it hard to accept at this time. Annette's parents passed away when she was eighteen within a few months of one another and she was an only child. She had been through a horrendous time and had a tough life, however it did not change her. Annette continued to be a loving, genuine person with a good heart, and she is one of few friends that I can trust.

I learnt how the Filipino community reacts when a relative dies. Kirk's family asked for photographic images of the deceased at all stages to be sent to them in the Philippines. I saw them capturing images of his coffin in the grave. We returned to the family home for the wake and sat around the dining room table reminiscing about Kirk's mischievous antics. Sadie stood near us cradling her heavily pregnant abdomen watching Kirk's brothers converse with his former fiancee. I knew her well as Kirk had dated her for years. The atmosphere was a little awkward but Sadie handled it well. Dan and I were the last ones to leave and decided to do so when the family decided to watch the movie *Salem's Lot* on television. I did not feel comfortable watching this immediately after Kirk's funeral and Sadie also decided to leave, commenting the movie would give her disturbing thoughts.

We visited Kirk's parents a few days after the funeral to see how they were. His mother had more time to discuss the accident and said she was home alone at the time of the accident. She heard a huge thud on the ceiling as though someone overturned a heavy piece of furniture at the time it happened and contacted her neighbour asking her to sit with her as the noise frightened her. While Dan and Marl were conversing, I saw a huge pile of photographs on the lounge coffee table. I picked them up and began to look through them. I saw images of Kirk's Ford Mini after the crash with the back wheels pushed up into the front seating area and the area where the accident occurred. Marl was about to speak to me but changed his mind. I discovered why when I found images of Kirk's body laid out in the chapel of rest. I previously declined the offer of visiting him as I preferred to remember him as he was. Seeing these shocked me, but I could not take my eyes off them. Kirk's complexion was grey and his neck was swollen from the spinal injury and the post mortem. His dark hair and eyebrows were neatly combed and the undertakers had dressed him in a new white shirt and a black suit with a mandarin collar. Kirk had wanted to own one of those for a long time, but I was accustomed to seeing him in casual clothes and looking dishevelled most of the time. His neat appearance was completely out of character for the person we knew and loved. His lively personality and good advice he often gave was a devastating loss for us all. Janice, the neighbour who spread false rumours when Tania was born also knew Kirk. I sent a message to her through someone else to let her know Kirk had died and she then approached me to thank me for letting her know. We began to converse again, but I kept the 'neighbourly friendship' more distant from them on.

Dan and I lived in our maisonette for about a year. Although I loved this period property, the windows of the lounge and kitchen were so large, we were unable to afford curtains to cover them or heat the rooms adequately in winter. I contacted Lady Murelle from the Church Housing Association and she offered us a newly built two bedroom apartment in Northfield, ten miles from our former home. Just before our move, Dan had acquired a three-wheel car that he could drive when owning a motorcycle licence. This helped him learn to drive a car and he was due to take his driving test. I received an anonymous letter supposedly from a 'schoolgirl' who said she was involved in a sexual relationship with Dan. They apparently arranged to meet during his lunch breaks at work. She described herself as big breasted and wrote that Dan enjoyed fondling them because he told her that mine were too small. The girl was supposedly pregnant and she wrote that Dan wanted to leave me for her. He had apparently told her he was unhappy and that I ill-treated my baby daughter. She advised me to let Dan go. This letter arrived on the morning of Dan's driving test, and when I presented him with it, he looked nervous when he read it. He explained it could have been from a colleague at work who did not want him to pass his driving test the first time, as they had failed their first one. I listened to what Dan had said as I knew his colleague from school and that he could be particularly nasty. Dan passed his driving test that day, however on reflection, I am still unsure if this was the truth as I recall him mentioning that schoolgirls loitering outside the shop near his place of work. I let a few of my friends read the letter and they thought its content was too ridiculous to be genuine.

Whenever I moved home, the local Jehovah's Witnesses called at our new property, as my mother had informed them of my new address. The negative experiences with Janice, my former neighbour, meant that I kept my distance from others in the new apartment block. She eventually had a child of her own and was moved into the apartment next to ours. I conversed with her but kept our relationship more distant, however she now had new neighbours to involve herself with. Dan left the place where he worked as an apprentice and began a new job at a jeweller's workshop. It was over twenty miles away from our home and there were evenings when he took change of clothes with him and stayed out until the early hours of the morning. Dan told me he was going to a bowling alley with colleagues from work, but I later heard from Marl's girlfriend that Dan visited nightclubs with them. She told me that one occasion he brought a sales assistant from the jewellery shop below his workshop. Dan had told me that the staff in the workshop did not see the sales assistants in the shop, but I discovered this was untrue. I did not immediately believe Marl's girlfriend as she had lied before, but she told me the name of the sales assistant and to check this out.

I took her to visit my friend Danielle and asked her to repeat her story. Danielle contacted the shop by telephone and the young woman answered the phone. I later confronted Dan about it and he did not deny it but said there was nothing between them both, only that he took her out for the evening. He then criticised her appearance, telling me she was ugly with protruding discoloured teeth. Apparently he became upset on his night out because Joel asked her for a slow dance. Dan felt inferior to him. I wanted to speak to the sales assistant myself to see what she had to say, so the following day I waited outside the jewellery shop at closing time. Dan pointed her out and then left me to confront her. I introduced myself and her hands began to shake while she held on to her umbrella. I asked her about the situation and discovered Dan told her the predictable story of 'my wife doesn't understand me'. She assured me she was not attracted to him and only accompanied him to the nightclub as a friend. She expressed her surprise to see how attractive I was, as she said Dan's description was totally different. Apparently he had also been transporting her home from work each day which explained why he was often late and she purchased cigarettes for him in payment. I later spoke to a friend of mine about this and they replied that they had seen a female in his car but decided not to say anything.

Dan and I had married far too young and he was jealous of the freedom his friends had. They dated many young girls and this was a constant reminder of the life he missed. The disagreements and fights with Dan escalated after this and our neighbours grew concerned when they heard my screams. They thought about contacting the police but had no desire to become involved. I eventually applied for a court injunction to stop his violent outbursts and on the day we attended court, Dan had been well behaved and kinder to me. I then regretted taking this step as I sensed life could become more volatile if I went through with it. At court, Dan sat in front of them with Tania on his lap acting like an affectionate devoted father and cited provocation on my part that caused his violent reactions. To keep the peace, I agreed to this so they would be lenient with him. The court then put a restraining order on him for violence and one on me for provocation.

The violence predictably continued and late one evening I could take no more and contacted the police. They escorted Dan to his car and advised him to stay with his mother for a while. This behaviour was distressing for Tania who was three years of age. She had grown into a 'highly strung', nervous child who constantly craved love and attention. I did not think it fair that Dan treated me this way when he was the only person I had a sexual relationship with. Two of his friends were attracted to me, so I had extra marital affairs with them to gain experience with other young men. I no longer wanted an abusive man to be the only one with access to my body. I also suspected that Dan had been unfaithful to me, as he had been deceitful about people he worked with and places he had visited. On the occasions we visited a nightclub together, he would leave me to walk around on his own. At times I stood back and watched him 'chat up' other women at the bar when he did not know I was there. Some evenings he would want to leave the clubs early, saying that there were men who would assault him outside. On reflection, he may may have been caught making advances to their girlfriends.

Dan's new occupation placed him in a better financial situation, so he decided to purchase a property nearer his place of work. We lived in Northfield for two years and then moved to a two-bedroom house in Chatford. Dan's relationship with his work colleagues was fraught, as the men insulted and teased him throughout the day. He would often return home in a bad mood and would take his anger out on Tania and me. Dan avoided fights with men and would not stand up to them, however he did not think twice about using physical violence on women.

CHAPTER 8

BAD ASSOCIATIONS SPOIL
USEFUL HABITS

The nightclubs we frequented had competitions and performances where scantily-clad women performed on stage. Dan made a point of standing at the front near the stage to observe them. I knew that when we returned home, he would use my body while talking to me about them. Dan admired the 'glamour models' and 'kissogram girls' which did not help my self esteem and I felt that I was not good enough.

I then discovered a local model agency and applied to join. I also joined a 'kissogram' company. I wanted to prove to myself that I was as attractive as the women he admired and if Dan stood at the front of the stage in nightclubs to watch these women, I may as well be on it. The positive outcome of this was that I grew in confidence, particularly when I visited 'stag nights' as a kissogram and learned to control a crowd of drunken men.

It was on one of my modelling assignments that I met Tifelle. She was a few years younger than I and married with two small daughters. Tifelle had more experience in the modelling world and gave me some useful advice. My image appeared in local newspapers when they published articles on local beauty competitions. Two young men were reading a newspaper that displayed one of these photographs while taking a break on their window cleaning round. They worked for Kevin who saw them looking at what he assumed was a photograph of a group of models in lingerie. He then recognised me. Kevin immediately visited my parents with the newspaper to show them. I also appeared in television commercials, fashion magazines and my image was displayed on boxes of new lingerie. These images give the purchaser the impression that the underwear inside the box fits the model perfectly, however they are unaware of the huge amount of pins holding the item in place to give that impression.

Faye, the manager of the model agency, had a daughter the same age as Tania. I stopped them playing together after a while, as I discovered that their family was promiscuous and the children were playing games together that disturbed me. It was so difficult to keep Tania safe as we seemed to be surrounded by an unhealthy sexual energy from most people we knew.

Faye escorted me and other girls to a nightclub in London frequented by influential men. She pointed them out to us and explained who they were. She added that if we wanted to progress in our modelling careers, it could mean offering sexual favours to some of them. I was not ambitious enough to go that far, but one of my stunning friends became a page three model for a well known tabloid newspaper. She took one of my photographs with her and they were interested, however accepting their offer meant I would be required to travel overseas for work assignments. I did not want to leave my daughter for long periods of time with people I did not trust. At this time I had part time work in a lingerie shop run by an older couple. They also sold fetish wear and told me that some of their customers were transvestites. I discovered that in the next building was an escort agency. The manager asked to see me and offered to pay me one thousand pounds if I agreed to spend an evening with a man. He said that he had many women he employed that he could ask, but for this booking he wanted someone with more class. I asked if it would mean spending the night with him and he replied that this was a possibility. Although it was a huge amount of money, I politely declined. It did not take long for me to discover how superficial, spiteful and abusive the modelling world could be. After speaking to many of the young women, I also discovered most were sexually abused as children and they learnt from a young age how to use their bodies to gain power and be successful in life.

Dan and I met a young couple who were involved in an American pyramid selling company that promised them wealth. The business initially interested us and they introduced us to the charismatic couple who recruited them. We attended some of their meetings and purchased a kit of cleaning products. We tried to sell these products to friends and relatives as instructed. Some of them initially purchased a few products to help us out but did not want them on a regular basis. We were invited to attend a district convention and I noticed how reminiscent it was to the way Jehovah's Witnesses organised their meetings and conventions. Those at the top of the pyramid were making a huge profit and invited some of their recruits to the stage. There were huge hugs and plenty of affection to make them feel important. The recruits were asked to relate their experiences and success, encouraging others to put extra effort into their businesses. Those at the bottom of the pyramid are then instructed to recruit others to work for them so that their earnings would increase.

Our friends began to distance themselves as they were uncomfortable about this business and no longer wanted to purchase products, let alone sign up for recruitment. On reflection and after research, I now know that this business is another form of cult organisation and I was fortunate to leave it after only two months.

Dan and I had stayed in contact with Ena and Percy who were our neighbours when we lived in the maisonette. We did not begin associating with them until after we had moved away. They invited us to their home on a few occasions and Percy revealed that they frequented a local naturist club. He invited us to attend one evening with them and at first we declined. I had enough difficulties with Dan's addiction and a naturist club could worsen this situation. Percy was persistent about this and one evening we arrived at their home to find them both naked. It seemed he hoped that we would also disrobe and when we did not, Ena began to feel a little self-conscious and left the room to put on a dress. After weeks of persistence, we eventually agreed to try it for one evening. Dan had wanted to go all along and I sensed that he asked them to persuade me. I was surprised to discover that the club members varied in age from eighteen to eighty. It was like a family atmosphere and their bodies were not as glamorous as I imagined them to be. The atmosphere was relaxed and I noticed less of a barrier as people without clothes conversed freely and honestly. There was also no class distinction as you could not tell who was more affluent, or who dressed better than another person. The venue did not charge a huge membership fee, so we joined. Ena introduced me to Monty, the owner who was middle aged, well spoken and quite a charmer with the ladies. He set up the naturist club in the 1960s and it had been popular for years. Ena said that Monty would like me and she was right! The venue organised a camera club for amateur photographers one Sunday afternoon each month and I was offered modelling work there. I also attended their Fun Day and won the International Naturist Beauty Competition in 1988. My image appeared in the famous *Health and Efficiency* magazine. Dan and I regularly attended the club and it soon became apparent there were many couples known as 'swingers'. Many of the women were bi-sexual, however most of them participated only to please their husbands. Dan noticed other women were attracted to me and used this to gradually become involved with them himself. He gave me a 'false sense of security' by setting rules that neither of us would participate in wife-swapping, however he gradually involved himself a little more with each visit. I had entered what could only be described as a ' murky swamp' of quick-sand that was pulling me in deeper and I felt I had no way out.

Tania was an anxious child. She was hyperactive and distressed from the fraught, violent life at home. This would often escalate at night and it reached the point where Dan threatened me with a broken lager bottle. Tania cried out to me from her bedroom, then I would rush to her room to hug and reassure her it would calm down. When Dan entered the room, Tania had learnt that if she sat on my lap, he would not hit me. Instead, he vomited over both of us and I had to change her bed and our nightclothes before I could make us both comfortable. Tania once had a mark on her abdomen as Dan would threaten to cane her with a stick of bamboo. She told me that he did cane her when he looked after her. Someone at our local Inn asked Tania about the mark and she told them I had hit her with the cane. Gossip spread within the Inn that I was being cruel to her and Dan backed up this story when they spoke to him about it. I noticed that many of the women in the

Inn were watching me and were unfriendly. When I heard about the gossip, I visited the landlady and told her the truth of the situation. The landlady replied it had puzzled her, as when Tania was with me she never cowered from me but was always affectionate. I also expressed my concerns to the social worker who warned me that it did not matter to them if I chose to stay with Dan, however they would investigate Tania's safety and consider taking her into social care.

I could have still returned to the Jehovah's Witnesses, as I no longer attended their meetings and had moved twice since then. However, if I returned again, the elders would want to know all details of the life I led since they last saw me and would use it against me. It seemed a hopeless situation, however something was about to happen that would provide a way out and change my life.

On New Years Eve of 1988, Dan and I were invited to a private party hosted by a member of the naturist club. We collected Tifelle from her home and visited the club-house first. A while after we arrived, she said that she had seen a handsome young man near the dance floor. Good looking men with muscular bodies were few at this venue, so seeing one was quite a novelty! Tifelle pointed him out when she saw him again and he was handsome, muscular and stockily built. He had dark hair and deep brown eyes that studied everyone around him. His arms were folded and he stood there totally naked apart from a pair of casual beige shoes. I approached Dan and suggested we invite this young man to accompany us at the private party. Tifelle wanted to have some fun as she was unhappy in her marriage and described her husband as boring. I witnessed him punch her in the breast on one occasion. Dan introduced himself to Patrick and then said: "You aren't one of those 'perverts' are you!" He conversed with Patrick for a while before

Tifelle and I joined them and we were introduced. Patrick accepted our invitation and Tifelle travelled with him in his car and followed us. She asked him about his occupation as she took out a large herbal cigarette known as a 'spliff' from her bag. He replied that he was a policeman and we thought this amusing! Tifelle said it did not bother him and he had a few 'puffs' on it. I felt a little envious of her travelling in his car, as Dan was shouting and swearing at me because I made a mistake with the directions. He stopped the car and Patrick got out of his to speak to us. He said that he knew the area well and told us to follow him. Before he left us we exchanged a smile and I was relieved he was there.

At the party, I asked Patrick more about his work in the police force. I also asked if he could suggest any self-defence moves and he was eager to demonstrate, not realising I needed them to defend myself from Dan. Patrick was a confident, informative man who took control of the situation and I found this extremely attractive. Dan was unsure of himself in the presence of other men and could not say 'no', to those who pressured him into something he did not really want to do. He thought he would lose friends if he did. It was only when we were at home that Dan exerted his control using manipulation, demands and violence. The parties we attended were mainly for 'wife-swapping' couples and although we attended, we had not participated in these activities. They respected this, but assumed it would only be a matter of time before we changed our minds as we had seen this happen with other couples. Dan disappeared at the party and Tifelle met a handsome young man in a soldier's camouflage uniform. Patrick and I were left on our own and he asked where the upstairs bathroom was. I explained and he left me momentarily. I stood in the lounge alone when two women I knew approached asking if we could discuss a matter with me. They explained that apparently Dan made it obvious he wanted to 'wife-swap' and cited me as the reason he had to decline. Both of these women lived with one man. One was his wife and the other was a friend who moved in with them. The wife was extremely attractive, slim with long dark hair and bright blue eyes. I could not understand why her husband was dissatisfied and wanted the other woman who was not so attractive. They both said that as their man was attractive and they were in no doubt that I would want him, there should be no problem with us taking it further. I replied that I was not attracted to their man in the slightest and the conversation ended there. I saw Dan a while later and related this conversation to him. He denied what they had said and walked away. Patrick returned from the bathroom in surprise at the activities going on when he passed the bedrooms. He thought that I did not know about it, but I explained that this was par for the course at these parties and I had a few encounters with women but avoided the men. Patrick and I conversed until midnight and we shared a new year kiss, but soon after that he disappeared. Tifelle said he had to work an early shift on New Year's Day so he had to leave. I did not get the chance to say goodbye to him and regretted that I had no contact details for him.

From the first day of 1989, my relationship with Dan changed dramatically. He often stayed out all night and I discovered years later that he met a woman at the new years eve party that developed into an extra marital affair. I sat up all night hugging Tania, crying and pleading with him to return. When he returned the next day, he hardly spoke to me. After ten years of hoping Dan would change, I then realised this would not happen. I remembered the conversation with my social worker who threatened to take Tania into social care if I stayed with him. I also remembered the time Tania cried and said; "Please find me a nice Daddy.". I knew it was time to leave, but I was unsure how to go about it. Tifelle and I began visiting nightclubs alone. We discussed the men we met on our nights out, but my mind constantly returned to Patrick. I asked Tifelle about their conversations in his car and if he had given any clues as to where he lived, but she could not remember. She was seeing the young soldier she met at the party and had no interest in Patrick.

On Valentine's Day, Dan received a mysterious card from someone. I did not know if it was sent by the same colleague who sent the other letter, but on reflection Dan was also having an affair at the time. He was often violent during the night and then he retired to bed leaving us upset and slept soundly. I understand why some women were driven to the point where they had murdered their violent husbands while they slept.

I was still in contact with Reginald, he took Tania and I out for the day on her birthday. We visited London and he bought her presents and took us out for a meal. He invited me to his home in Graveton for lunch and told me to hire a taxi and he would pay the fare when I arrived. Reginald still lived with the same woman and on one occasion when Tania was a baby, I boarded a bus and saw them both seated on it as passengers. She looked at me with daggers and Reginald looked the other way. I was concerned about visiting his home and having a twenty mile journey in a taxi, where I would not have the money for the huge fare if anything went wrong. I did not arrive that day and he was upset about it.

My mother contacted me by telephone distressed saying she did not like to think about me being abused by Dan. On one occasion when we visited her Dan hit me in her presence. He also swore at her and this shocked her. He took advantage of my father's absence that evening as he would not have dared to behave that way in his presence. My mother spoke of the times she was violent towards me and that I was the only child who did not retaliate whenever she hit me. My father was much bigger and I would have been in trouble if I had! She begged me to leave Dan. On reflection, maybe she realised that I accepted Dan's violence as she behaved the same way towards me. It was something I was used to throughout my life.

I contacted Linsey by telephone when I was upset about Dan's treatment of me. She replied she was fed up with hearing about it and soon everyone else would also feel the same. Linsey told me to leave him before everyone stopped listening to me. Dan's brother's wife also told me that I was young enough to start a new relationship, whereas she was too old to do the same. She decided to stay with Dan's brother and tolerate the abuse she received. Three female family members in a short space of time told me that I should leave. I then reflected on my life with Dan and concluded there was nothing in our marriage worth saving. I realised I had wasted too much time already by hoping he would change and the time had come to let it go.

At the end of March 1989, Tifelle and I attended an Easter event at the naturist club. We had limited funds for nightclubs and women at this venue were not required to pay an entry fee. As there was no licensed bar, all club members brought their own drinks with them. These factors resulted in a cheap night out! Tifelle and I entered the clubhouse and conversed with people we knew. I approached the disc jockey to request a tune and felt a firm hand upon my shoulder. I turned and was delighted to see Patrick smiling at me. We spent the evening together and I told him about my unhappy marriage, the violent situation and my concerns for Tania. I explained that I wanted a divorce and Patrick seemed understanding and sympathetic. He shocked me when he asked if we could become a couple, however I later discovered that he asked in haste as he noticed that another man was attracted to me. I was a little unsure at first, but Tifelle persuaded me to date him as she said he was a good looking man with a good body, his own home and had a good career.

On Sunday I arranged to see Patrick again so I told Dan he could make his own arrangements that day as I had other plans. I walked to the train station with Tania and Patrick arrived in his car to transport us to his cottage. Patrick tried to converse with Tania in the car, but she decided to ignore him which was rather embarrassing. We arrived at Patrick's cottage, a typical 'bachelor pad' that needed a clean-up and a vacuum. There were dirty dishes in the kitchen sink, at least a few days old. I offered to clean them which pleased him and as I did so, I could not remember a time when I felt so relaxed. When I tidied the lounge, I noticed a tabloid newspaper behind the couch that usually featured topless women. He explained that he had purchased it because of the front page story. It was about someone breaking into Buckingham Palace and the police re-enacting another break-in to test the security. I then discovered Patrick worked at the palace as a police guard. I spent the Easter weekend with him and we visited an Inn where I met his sisters and a couple of his friends. Patrick advised me to legally separate from Dan by asking him to move out of the property. I would then need to contact a solicitor to begin divorce proceedings. It seemed quite a daunting step to take but I knew it was time to do so.

On Tuesday, Dan contacted my parents and other members of my family asking if they knew my whereabouts. I had stayed overnight at

Patrick's home and my relatives were concerned as my disappearance was out of character and they were aware of our volatile relationship. Our home had a cellar and they feared he may have murdered me and hid me there, saying that I was missing. Patrick transported me to Tifelle's home, and after staying a while, he left and she transported me home. Dan was outside the house in his car about to drive away with his sixteen-year-old work apprentice. He looked pale as if he had not slept. After all the nights he spent away from home without telling me, he had a taste of how it felt. I explained to Dan I had given a lot of thought to the future of our relationship and decided it was time to separate. I suggested he packed his clothes and moved in with his mother. Dan and his apprentice were shocked at first, but Dan replied that they were about to go out for the evening, so he would discuss the matter on his return. I immediately contacted Patrick to update him on the conversation and he said that I should not stay there, as Dan would likely be intoxicated on his return. He thought the violence could become extreme if Dan believed I planned to leave. Patrick then added what I needed to hear, that he wanted Tania and I to move in with him. I thought we would both be safer with a policeman. I asked Tifelle to help me pack my clothes and transport me to Patrick's home. She panicked as she did not know how to get there and was afraid of how Dan would react if she helped me. I picked up the telephone and contacted the woman I worked for at the kissogram agency. She told me she was once in a similar situation and offered to help. As I packed our clothes into a few dustbin liners, Dan unexpectedly returned. He saw the bags and said: "Leaving are we?". I replied that as he would not leave, I had to. Tifelle and I were relieved when he bent down and kissed Tania goodbye before leaving the house. He made no attempt to ask us to stay or stop us from leaving, as on reflection, he may not have believed I meant it.

When I arrived at Patrick's home he was surprised how much luggage I brought with me, as I had no intention of returning. I was unfamiliar with the area and the next day he suggested I explore the town while he returned to work. Patrick suggested that I contacted the local school so Tania could attend after the Easter holidays. Most importantly, he advised me to also contact a solicitor and begin divorce proceedings. The first phone call I made was to my parents and Waverley to let them know Tania and I were alive and well. Waverley was excited I had done this and my parents asked where I was. I replied that I was staying with female friends as I knew they would not approve of me living with Patrick. A few days later, Patrick transported me to my parents home and waited for me in the car. I explained to them that we were dating and when I told my father that Patrick was a policeman and we would be safe with him, he replied that being a policeman does not necessarily mean he is a good man. Waverley's first reaction was: "Trust YOU to date a policeman"!, as she admired men who were bad boys with criminal records. When Patrick worked night shifts, I received silent phone calls at four in the morning. I heard a budgie tweeting in the background and wondered if my mother suspected I was living with Patrick and phoned at this time to see if he answered. When I told her about the silent calls and mentioned that I heard a budgie, she laughed, but did not deny it was her who called. On reflection, Waverley had visited me there, so I would not be surprised if she had told my parents exactly what was going on.

The governing body of Jehovah's Witnesses will only agree to a couple divorcing if one has committed adultery. Patrick was adamant

Dan had been unfaithful, but I was uncertain as I did not know he was having an affair. Although I had two affairs myself, I would rather tell the elders that he had committed adultery as I knew it would create further trouble for me. I met with Dan one afternoon as he wanted to see Tania and he confessed to me about the affair he had from New Years Eve, so Patrick was right. I was then glad that I had affairs, as it would have been more devastating for me if I was faithful throughout our abusive marriage.

Patrick's neighbour was Alice, a single policewoman in the Kent constabulary. There were signs that she was attracted to him as when I first visited his home, an Easter egg was placed on his doorstep with a note that read: "From Me to You". He had received a local anonymous Valentines card too. Patrick said he had helped Alice when her horse was put to sleep. She wanted to thank him and invited him out for a meal with her parents. She also gave Patrick 'dressage' horse riding lessons that did not last long as he found her too serious and abrupt. Her resentment was obvious when I moved in as Patrick had not told his parents immediately. Alice contacted them to break the news and told Matilda his mother I was living there and abusing his hospitality. Soon after that, Matilda unexpectedly visited the cottage and let herself in while Patrick was at work. I was upstairs in the bathroom and when I descended the stairs I was surprised to see her standing there. We sat down together and conversed for quite a while. Matilda realised that I was not the type of person Alice had described and this put her mind at rest. She told Patrick that she approved and thought I would get on well with his eldest sister. Patrick arrived home from work one evening and asked if Dan had visited the house. I assured him no one had called that evening and we had a peaceful time watching television. He seemed puzzled and I later discovered Alice contacted Patrick at work, telling him there was a strange car outside the cottage and she heard screams and raised voices. It seemed she wanted to give the impression I was causing problems, hoping it would end our relationship and he would ask me to move out.

I resumed my usual routine of housework and caring for Tania in the home. When I hung Patrick's working shirts on the rotary washing line, Alice took out her garden hose to water her plants by late afternoon and sprayed it over the garden fence, soaking all the dry shirts. We received telephone calls during the night where someone quickly hung up when we answered. Dan did not know where we were at this time, so I did not suspect him. This also happened while I was sunbathing in the garden. Alice disappeared into her house from the garden and the phone began to ring. I went into the house to answer it and the caller hung up. I returned to the garden and Alice was outside again. The phone rang again and before I answered it I glanced over the fence to see if Alice was in her garden. She physically jumped when she heard the phone ring and I looked at her. On this occasion it was someone else. Patrick had explained to Alice about the problems I had with Dan and maybe she thought I would leave if I suspected he had found me. I am relieved he did not tell her Dan's whereabouts as she may have informed him. When Alice's meddling was unsuccessful, she sold her cottage and moved away, leaving Patrick a card to say goodbye and that she was sorry they were unable to continue being good neighbours!

My divorce took seven months to complete, as Dan was cooperative and stated that if I did not ask for child maintenance, he would not ask for visiting rights to Tania. I agreed to these terms as Dan was not in the right frame of mind to be a responsible father and I did not think

Tania would be safe with his violent rages. Dan was never admitted to a psychiatric ward when I met him, unlike his mother and brothers, but three weeks after I left and he realised I was not returning, he was then admitted. He told the staff I had left him and taken his daughter away, but did not tell them about his behaviour. On the occasions I contacted the hospital during our divorce, the staff were hostile and treated me as the person at fault. I had always got on well with his mother Jenny, but my mother warned me that when you upset a mother's son, they will change towards you. Of course, my mother would have known that.

CHAPTER 9

SECOND MARRIAGE

Patrick and I married three weeks after I received my decree absolute. We booked our marriage date for the first week in December of 1989. We decided to marry at a registry office, as my parents and Patrick's friends would only agree to attend a non-religious ceremony. The reason for marrying in haste was that my parents wanted to know my place of residence. However, after we had married, my mother continued to contact me on the same telephone number and said nothing about it.

Patrick had apparently played horrendous tricks on his friends when they had their' stag nights, so they were eager for revenge. As I was concerned about what they may do to him, we arranged a joint 'stag and hen' night two days before the wedding. His friends accused him of 'hiding behind my skirts', but I did not trust them. I had visions of them putting him naked on a train while intoxicated and him ending up somewhere far away before the wedding. His friends brought along two 'ball and chain' attachments and fastened them to our ankles. My plastic ball was light and easy to wear but they had filled Patrick's with concrete. We were then chained together which meant we had to visit the male and female lavatories together. Patrick's friends plied him with triple measures of rum and they added raw chillies that were floating in his drinks. He also drank a 'yard of ale' and a huge bowl of peanuts. At the end of the evening he became so ill they had to separate us. As we passed the local graveyard. Patrick jumped over the wall and fell to the ground unconscious and looking like a grey corpse amongst the graves. His friends took me home first and then returned for him to carry him home. I sat up all night nursing him. The next day he was ill and still vomiting. This angered me as I also had Tania to care for and she was in a lively mood. I expressed my feelings to Pete, Patrick's closest friend and best man. He offered to take care of Tania for the day with his wife while I nursed Patrick. I disliked Pete because he constantly spoke of Patrick's former girlfriends, particularly the one he was once engaged to. He had a photo album dedicated to Patrick with images of his former girlfriends that he had shown me. Pete married very young and seemed quite jealous that Patrick was now getting married. He felt he was losing his friend and also warned me I would have problems within my marriage if I was jealous, as a lot of women were attracted to him. Pete and his wife had a lot of influence over Patrick's life as they helped him to renovate and decorate his home. They also had a key to his home and on one occasion they collected piles of coins he had left around his home and used them to purchase groceries for him. Patrick would discuss all his life choices with them and they expected this to continue.

Patrick's father was loving and welcoming to Tania and I, but he commented I may find him boring after being married to a 'bad boy' which could be more exciting. I assured him I was happy with Patrick and that my first experience of marriage was far from exciting.

The registry office ceremony was formal and took about twenty minutes. We had our wedding meal in a small chapel that was converted into a hall. Matilda had hired this out as she was a member of the Red

Cross organisation that met there. Although Patrick and I planned to keep religion out of our wedding, my father stood up to make a 'father of the bride' speech and brought his bible with him. Fathers usually talk about their daughters and memories of them growing up. They also speak about the relationship they had. My father said nothing about this and decided to talk about how unbreakable a threefold cord would be if a man and woman included God within their married lives. He read out Ecclesiastes 4:12: *"And some may overpower one alone, but two together can take a stand against him. And a threefold cord cannot quickly be torn apart."* This did not please the friends of Patrick and I felt rather embarrassed. We tried to mix both sides of relatives and friends together at tables so they could get to know one another. Waverley announced to Patrick she did not want to be seated with a couple who were smokers. The couple concerned overheard this and were upset about it as they would not have smoked while sitting with her. Patrick's friends then decided to all sit together on a long table and smoked constantly throughout the wedding meal, to make a statement.

Patrick's parents hosted an evening reception at their home. My family members stayed in the dining room while Patrick's friends were in the lounge. Most of the wedding guests got on well together with an evening of dancing and singing. Tom and Amy Sheldon were there as they were like close family to me. They enjoyed being with Patrick's father who was quite the entertainer. Pete tried to get me to sing a backing chorus to his song and I refused, as I did not want to go along with his instructions. Before leaving the reception that evening, my mother stood in the doorway of the lounge to say farewell to Patrick's family and friends. She explained that she hadn't joined them in the lounge as she didn't want to inhale their cigarette smoke. As she left, the boyfriend of Patrick's youngest sister shouted "Well, we had to have your religion!!"

In January of 1990 we moved out of Patrick's tiny cottage. Tania had slept on a fold-down armchair-bed in the lounge for a year without complaint, so it was time she had a bedroom of her own again. Tania however, resented sharing my affection with Patrick as she had received all my love while I was married to Dan. Patrick sold his cottage and purchased a newly built three-bedroom house in a rural setting about ten miles from where we were . It was a beautiful terraced house in a good location. Patrick observed my relationship with Tania and had difficulty in understanding physical motherly affection. He referred to it as strange, and claimed he did not receive it from his own mother and could not understand the unusual relationship I had with my family. As I was now within a secure environment with less problems however, buried issues from my past began to surface.

One afternoon while visiting my parents, my mother discussed Waverley's second marriage. This occurred before I met Patrick, as her first marriage had lasted three years and she had two sons with her first husband. Waverley was pressured by my mother to become a baptised member of the Jehovah's Witnesses religion. She eventually agreed to do so at the age of twenty one. Waverley stated she would never marry within their religion as she thought the brothers were 'wimps'. Terry, a friend of her second husband attended their wedding and he was attracted to me. I had deliberately worn a black PVC dress to the wedding as I knew that my cousin Carmel and her daughter always had something negative to say about me, so I decided to give them something to talk about. It had the desired effect as they disliked my dress and commented that I looked like a 'tart'. While conversing with Terry, he said he had not yet purchased a wedding gift for them, so I offered to accompany him into town to help him choose one. Terry and I left the wedding reception and while we were in town, he met his mother who invited us to an Inn for a drink. We were absent from the wedding reception longer than expected and when we returned with a newly purchased gift, there were disapproving looks from my mother and Kevin.

My mother told me a few days later that the abusive family member commented that I wore the attire of a whore to the wedding and Terry and I were absent long enough to engage in sexual activity. This angered me, so I wrote a letter to him, relating what I heard and reminded him he had no right to judge me after the abuse he inflicted on me when he was seventeen years of age and I was six. I added that he sickened me.

On receiving this letter, he panicked and took the letter to my parents who immediately visited our home. We were in the middle of hosting a dinner party with his friend Pete and his wife, but they insisted their discussion could not wait. Patrick asked them to wait in our kitchen while we discussed this. The abusive family member's eyes were red and swollen from crying and they pleaded with me not to take the matter further, as he was only seventeen at the time and not aware of what he was doing. Patrick stated that at seventeen, he would be fully aware of his actions. My father and I later had a conversation about this when we were alone and he said the abuse had not bothered Waverley, so why should it bother me. He added that he would not have his name 'dragged through the mud'. I softened towards the abusive family member when he cried, saying that maybe he did not deserve to be my relative. I told him that I would take the matter no further and then they left us. Pete and his wife heard the whole conversation from our kitchen and were appalled that the abusive family member admitted his actions. I had already discussed the matter with local police officers who said that as the case was historical, they would be reluctant to pursue it as a prosecution would be unlikely.

I explained to Patrick how Jehovah's Witnesses lived their lives and viewed certain things, as he had no previous knowledge of this religion. He had a small circle of friends and some he had known from school. His friends were childless couples who eventually excluded Patrick and I from their social activities. Patrick enjoyed being unpredictable and purposely involved himself in unusual activities to gain attention, hence the reason we met. He was no longer keen on attending social evenings at the naturist club when he discovered the 'swinging scene' there. I continued to go with my friends because it was a night out that did not cost a huge amount of money, as it would when frequenting nightclubs. I was relieved to discover That Patrick was completely different to Dan with no pornography addiction, or anger issues which meant I could relax more. These were two reasons I fell deeply in love with him.

Patrick decided to attend the Jehovah's Witness meetings and learn more about it. He also agreed to a bible study. Two elders visited me to ensure that my divorce had met with their requirements and adultery had been committed. The information I gave satisfied them and they were pleased my second marriage was suitable 'in God's eyes'. My parents then assumed Patrick would become a new recruit and were delighted about this. He had an 'air of authority' about him because of his occupation and some members of the congregation thought that he was a visiting elder. My parents praised Patrick and spoke of him constantly. Linsey commented that this upset Waverley as she told her she was sick of hearing about us. Kevin said that Waverley was jealous because I lived in a beautiful mortgaged house in a good location, while she had a rented council house on a rough estate. As the years passed I could see this was true. As Patrick's bible study continued, his family and friends grew concerned that he would join the religion. Patrick enjoyed the extra attention that this generated.

Ian, a cousin of Clark (who was once the teenage bottom pincher) visited us each week with his wife Gaynor to conduct Patrick's bible study in the dining room. Gaynor conducted a bible study with me in the lounge. There was something about reading scriptures aloud from the bible that made me emotional and to this day I cannot explain why. On reflection, it may go back to the abusive family who made me read the scripture aloud about being a liar when I knew that I was telling the truth. Questions that I had about religion for years, with no satisfactory answers still bothered me as well as the hidden abuse. Gaynor asked me to read a scripture and I became emotional, so we had a long conversation about it. I asked her the questions that had remained unanswered for years and revealed the abuse I experienced in childhood. Although it shocked her, she advised me to leave the past behind and put those memories out of my mind.

At the next meeting, one of the elders asked Patrick about his occupation and when he replied that he was a police officer, the elder intimated that this would not be permanent if he was to join their religion. Patrick later discussed the matter with Ian, and he confirmed that to join their religion he would be required to leave the police force. Patrick immediately cancelled his bible study and after the response I received from Gaynor who offered no help, I sent a letter to the elders disassociating myself from the Jehovah's Witnesses. This meant that I would once again be treated as a disfellowshipped person and shunned.

CHAPTER 10

SECOND CHILD

Patrick's parents often asked me about my plans for pursuing a career, as all women in their family had one. I felt pressured and did not feel ready or confident enough to take this step. I discussed having a second child with Patrick as I thought it would be fair for him to have a child of his own as he was raising Tania. He agreed and we planned a conception so that I would give birth in the spring. I researched a method of how to conceive a male child as I sensed that Tania would resent it if Patrick had a daughter. Within a few months, I conceived and my twenty-week scan confirmed that the foetus was male.

I once again had the misfortune of having another neighbour who had difficulty conceiving. When my pregnancy was confirmed I asked Patrick not to tell our neighbours as I did not want a repetition of the last time I became pregnant, however, in his excitement he told them the news. After a while the neighbours turned against us as we asked them not to play loud music until the early hours of the morning. They stayed up late and slept until midday while their small children were locked in the bedroom. They continuously thumped on the walls to wake their parents and this was heard by our neighbours on the other side of our property. Despite these problems, my pregnancy was still more relaxed than the first one because I had a caring husband.

A mother who took her child to Tania's school warned me that the community believed I was carrying a dead baby. Apparently Tania told her school friends that my baby had died. We were shocked about this and I assured the mother that this was not true. As Tania had experienced abuse from Dan, I was concerned how she may treat our son if she wanted the baby to die.

When the time arrived for me to give birth, my nineteen-hour labour resulted in another emergency caesarean. I once again refused a blood transfusion although I was no longer a Jehovah's Witness at this time but the staff did not seem concerned about it. After the surgery, they said there was minimal blood loss, however the blood count was low so I was prescribed iron tablets to raise the levels. Ryan, our son spent five days in a special care baby unit with breathing problems, but he was a hefty nine pounds in weight and strong enough to survive. He returned to the ward with me and was ravenous for food. It seemed my breast milk was not enough for him and after two days and nights with no sleep and trying to recover from surgery, the nurses advised me to bottle-feed him. I noticed during my labour that one of the student nurses had a 'crush' on Patrick. She was in the labour ward when Ryan was born and cried when he had difficulties. The nurse visited me often in the ward when Patrick was there. Patrick's mother was unusually nice to me after the birth and gave me a gift of beautiful ivory satin nightwear. I left it on my bed when visiting the special care unit and when I returned, a lady in the bed opposite said that a young woman cleaned the area around my bed and she closed the curtains. I found that the nightwear was missing and this saddened me as it had meant a lot to receive this gift from my mother in law. I purposely chose to give birth at the training hospital where she worked, hoping it would please her, however there were a few incidents during my stay that caused me to regret it.

Our neighbours were more considerate on my return home as they heard that Ryan and I had a difficult time. We then had a relaxed and peaceful atmosphere to settle into our routine. In the first two months of his life, Ryan received a lot of attention from my family who had visited me after the difficult birth. Tom, Amy, Mary and Philip Shelden also visited us frequently to see Ryan and this meant a lot to me. One evening, Tania suddenly disclosed that Albert had inappropriately touched her three years ago when she was five and he was fifteen. I remembered an occasion while visiting my parents that Albert brought his nightwear into the lounge and changed from his day clothes by the gas fire. Tania was a toddler at this time and when she ran to him, I saw him take her hand and pull it towards him when he had nothing on from the waist down. She pulled her hand from his and walked away. I immediately told my mother what I had seen and she said the beaded curtain separating the lounge and dining room would have prevented me from seeing this clearly. At this time, the curtain was tied back.

When I had disclosed my abuse, it was kept within the family and I was labelled a liar. I did not want the same to happen to my daughter, so I chose not to ignore her disclosure and do nothing. Patrick then arranged for Tania to be interviewed by two police officers from Child Protection. Tania was already attending regular sessions with a child psychologist as there were aspects of her behaviour that were rather disturbing. We hoped these sessions would help us discover the reasons she acted this way. Tania enjoyed the attention she received from three police officers during her interview and when they asked her to demonstrate what occurred by the use of dolls, I noticed their puzzled expressions as maybe she did not act or describe the abuse in a way that other victims had.

After Tania's interview, the police officers planned to interview Albert. I had made the mistake of confiding in a friend who then passed this information to Selene. She passed it on to Waverley and my parents immediately visited us to persuade us not to pursue this. My mother began to cry the moment she entered the room, but her tears did not have the desired effect. It was as though she 'flipped a switch', and then her distress turned to anger and she began making threats. Patrick opened the door and ordered her to leave, so she sat in my father's car. Patrick then told my father the matter was with the police and out of our hands. When Albert was eventually interviewed, Waverley, who had in the past defended the abusive family member's behaviour, accompanied him. He was considered a 'vulnerable adult' with traits of Asperger's syndrome so a 'responsible adult' is allowed to be present for the interview. When Patrick asked the police officers about the interview the apparently told him it was well-rehearsed by the family because they had been forewarned. Albert denied the accusations and as it was Tania's word against his, there was nothing they could do. Patrick also said that before leaving the interview, Waverley said that if Tania had been abused it was by us rather than members of her family. It was no surprise that my family cut off all contact with us from them on.

As the years passed there was a disturbing outcome and we discovered that Tania had told many 'stories' at school that were untrue. She had listened to all our conversations and knew that I was abused as a child. This meant she could use my concerns about protecting my children as a tool for manipulation. I had difficulty in keeping Tania away from predators as on reflection she inherited her father's addictive personality and was drawn to them. I was also concerned about her behaviour with Ryan as I did not want him to be abused by her. The truth of the matter between Tania and Albert remains unresolved.

To understand more about my past and childhood abuse, I enrolled in a voluntary counselling course with an organisation that assists survivors of sexual abuse. It was a difficult course for me, as a student is required to re-visit and relate their own experiences. The hardest part was when we were asked to draw an illustration of our traumatic life experiences. Each member of the group took it in turn to place their illustration on a board supported by an easel and explain their illustrations to the group. It was an emotional experience and I was unable to complete it. The group were visited by police officers from the local child protection team who related horrific stories of the lengths that abusers go in order to control and silence their child victims. These stories are impossible to forget. When I completed the course, I received a counselling Diploma and provided assistance for victims who contacted the organisation by telephone. It was similar to the way in which the Samaritan organisation operates.

CHAPTER 11

COLLEGE EDUCATION

Patrick suggested that I enrolled in a college course to embark on a new career. My ambition from childhood was to be a professional dancer but in my mid thirties, I felt too old to go into this. I would have been in competition with teenage students who had more energy and flexibility. I told Patrick that I would like to do a Psychology course as I had a fascination for how the human mind works. Patrick advised against this saying that the course would take over four years for me to complete. I then remembered the conversation I had with Dana the American *sister,* about her regular manicures and how popular the beauty industry is. I then enrolled in a two-year Beauty Therapy course. My college courses were intense and in the evenings, I would walk to the car park exhausted and noticed the moon shining down on me. It felt like a motherly presence, as if she were saying: "I am here". She followed me all the way home each night and my connection with her deepened. Patrick had also advised me to meditate as he said it would help with my stress levels. At first I was reluctant because of the warnings from my parents. I eventually put those thoughts aside and followed beginners instructions that I found on the internet. I began to notice positive changes and my stress levels were not as high. I began to think more about my mortality and the meaning of life as I had avoided all spirituality and religions after my experience with the Jehovah's Witnesses. I was curious about the 'new age' scene and Witchcraft, but at this time, information on these subjects was not readily available.

Although I was a mature student, these college courses made me feel young again. The younger students in my class were fascinated by my spiritual interest in Witchcraft and my fun, mischievous energy as I did not act like an older woman. On reflection, I believe that being raised in a cult keeps a person's mind undeveloped, so they are behind when it comes to maturity.. The other older female students were competitive and resentful when many of the treatments came naturally to me and I received high marks for them. They began to spread rumours about me because the younger students were drawn to me and accused me of seduction. Patrick and I spoke to the tutors about this and they advised me not to worry about it and spoke to the students who were spreading the rumours. I won a Student of the Year Award for 1997 and also the College make-up competition. I went on to represent our college at the International Make Up Competition in Brighton. I discovered at this event how highly competitive my tutors were against other local colleges and this placed extra pressure on me. I wanted to finish the cosmetic image for my model with a few silver face stickers, but my tutors said that using these was against the rules. I felt a little dissatisfied with my work as I could not complete the look I had visualised without them. Ironically, the winner of the competition had used facial stickers. The teachers said that the work I had done that evening made me a strong contender for a winning place. During the final year of the course I noticed how clients would confide in their therapists about personal problems. I then decided that instead of working on a client's outer appearance, I wanted to go on to study treatments that calmed the mind and helped to heal emotions. I enrolled in courses for Aromatherapy, Reflexology, and Indian Head massage.

My parents resumed contact with me after a period of six years without it. I cannot recall the reason for this, but my mother sent me a card adding the usual scriptures and enclosed a recent photograph of her and my father at the age of sixty five. I agreed to visit them and my mother cried out as she hugged me, saying that her arms had ached to hold me. I saw tears in her eyes as she looked at me and she expected me to have the same reaction, but at this time I felt numb. I told my parents about my ongoing college courses and they both volunteered to be case studies. I provided Reflexology treatments for my father, and Aromatherapy for my mother. On one occasion when I had arranged to visit them, the abusive family member arrived and immediately approached me saying: "Give us a hug"! I did not respond and he still hugged me without my permission. My parents quietly exchanged glances but said nothing. He then sat at the dining room table opposite my father and conversed with him about their religion. As he did so, I fixed my gaze upon him, that conveyed I could see right through him while listening to the hypocritical conversation. He did not stay for long and when my mother walked with him to the front door, I heard a whispered conversation between them. I wondered whether my mother had told him I was visiting that afternoon.

When I returned the following week, the abusive family member was already there and I sensed I had interrupted a serious conversation between him and my parents. On this occasion his reaction towards me was cold and distant. He left soon after my arrival and although my parents sat with me, they were deep in thought and quiet after this conversation. I did not ask them about it and did not discover what it was about until a few years had passed. I felt uncomfortable that he had visited them twice on days I had arranged to be there. That day I had completed the case studies, so I wrote to my mother saying that I thought it better not to continue my visits. She promptly replied by letter saying she felt the same way and her arms had stopped aching for me now. She never failed to end her letters with 'Christian Love' and a scripture from the bible, as she could then record the time it took her to write the letter. They filled in a report form of hours they had preached at the end of each month before handing it in to the organisation. My mother once said that if I spoke to a person for two hours and mentioned one scripture or sentence related to the religion, I could record all that time on my report. I am sure there were many pioneers who took advantage of that!

Patrick arranged a family vacation for us in the north of Cornwall. I was accustomed to visiting places I knew from my childhood, but he assured me I would love this area and he was right. During our vacation, Patrick's colleague suggested we visit a Witchcraft Museum in Boscastle. It was there I read about the horrific tortures people accused of Witchcraft suffered at the hands of Christian believers. Many were innocent of these allegations. I concluded that if Christians were guilty of these horrific actions towards their fellow man and cited people who practised witchcraft as evil, maybe the occult was not really the evil practise they portrayed it to be. This inspired me to search for Witchcraft, although I did not know where to begin. At this time Matilda invited us to her August birthday barbecue and she coincidentally introduced me to Stella, not knowing that she was a practising Witch. Stella invited me to her home and provided me with literature to study. I found an advertisement for a Reiki course in one of the magazines that taught students healing treatments. The healing energy also worked on practitioners while they channelled it for the recipient. This sounded ideal for me and within five years I qualified in all three levels of Reiki and have taught these courses to many others.

It was easier to connect with Pagan practices, as the elements of nature were an ideal focus for rituals. Jehovah's Witnesses forbid using any type of imagery describing it as idol worship. This is not true as I discovered people do not actually worship these physical images, but use them as a focus for connecting with God or the Almighty Spirit. I researched the subject of life after death, as Jehovah's Witnesses believe that our bodies do not have a spirit, so when a person dies, there is no 'afterlife'. They did however make an exception for anointed members of the congregation who apparently transformed into spirit beings after death to reside in heaven. I sensed from childhood that there was something more than a physical life and was determined to find out exactly what that is.

There were certain incidents of the past that my family would not discuss. An elderly man regularly visited my grandmother and when I asked who he was, she replied he was her 'sweetheart'. I sensed he was my grandfather, and it shocked my parents when they spoke to my school teacher and heard that I was recently upset at school because my Grandfather had passed away. I expected them to scold me about this on the way home, but they remained silent and many glances were exchanged between them. There were some things in life that had not been revealed to me that I already knew and this frightened my parents.

My mother had described the local spiritualist church and its members as evil. We passed it in our car every Tuesday and Thursday evening as it was near the Kingdom Hall. I often dreamt of this place in my childhood and it was there I attended my first spiritualist service. I wanted to know if this place and the people were as evil as my mother had said. I was pleased to find that they were warm and welcoming. The service was an emotional experience for many as I listened to spirit messages given by mediums to the attendees which provided comfort. After the service, we were all invited to the basement kitchen for a cup of tea and a biscuit. A lady who organised the services introduced herself and explained it did not matter what we believed, as God and the spirit world connected us all. This made sense to me, so I visited the church regularly and attended one of their workshops. A young woman invited me to attend a new psychic development circle as she observed my participation in a psychic exercise. I gave accurate information to a woman unknown to me. This surprised and delighted me and members of the group. I have attended many development circles over the years and encountered no demons or evil spirits I had been warned about.

I also attended Yoga classes that promote fitness of the mind and body. I was also warned against these, as they were supposedly part of a religious practice that imitates the movements of a 'snake God'. The meditations are supposed to empty one's mind and would apparently leave it open to demonic possession. I experienced nothing negative from these practices either and became physically fitter, calmer and happier within myself. I continued my spiritual development and also worked as a mobile therapist.

Being the wife of a police sergeant was not easy, particularly during the poll tax riots in London. I watched them on a live television news broadcast and this was distressing because my husband was there.

We tried on one occasion to meet Dan at a local Inn so that he could see Tania and this did not go well. Dan was thirty years of age and dating a girl of fifteen. He arrived at the Inn with large 'love-bites' on his neck and Tania asked what he had done to his neck and he seemed embarrassed. He also wore an engagement ring, but in the past Dan said he did not want to wear a wedding ring as it emphasised his amputated finger.. When Patrick and I visited Dan's home to collect the rest of my belongings, the bed sheets were soaked in baby oil from a large bottle that stood on the bedside table. There was a book on sensual massage, hard core pornographic magazines, used sanitary wear in the open bin and a photo of his girlfriend in bed cuddling her teddy bear. Dan had told us his girlfriend was eighteen, but there was a letter in the lounge from Jenny telling Dan she would let them move in with her, but his girlfriend was underage. We decided that it was not wise to let Tania have contact as she would not be in a safe environment. When the relationship ended, Dan's girlfriend contacted Patrick, saying that she stopped seeing him after he pushed her down the stairs.

Dan later entered into a relationship with a woman nearer his age. She persuaded him to apply for contact with Tania as she had a daughter of the same age. They drove to our home and loitered outside one Sunday afternoon. Tania was riding her bicycle around the cul-de-sac and they attempted to speak to her. She burst through the door crying and threw herself into my arms. Patrick and I approached them, but rather than have it out in front of the neighbours, Patrick invited Dan and his girlfriend into our home to discuss the matter. His girlfriend was shocked when she heard that Dan said he would not see Tania if I did not apply for child maintenance. He also began to act in an immature way in front of me and his girlfriend saw a different side to him. When he noticed Tania wore spectacles and had protruding teeth, he demanded that I get her eyes and teeth corrected. Tania calmed down after a while and began to talk to Dan, so we allowed him supervised contact. When I applied for child support Dan signed on for unemployment benefit and informed the agency he was unable to pay maintenance because he was unemployed. We later discovered he had full time work as a Goldsmith, so Patrick reported him for fraud. After one supervised meeting, we refused further contact as my friend and I had been receiving sexual phone calls that we believed were from him. I had witnessed him giving silent harassment phone calls to others who had upset him in the past. Although I could not prove it was him, I also knew that I could not trust him.

Dan then took the application for contact to court and Patrick had to pay to fight this case as we were married. Dan's lifestyle was too unstable for a sensitive child and at this time Tania was regularly seeing a child psychologist for counselling. The court procedure was draining for me, as Ryan was only six months of age and I was recovering from a traumatic birth. Eventually social services stepped in and declined his application, placing Tania on the 'at risk' register. Patrick seemed happy to raise Tania as his own child, however as years passed, the negative personality traits of her biological father became more prominent within her and resulted in further behavioural problems during adolescence.

I had been extremely protective of my children, so that their childhoods were not ruined by sexual abuse. Tania seemed to take after her father with a fascination for this activity. It was difficult to protect her as she was constantly attracted to potential abusers. I had saved my children from predators on many occasions as I sensed something about their energy and a look deep within their eyes. I distanced my children from them and although others doubted my intuition, in a short time it was proved that I was right. Some were arrested for possession of child pornography or were caught abusing other children. I met a male model through my modelling agency who could have had any woman he wanted, however it became apparent that he wanted children. I stopped any interaction between him and Tania, however she was mesmerised by him and I was relieved when he returned to Germany.

Patrick was aware of Tania's disturbing preoccupation and made a concerted effort to distract her by giving her other interests. On reflection, witnessing Dan's constant interest in pornography and then being with Patrick and I during our courtship and honeymoon period of living together did not help matters. I enrolled her in a dancing school and Patrick funded horse riding lessons for her. She also developed a wonderful operatic singing voice and at twelve she performed in the chorus of the Kent opera company. Patrick also financed her singing lessons and took her to the opera rehearsals and performances. Despite her having potential to become a professional singer with a unique voice for her age, Tania began dating a boy at school when she was fifteen and gave up her singing lessons and performances for him. She often stayed out all night without letting us know where she was, just as her biological father had. Her relationship with her boyfriend was obsessive and intense. In a short time she became pregnant, but said she did not want the child. I did not influence her choices as it was her body and her decision. Her boyfriend's mother also told her to terminate the pregnancy. Soon after this, she unexpectedly left home at sixteen to live with her boyfriend. I did not stop her as I knew it was the only way they would truly get to know one another and it would test their relationship.

Patrick and I discovered that Tania had been secretly meeting Dan, as her boyfriend said they could get money out of him because he had not paid child maintenance throughout her life. Patrick was at this time still paying back the ten year loan he arranged to fight Dan's contact application when Tania was eight. This debt had made our financial situation at home more difficult and it was no surprise that Patrick began to resent Tania. When she left home, Patrick said that her name must not be mentioned within our home.

Ryan was an easier child to raise in some aspects and there were signs of him being extremely intelligent. Patrick and I involved him in most of our activities and interests. At the time, I thought he was different from other children as he liked unusual things that others his age were not interested in. I was in a more relaxed environment and able to enjoy Ryan's development and had a close relationship.

CHAPTER 12

RELIGIOUS EXPLORATION

I studied witchcraft for a year and then took the step of self-initiation by following a ritual from a book I had borrowed. After experiencing the energy that I could raise alone, I was curious to experience working within a group. I joined an Egyptian magical group with Patrick and learnt about Egyptian history and ritual. I remembered some of the information that was mentioned in the bible. After a few months we left this group as the Priestess was disorganised and we were let down on a few occasions when events were arranged.

We visited a local folk festival where I was attracted to a gothic Morris dancing team. The same team performed at one of the Pagan events in London and were asking for new members. As I enjoyed dancing, I persuaded Patrick to join the team with me. Through our association with them I met a Gardnerian Wiccan Priestess and we soon formed a training group with two other Morris team members. A friendship then developed with the couple who led the Morris team and I discovered they were high priest and priestess of an Alexandrian Wiccan coven. We left the training group and after a while, were initiated members of the Alexandrian coven. I trained and worked for a year within this coven, however it soon became apparent the priest and priestess were fanatical believers with cultish behaviour. They were only a few months older than myself, their words and actions reminded me of the behaviour of my parents. Patrick left the coven and I followed soon after. It meant we also had to leave the Morris team, as the atmosphere would be difficult. We worked hard performing with the team for three years, but after resigning. We received a letter from the couple stating there would be no further contact between us. They shunned us in the same way my parents did. Disappointed and disillusioned, I took a break from all Wiccan associations and kept busy with therapy and psychic work.

I applied for a position as a volunteer visitor at the local nursing home Visiting the elderly helped to fill a void while being shunned by my parents. I visited the residents weekly which gave them something to look forward to if they had no other visitors. I befriended Arthur an elderly man. We played card games together as I once had with my father. On my last visit to him when I realised he was dying, I spoke about life after death when we were alone in his room and assured him his wife would be waiting for him. I added that he would meet up with his friends for a huge reunion party in the spirit world. It gave him comfort and that afternoon, I was rewarded with some astounding spiritual activity. It proved to me without a doubt that someone in the spirit world awaited him. He promised me he would let me know that he had arrived safely after passing away and he did so shortly after his death. I will always have special affection and wonderful memories of Arthur.

One morning while working as a mobile therapist, I called at the home of a client in my home town to provide a reflexology treatment. When I left the client's home and placed the treatment couch in the back of my car, I saw uncle Brandon walking along the road. I was unsure of what his reaction would be if I spoke to him, as he too, was a Jehovah's Witness. I crossed the road to approach him and it took a minute or so for him to recognise me. Brandon asked if I was on my way to visit my father, as he did not seem to remember I was disfellowshipped and shunned by them. I replied I was not visiting him that day as I was working. I updated him on my family and how they were getting on. When I told him I had grandchildren, he commented that my father was a great-granddad. Uncle Brandon then sidled up to me asking for a hug which I gladly gave him. We said goodbye and he walked away smiling to himself. I sat in the car wiping away tears from my face. I hadn't seen him for years and was moved he spoke to me and gave me a hug.

I had visited Tom and Amy Shelden all these years as I enjoyed being with them. They commented that I was like another daughter to them. I had confided in them about being shunned by my parents and when my father called to see them one afternoon, Tom said how well I was doing and that my children were growing beautifully. He said my father's eyes filled with tears on hearing this, which revealed that he found the shunning difficult. I felt anger towards my parents for doing this, so hearing what Tom had to say did not soften my feelings towards them.

I visited Tom and Amy one afternoon and sensed that someone had passed away. I did not mention it to them as I felt a sad atmosphere within their home. I stayed with them for two hours and on leaving, Tom followed me to my car, opened the passenger door, got in and sat beside me. He explained that he had some bad news and a feeling of dread came over me. Tom told me someone had passed away and I immediately asked if it was my father. He shook his head and revealed it was uncle Brandon. This was a shock as it was only two months ago that I hugged him. Amy had asked Tom not to tell me in her presence as she couldn't bear to see my reaction. Tom's daughter Mary was a florist and provided flowers for the funeral so they were also able to tell me the name of the funeral director.

On my return home, I contacted the funeral director and discovered Brandon's funeral occurred the previous week. The next day I purchased a bouquet of flowers and visited the local cemetery alone. As I walked through the gates, my legs suddenly felt weak as I realised that one day my parents would also be buried there. I did not know how I would handle that. I found the caretaker at the cemetery and asked him the location of Brandon's grave. He left for a moment to find a document and then escorted me to the grave. It was covered in flowers from the funeral and most of them had died. Cards were still attached to the flowers and I read some of them and thought about the last time I saw him. I thought about my family who stood there a week ago and how upset my father and aunt Verity would have been. I wondered how she was coping without him as she depended heavily on him. I wrote a letter to my parents expressing how upset I was that they did not contact me and let me know. I received a prompt reply with a quoted scripture and the hope of seeing Brandon again in the 'the resurrection' if I returned to the Jehovah's Witnesses.

A year later on Good Friday of the Easter weekend in April 2003, I had an unexpected telephone call from my father. He said the staff from Carl's residential hospital contacted him early that morning to let him know that Carl had passed away. He apparently died from a twisted intestine and as he could not communicate, they were unable to work out what was wrong. Fluids filled his body and eventually drowned him. My parents were understandably in shock and my father had to sort out the necessary arrangements. He told me the date of Carl's funeral and spoke kindly to me, as he knew I too would be shocked by this news. Dartfleet council had agreed to allow Carl's body to be buried in my parents' local cemetery. The funeral service was held in the small cemetery chapel. It did not surprise me that they were not having it at the Kingdom Hall, as Carl was not able to be a member of any religious organisation with severe autism.

Knowing how distraught my parents would be about Carl,, I called at their home with a huge bouquet of flowers. Albert answered the door and was shocked to see me standing there. I asked for one of our parents, he nodded and disappeared to fetch my father. I saw Waverley's car parked outside and it did not surprise me she was there. My father came to the door, and I gave him a bouquet of flowers. I reached up to hug him and gently pulled his head towards me to kiss his cheek. I could feel the resistance as he was a strong man and it was difficult for me to do. He did not invite me into their home, but as I left him, he smiled holding the bouquet while looking at the neighbour's houses. I hoped that he wanted them to see the flowers I had brought rather than doing it for appearances to make the family look good, but I will never know for sure.

It was a warm, sunny spring day when I attended Carl's funeral. I wore my sunglasses to shield my eyes from the sun, but also to hide any emotion I was feeling. It was likely that I would be shunned by any Jehovah's Witnesses who attended as well as my family, therefore I did not want them to see any hurt feelings I had. Patrick and I entered the cemetery gates, where I immediately saw a crowd of Jehovah's Witnesses outside the chapel chatting and laughing together. As we walked towards them, they saw us and fell silent. I told Patrick that I did not want to be there. We kept our distance from them as I watched my family process in line towards the chapel. My mother clung to Waverley as her main comforter as they walked at the front with my father beside them. Kevin was behind them with Albert and when he saw me, he bit his lip uncomfortably and looked in the other direction. Linsey was at the rear of the procession with two of her children and Waverley's sons. They all entered the chapel and the Jehovah's Witnesses paused and looked over at me waiting for me to follow.. I shook my head and they entered the chapel. Kevin's daughter Merea arrived late, and was about to approach me when he ran out and ushered her into the chapel. His other daughter Louise did not attend as Kevin had not told her about the funeral. A few years passed before I discovered that he did not want us both to meet at family events and why. The chapel was full and some of the attendees stood outside listening to the funeral service from a speaker that was placed outside the door. Brett was the usher and he asked me if I wanted to sit inside with the rest of my family and I refused. It angered me that so many Jehovah's Witnesses were there, as most of them did not know my brother and few had visited him. I knew they were there to support my parents mainly for appearances to make the religion look good and to seize an opportunity to preach to non-believers. I heard an elder begin the service and Brett stood outside the door of the chapel watching me as I sat on the wall. He heard Patrick say that we should walk around the cemetery rather than listen to their 'rubbish'. At the far end of the cemetery, a hearse was parked by an open grave. As we drew closer, I saw Carl's coffin laid by the grave. My mother did not want it in the chapel being the type of person who 'buried her head in the sand' in certain situations. If she did not see it, she could deny it was happening. In one way this decision was a positive one for me. Patrick approached the undertakers to say that we were members of the family that no one spoke to and that I would like to spend time with my brother. They allowed me to sit on the lawn beside Carl's coffin, so I laid my hand upon it and conversed with him for a while before the rest of my family left the chapel. As they approached, I stood back and observed my father, Kevin and Albert as they stood at the edge of the grave. One of the elders read out scriptures from his bible as my father wiped tears from his eyes. I wanted to approach and hug him but I knew he would not respond to me while all the congregation members were watching. When the burial was over, he approached each person in turn to shake their hand and thank them for attending. I had sent a beautiful spray of flowers that were laid by the grave with all the others. On the card I wrote: *'I wish we had known the 'real you' locked away inside. You are now free and at peace. I will always remember you my darling brother'*. As no one approached me, Patrick said we should not stay around any longer and as we turned to leave the cemetery, my father looked over at us.. I was not told where the gathering after the funeral was, but later discovered it was at the home of Brett and Rosie. My parents still had a close relationship with them. I also discovered that Rosie's mother Vivien had passed away a few years ago and I was saddened to hear of this.

That evening I conducted a Requiem ritual for Carl on my own. The following day I wrote a letter to my mother informing her I attended the funeral. I expressed how upset I was to see Carl's coffin left outside the chapel and to be shunned at my brother's funeral. She responded quickly with a letter explaining that she could not handle seeing the coffin there and wrote how wonderful the *brothers and sisters* had been to them. My mother mentioned that someone saw me there and commented on how beautiful my long hair was! I knew my mother had seen me there when she stood at a distance from the grave. She had buried her face in Waverley's chest and at one point she raised her head to speak to her. Waverley nodded her head in my direction and my mother turned to look at me and once again buried her head and continued crying. I heard from a relative that after the funeral, Kevin commented on my sunglasses saying that I apparently wore them to look like a movie star!

Shortly before our move, Kevin's daughter Louise contacted me asking to visit. I had not seen her for about ten years, but discovered she had left the Jehovah's Witnesses. Louise arrived with her boyfriend and as it was a warm sunny day, we provided food from the barbecue. Louise wanted to discuss something with me and I was shocked to hear her disclosure of sexual abuse by the same abusive family member.. It occurred when she was a small child and she added he had also abused her sister Merea. Louise described how he would take her to the Kingdom Hall toilets during religious meetings and abuse her there. I recall one occasion when we attended their Kingdom Hall and he took her out of the hall to the toilets. They were gone quite a while before he carried her back into the hall and I noticed her hair stuck to her face with sweat as she was extremely flushed. This memory confirmed a strong possibility that Louise was telling the truth. People often commented how Louise and Merea were reminiscent of Waverley and I when we were children. Linsey's sight had reduced considerably so there were many things she would not have seen during their childhood. Louise was seeing a counsellor and had spent time in psychiatric hospitals to come to terms with her abuse. She revealed that since childhood, the abusive family member told them my brain had been affected by meningitis and this had caused me to lie about many things. As I had disclosed the abuse to my parents, he used this story to cover himself in case I disclosed it to others. My nieces and nephews then believed I was brain-damaged. I then realised the abusive family member had arranged it so that Louise and I did not meet at family events.

Louise told me that in her anger she threw a brick through his lounge window. He had her arrested and prosecuted at court for criminal damage. Louise gave a statement to the police about the abuse, but later withdrew it. The abusive family member repeatedly told her she was sick, mentally ill and a liar. Linsey said the same and her sister Merea did not support her claims. Merea apparently defended the abuser in the same way that Waverley and my mother had. I explained to Louise what occurred in my childhood and the memories I had of my abuser. She later confronted him with this and he advised her not to listen to me, describing me as a 'black witch' .He persuaded Louise she had imagined it all and that I was lying. Louise became confused wondering if the abuse had actually happened or whether it was all in her mind. I contacted the police and they said they would only take action on my evidence if Louise came forward to prosecute. Linsey's sisters who were near my age, told me he had also abused them as children, but although they spoke about it, they were not willing to take legal action. I pitied and understood Louise's distress as sexual abuse from someone close and in a position of trust is worse than it is from a stranger. It would also affect how she related to men in her life. After Louise conversed with the abusive family member and he manipulated her mind, she did not contact me again.

Uncle Vernon had visited me regularly. I thought we had a close relationship throughout my life where I could speak to him about anything. After Louise's visit, I confided in him about the childhood abuse. He was initially shocked and he cried, saying that he wanted to strike the abuser. After this visit, Vernon spent a few days thinking about the conversation and then Patrick received a letter from him stating that he would no longer visit me. Vernon said I was a liar and that my parents had been right about me all along. He quoted scriptures and ended the letter by telling Patrick he would be better off without me. I sensed that he realised that if he sided with me on this matter, he would lose the rest of his family. By siding with them he would keep all the family and sacrifice his relationship with me, Vernon put his own needs of being with his family first, meaning that we were not as close as I believed we were. My mother had also sacrificed her relationship with me to protect the abusive family member.

Patrick and I put our home on the property market. We discussed moving to Cornwall and put plans in place to do so after his retirement. Our property eventually sold in 2006 and we moved into a rented property in Dartfleet while Ryan finished his education at the local Grammar school and we planned to move after his examinations.. We then began our search for a property in Cornwall. I continued hosting psychic development circles and experienced fascinating occurrences within the home. The property was owned by Perry, a colleague of Patrick whose mother recently passed away. I wrote to my parents once a month updating them on our lives but eventually my mother wrote to Patrick explaining they did not want contact because of their religions and to tell me not to write to them.

As I mentioned before, Tania had been seeing her biological father since the age of fifteen without my knowledge. As I lived near her, I unexpectedly called on two occasions as I was passing her home. I also contacted her by phone once a week to check if her family was okay. She later contacted me by telephone, shouting, swearing, accusing me of checking up on her. I was appalled at her disgusting language to me that was reminiscent of her biological father. After this call I decided to have no more contact with her. I then had no connection with any of my family and no good reason to stay in the area. The only people that I would miss were Tom and Amy Shelden as they were more like family to me. It was time for me to move away and begin a new life in Cornwall.

CHAPTER 13

MOVING TO CORNWALL

In June of 2008, Ryan completed his final examinations and we began our final journey to our new home in Cornwall. There were a few friends within my psychic development circles and Reiki courses that I would miss. Tom and Amy Shelden contacted me shortly before the move and said my Auntie Mary may have passed away, as my parents ordered flowers from their daughter's florist shop for my mother's sister and were extremely upset. At this time I was unable to make further enquiries as we were moving home. Mary had severe arthritis throughout her life and in the last few years she moved to council accommodation four properties away from my parents. My mother had tried to recruit Mary into the Jehovah's Witnesses for many years. Her husband worshipped her and gave her everything she desired, however, the one thing he did not agree with was joining the religion. On one occasion she attended her local Kingdom Hall without him knowing, He worked out where she had gone and walked into the hall asking her to leave with him. They had been happy together throughout their lives, but this affected their close relationship as Mary was adamant she wanted to join the religion. Her husband eventually relented when Mary's health deteriorated as it seemed to help her. My parents did not contact me about her death as unbeknown to them, I was in the process of moving. I did write to them with my new address when I had settled in, as I had each time I moved, but they did not reply. I will always remember the days when Aunt Mary and I were close, however this changed in my teenage years when she believed my mother's negative embellished negative stories about me.. I understandably rebelled in reaction to the scapegoating role but unfortunately this gave credence to the stories she and the abusive family member spread to everyone they knew.

I contacted Gavin, my 'childhood sweetheart' in Cornwall, who at this time was out of the religion. He invited Patrick and I to his home for a barbecue with his family one Sunday afternoon. Gavin and Marna had been together since they were sixteen and had four grown children. She may have been the girlfriend Gavin broke up with for two weeks on my last holiday with my parents. Marna felt a little uncomfortable about us meeting as Gavin had shown a photograph of me to his family and described me as his former girlfriend. Marna and I conversed easily and I assured her that we did not have a sexual relationship.. Marna relaxed more after hearing this and discussed her married life, telling me that although Gavin had left the Jehovah's Witnesses at sixteen, his family and their beliefs strongly influenced him. He lived life as though he was still a member of the religion and this caused difficulties within their marriage. Marna also revealed other relationship problems they had. Patrick and I visited them again a week before Christmas. The only decoration in their home was a small Christmas tree. I loved my decorations, compensating for all the Christmases I missed throughout my childhood. I also wanted to make it exciting and magical, to give my children the Christmases I would have loved to have at their age. Marna explained how difficult it was to persuade Gavin to have a tree in their home. but he eventually relented under family pressure. Ryan later told me that he and Gavin's daughter were watching television in the lounge and he changed the channel to see an episode of *Most Haunted*. Gavin entered the room and angrily told him to change the television channel as he did not want his daughter watching demonic programs. Gavin's parents visited that afternoon. I did not expect them to speak to me, but his mother did. She stood there for a while waiting for me to approach her but I did not as I knew they would preach to me. It surprised me when Gavin used foul language in front of his parents although he lived most of his life as though he were still in the religion. He told me that he came out of the religion as he could not behave in the way that they wanted him to. Gavin adhered to some of the rules, but did not see anything wrong in lusting over other women. Marna said he was not satisfied with the size of her breasts but she refused to have cosmetic surgery to make them larger for him. Patrick and I visited a local Inn with them and while Patrick conversed with Marna giving her advice on her relationship, Gavin, who was a little intoxicated, conversed with me and said he found me exciting when we were teenagers and I visited the Kingdom Hall with my parents. He said I was everything he wanted in a woman. When I did not respond to this, he told me to ignore his ramblings as he had drunk more than he should have.

The last time we went out with Gavin was when he invited us to join him and Marna at an Inn for an evening meal. His sister Lynette would also be there and as she was still a Jehovah's Witness, Marna commented that 'I knew the score' and Lynette would shun me. There was an awkward atmosphere that evening as she conversed with Patrick and Ryan, but not me, so we did not stay there for long.

A few months later we heard that Gavin and Marna had divorced. He attended the funeral of one of Jehovah's Witnesses that he knew and while he was there, had a long conversation with one of the *brothers*. Gavin felt alone after his divorce and returned to the Jehovah's Witnesses. He immediately met a single *sister*, went through the baptism process and married her within two months. Gavin contacted me a few years later although he was not supposed to. He seemed happy with his relationship as he thought Jehovah had rewarded him by giving him a wife with larger breasts who was an active member of the religion. As his marriage continued, he said his wife suffered from depression and this affected their sexual relationship. Gavin said he would 'remain within the marriage for Jehovah', but he attempted to instigate sexual conversations with me via mobile phone texts. I then ceased all contact with him.

I diligently networked in Cornwall and met a few like-minded people that resided in the west of Cornwall. They invited me to a Folk Festival and asked if I would like to become more involved within it. When I accepted the offer, they put me in contact with Clarissa who agreed to train me in a Teazer role to perform with the town's 'Obby 'Oss. I discovered Clarissa also needed an apprentice to hand on her business to after retiring. I agreed to an apprenticeship for her Wisewoman business and we worked intensely together for many hours each day. Patrick was nearing the time of his retirement from the police force after commuting to London for eighteen months. Ryan was at college, so they were both occupied with their work and I had time to train in these skills. Patrick agreed to my training with Clarissa on condition it did not encroach on my roles as wife and mother. The training was intense and I spent most of my time with Clarissa causing gossip amongst our local acquaintances. A few weeks before Patrick was due to retire, he revealed his plan to rent out our cottage as a guest house for tourists. He instructed me to find a property we could rent. I searched for one in west Cornwall as I would be working in that area and eventually found a mill house one mile away from Clarissa's village.

By mid-January of 2010, we moved all our belongings into the mill house so Patrick could arrange the renovations on our cottage required by the letting agency. Although Patrick moved his clothes into the mill house, he did not live there as he said he needed to be near the cottage and two caravans he purchased with part of the 'lump sum' he received on retirement. Patrick had revealed all details of his life to local residents including the large sum of money he acquired after retiring. It was no surprise that new 'friends' suddenly entered his life. Ryan enrolled at university and lived on campus and I was alone in a secluded rental property. Clarissa loved the grounds of the mill house and volunteered to move in, as she was concerned about me being alone at nights. My friendship and working relationship with Clarissa grew closer and I admired her. Patrick said this did not bother him, but little did I know it was part of a plan. Patrick gradually distanced himself from me and this was obvious at Ryan's eighteenth birthday party. Clarissa was the only one who offered support when Patrick suddenly announced he wanted a divorce. He removed all financial support and I sold most of my belongings to pay my share of the rent. He said he wanted a quick divorce that could be done on the internet with no solicitors or division of finances. He gave an ultimatum by promising support and friendship if I agreed to this his way. If however, I used solicitors and asked for a division of finances, I would never see him again. I thought about this for while and did not immediately apply for a divorce. As time passed, it was obvious that Patrick offered no friendship or support and he entered a relationship with a woman who was a 'fan' of the band Ryan performed with. When I could no longer afford to pay my share of the rent, Clarissa suggested I move into her cottage where she assured me that I would be safe and in a position to proceed with the divorce.

I re-connected with Waverley in 2013 after twenty-two years apart. It was I who first contacted her when I noticed she displayed a childhood photograph of us both on social media. I discovered she left the Jehovah's Witnesses after recovering from a serious car accident that caused her to reflect on her life. She no longer wanted to live her life for other people and she became a manager of a nightclub with her friend Lena. Waverley heard from Tania, that I had lost everything, my husband and my home. She however had plenty of money and was living with her boyfriend in his mortgaged house in the 'posh' area of Graveton. As Waverley was now in a better position than me, she was happy to reconnect again. Lena imitated Waverley's appearance and personality, telling people they were blood sisters. When I saw photographs of them hugging, Waverley looked really happy and I felt that it should have been me having this relationship with her. I was unsure whether Lena was truly happy about my re-appearance into my sister's life although she seemed supportive at the time. I later heard from Lena their relationship was not what it appeared to be and at times Waverley spoke to her like 'dirt'. At the start of our reconnection, Waverley said that even though we were in contact again, our relationship as sisters would not be what I hoped for.

She reconnected me with uncle Vernon who seemed overjoyed to be in contact again after twenty-five years. He was still viewed as an apostate by the Jehovah's Witnesses and had no contact with my mother. Vernon did not speak of the time we stopped seeing one another or about the letter he wrote to Patrick, but said he would do anything for me to make up for the time we were apart.

CHAPTER 14

DIVORCE

I contacted a solicitor and filed for divorce. Patrick contacted me by phone when he received the letter, shocked and angry. I explained that I needed some financial security and he did not reply and ended the conversation by slamming the receiver down. Divorce proceedings continued for eighteen months and were taken to a final hearing. I discovered that Patrick stripped all assets and was slow to declare his financial situation. As there were no assets, the court awarded me seventy five percent from the sale of our marital home. Patrick then stopped the mortgage payments and I applied to the court to gain possession of the keys as he refused to sell the property. It took four years to sell the cottage and the arrears had risen considerably. After Legal Aid took their fee for representing me, there was nothing left. Clarissa let me stay in her cottage and we worked together on the Wisewoman business. I worked hard promoting and networking, which meant the business situation improved. I managed to secure a percentage of the police pension when Waverley loaned the fee needed to put the pension order in place. This provided future security as the spouses of police officers do not receive it until they reach sixty years of age. I worked hard for ten years until then, Ryan was upset and he said I had no right to one penny of Patrick's money. He did not agree with the division of finances in a divorce and sided with his father. Patrick had told him that his inheritance would be less because of our divorce, as he also said that one day the cottage would belong to Ryan. This was not true as Patrick had only paid the interest payments on the property and not the actual mortgage. Patrick and Ryan revealed all the information to those who were members of our dance team. They turned out to be 'false friends' and joined Ryan in his negativity and formed a vendetta group against us. The group was led by a person who was once an 'obsessed fan' of Clarissa's but when she refused to teach them her Craft and gave them constructive criticism on their work, the obsession remained but turned toxic. Patrick was determined to ruin my life in Cornwall by spreading false information about my past and the group used this against me. In the year of 2012 Clarissa and I lost twenty people who we believed were genuine friends. Among them were long term acquaintances from Kent who I didn't expect to turn against me.

I visited Kent in 2013 to perform at a Kent Folk Festival with my Cornish Guise team and arranged to meet Waverley for the first time in twenty-two years. I met Ron, Waverley's partner who she had lived with for about fifteen years without my parent's knowledge, She was an inactive member of the Jehovah's Witnesses and if her true lifestyle was discovered, the elders would usually disfellowship her. However it seemed they 'turned a blind eye' to her living out of wedlock and running a nightclub that included 'gay nights', because she supported my parents financially and assisted them in many ways. They knew the responsibility of caring for my parents would become theirs if Waverley was unable to have contact with them. While in Kent, I would take flowers to my home-town cemetery to put on Carl's grave. I would also place one of the flowers on Uncle Brandon's grave that was nearby. I thought about my parents as I stood there and on impulse, sent a mobile phone text message letting them know I was at the cemetery. I did not expect a reply, so I continued to arrange flowers on Carl's grave while Clarissa explored the graveyard. My mother suddenly appeared at the gate and walked along the path towards me. I immediately stood up and smiled, but I could see her muttering something quietly and guessed that she was praying to Jehovah. She stood in front of me and as our eyes met, it shocked me to see the dramatic change in her appearance. My mother had severely aged since I last saw her. She said: "I cannot hug you" and then my father appeared. He looked a little older, but was still a fine, tall, upright man. His voice had a small tremor as he spoke, and his neatly combed strawberry-blonde hair was almost white. Clarissa joined us and I introduced them. After not seeing me for years, my mother aggressively expressed her disapproval of my dark brown hair and appearance. She told me that I looked ill with dark hair and black clothes. I wore an amber pendant that I later heard she assumed was a talisman. I sensed the underlying reason for her anger about my hair was she once had long dark hair and as I look like her, I reminded her of a younger version of herself. My father could not take his eyes off me, and I returned his gaze with so much love that he reacted by reaching his hand out to me on a few occasions. He then remembered it was against religious rules and retracted it. My mother's expression as she looked at me was of jealousy and anger. She announced that they were both old and in their eighties as though I had forgotten. This could not be further from the truth, as every year I remembered their anniversaries, birthdays and their age. My mother was embittered about reaching old age, as she believed that this would not happen to her. She also said that we would never grow old or die, as Armageddon would soon arrive and save us from this.

I did not think Clarissa would ever have the opportunity to meet them, so that was a surreal moment. They stayed for about fifteen minutes and I watched as they left the cemetery and it was only my father who looked back.

Before our journey back to Cornwall, Waverley suggested we meet for a substantial breakfast at a local restaurant. As we sat together at one of the tables, I noticed my parents seated two tables away with Albert and Pamela Lovell. Waverley assured me it would not be a problem and approached their table to converse with them. She returned and said they were happy for me to approach them. As I did so, Pamela rose from her seat and hugged me. The last time I saw her was when I visited her in the 1980s. She invited me to her apartment for lunch and at this time was an inactive Jehovah's Witness I remembered. Pamela was a tall, slim well-dressed woman and was surprised she had put on extra weight, but she was still extremely attractive with a lively personality. While she prepared our lunch, she updated me on the lives of Hattie and Honour as well as her own. There were framed photographs of their weddings on her wall. I knew that Honour had been visiting Waverley as I met her during one of my visits. Pamela commented that these visits were short-lived and that Honour would not have been interested in Waverley's husband! She still disliked members of the congregation and imitated the elders' voices and mannerisms so well.

I stood by my parents table at the restaurant and Albert did not speak to me, but smiled when our eyes met. I stood behind my father's chair and my mother looked at me with a blank expression. It was only Pamela who greeted me, so after conversing with her for a minute or so my mother stated that I had been there long enough and instructed me to return to my table. Before I turned to leave, I placed my hands upon my father's shoulders and gave them an affectionate squeeze and stroked the back of his head. He did not turn around but I sensed he would have liked to. I returned to our table where Waverley, Clarissa and I conversed about a few things. I wanted to capture an image of my parents with my camera, so Clarissa posed for a photograph positioning herself so that my mother and Pamela were in the background. I saw them having a serious conversation and my mother frequently looked at us. When my parents got up to leave, they approached us. My mother stood very close to me, looking up into my eyes. I then realised she was not allowed to reach out and hug me because of religious rules and hoped I would reach out to her. I then did so. Pamela asked Waverley and I to stand with our parents while she took a photograph, but my mother refused to be part of it and left the restaurant with Albert. Waverley and I stood either side of my father and I jokingly told him to pose like a male model and he chuckled. Pamela captured a lovely image of us that day and it is one that I treasure.

Waverley visited my parents the next day and heard that Pamela said to my mother it was such a pity that Clarissa and I were in a relationship. Pamela apparently heard about this from Hattie as we were both in regular contact and I spoke to her about many things. Waverley replied that my connection with Clarissa was more about having a 'mother figure' because I had no contact with my own! On reflection she was right. My parents then resumed contact with me through occasional telephone calls.

CHAPTER 15

TERMINAL ILLNESS

In the spring of 2014, Waverley contacted me to let me know our father had undergone surgery for a blocked colon. They discovered a cancerous tumour and further tests revealed there were secondary tumours in his lungs and liver. In cases of terminal illness, Jehovah's Witnesses allow contact with disfellowshipped family members. On reflection, I wonder if this decision is made so that all family members can help with caring for them, thus releasing the organisation from this responsibility. They are aware that after having no contact for a long period of time, unbelievers would be so grateful, they would do anything to help their family members. My father and I conversed regularly by telephone and I travelled the three hundred and forty mile journey a few times that year. The doctors prescribed a mild dose of chemotherapy as he was in his eighties, but sadly it did not improve his condition.

This caused me to reflect on my life as a rebellious child and I felt guilty about the added stress I had given him over the years. Instead of focusing on negative aspects of my past, I decided to concentrate more on the positive, such as the area we lived in, how hard my father had worked to care for us and took us on some wonderful vacations. He had been a constant reliable figure in our lives. I was so pleased to have the opportunity to tell him these thoughts when I sent him a beautiful card near Father's Day with a letter enclosed, expressing my appreciation for all he had done. My mother said that he became emotional while reading it and wanted me to know I successfully 'reached' through the barrier that had been there for years. Although she told me, she didn't seem happy about it.

I searched for the Kingdom Hall in Cornwall that we visited on our yearly vacations as I wanted to let the Jehovah's Witnesses who remembered him, know about his terminal illness. I thought I would ask them to contact him as it would be a wonderful surprise. I could not remember exactly where the hall was as they had built a new one on the outskirts of Fowey that I had only visited on one occasion at sixteen. I drove around the area asking local residents who did not know and then I saw a woman walking her dog. She also had not heard of a kingdom hall in the area and as she walked away, I paused to study the map. I then noticed her returning to my car and she bent down beside the open passenger window and stared at me with wide eyes. In a slow, determined voice she said "Don't go!!" and repeated this twice more! I assured not to worry as I knew all about the religion explaining that my parents were members and I needed to contact the congregation on their behalf. The woman had heard disturbing stories about them and was concerned I may be naively visiting it for the first time. I eventually found a Kingdom Hall but discovered that it was on the other side of the main town and their meeting was about to begin. One of the *sisters* welcomed me with a warm hug and kissed my cheek which felt so comforting. I explained that I was searching for the Fowey congregation and the *brother* who stood beside her began to laugh. They gave me directions and I eventually found the hall but had missed half of their meeting, not that this mattered to me. When the meeting was over Gavin approached me and I cried as I told him about my father. He asked if I wanted to see the elders and fetched two that I knew from the past. They spoke to me in the back room and I asked them to contact my father as it would lift his spirits. I added that I was considering returning to the religion. One of them gave me their latest translation of the bible as a gift and looked to the other elder for approval, but he did not react. My father was extremely delighted when he heard from them and Waverley was delighted, commenting that I had done a wonderful thing for them and thanked me for arranging this.

On my next visit to Kent I called at my parents' home early one morning. There was no answer so I was about to get into my car and my father opened the door. He stood there looking wonderful in a clean white shirt as he fastened his cuffs. He always was a well dressed man and still looked so handsome as an elderly man. I asked if I should return later as I could see he was getting ready, but he invited me in. I walked through the door and as he stood there waiting in the hallway, I reached up to hug him, covering his face with kisses. I purchased two huge Cornish pasties for my parents and Albert which they all enjoyed. I gifted my father a Cornish mug and my mother some ornaments to add to her Cornwall collection. They had asked me to find a ship in a bottle for them and I brought one with me. I will always remember how happy my father looked that day.

Waverley had contacted me before my visit to tell me that Kenneth, who was once in my class at school, had visited the local Kingdom Hall. He asked for a bible study and explained to the elders he felt guilty about an incident that occurred when we were fourteen years of age. Kenneth was a new pupil at our school and extremely quiet. He

appeared troubled and as I liked him, I wrote a letter to him and left
it on his desk. I explained that I liked him and I was one of Jehovah's
Witnesses. I also gave him information about the religion. He found
the letter on his desk and began to read it until the boy sitting next to
him snatched it and tore it into small pieces. Kenneth did not react. The
other boy walked to the front of the classroom and sprinkled pieces of
the letter over my head while I was busy with my schoolwork. I saw the
paper as it fell on my desk, but did not react or look up at him. Kenneth
was shocked that I did not respond but he was afraid to say anything.
This incident had apparently haunted him for years, and he wanted to
apologise. Kenneth introduced himself to my parents and asked them
about me, so Waverley passed on his details suggesting I contacted him.

I arranged to meet him during this visit. The years had been kind
to Kenneth as he had grown into quite a handsome man compared to
the boy I remembered at school. He arrived at the Bed and Breakfast
accommodation and we both walked to a nearby Inn. On the way, he
made a video call to his sister and asked her to guess who accompanied
him. He pointed the phone camera in my direction and when she saw
me, she asked him if this was the girl he spoke of for many years. At
the Inn, we discussed many things, and he apologised for the incident
at school. Kenneth thought it had also troubled me, but I explained
that I was accustomed to this type of behaviour at school, and rose
above it. Kenneth explained that he had been helping my family out by
transporting my mother and Albert to their religious meetings. He had
also taken my father to his hospital appointments.

My father spent most of his time in bed as his health was
deteriorating. I called at my parent's home to visit him and Waverley
was there with my mother. I asked if it was convenient to see him in

the bedroom and my father was delighted to see me. We conversed for a while and I said that I was contemplating moving back to Kent. He replied that he did not think he would still be here when that occurred. I reminded him how wonderful it would be when he met his parents again after fifty years. He quietly thought about that as I listed other family members and friends he would meet again. I believed they would reunite in the spirit world, but my father believed this would happen when he was resurrected on a paradise earth. I expected him to say something about this as I had given him the opportunity to preach, but he did not continue the conversation and this surprised me. I had my melodeon with me and played tunes for him and he enjoyed them. My mother explained that he had lost his appetite, so I took half of a large warm Cornish pasty to his room and fed him. He thoroughly enjoyed it and blew kisses to me between each mouthful. As I fed him, I thought about the times he had fed me in my infancy and now it was my turn to feed him. He asked to sit in his armchair in the lounge for a while, so we helped him to get out of bed. My father was a tall, well-built man and it was difficult to move him despite his weight loss. I showed Albert an easier method of lifting him as he was having difficulty.

When I returned to visit my father the following day, there was an ambulance parked outside. My mother explained the doctor had examined my father and suspected a stroke as one side of his body was not functioning as it should. He had been admitted to hospital for further tests. Kevin and his second wife Mavis were there and he was about to get into the ambulance when my mother asked me to go instead as I joked with my father and made him laugh. Kevin was only too happy to let me go in his place and laughed as he waved us goodbye.

It was the first time I had met Mavis and as we conversed later that day, I wondered what Kevin had told her about me. I then discovered how perceptive Mavis was as she did not know my mother too well, but noticed the high level of control she exerted over her family. She said that my father signed a letter for non-resuscitation in the case of heart failure. My mother had apparently hidden it. I understood why she would have done this, as she relied heavily on him throughout their married life and did not want to lose him. I wondered how she would react and cope when he did pass away having to continue without him.

My father was placed in the accident and emergency ward of the hospital with many other patients. My mother and I sat by his bed, hearing other patients screaming, vomiting, and shouting while doctors and nurses bustled to and fro. My father was extremely tired and slept through most of it until the doctor arrived to take him for a brain scan. I sat there stunned as I listened to the stressful activity surrounding us. I remembered my father as a tall, strong man with a powerful presence and seeing him lying on a hospital bed, elderly, frail, terminally ill and helpless was devastating. Years before this my father had a minor stroke on the day I visited him. He tried to assemble a globe for Albert and fix it to a stand, but as he reached out to pick it up, he repeatedly missed, so I assisted him in putting it together. Many years had passed with little contact between us after I left the Jehovah's Witnesses and I knew it would not be long before we said our final goodbye.

Waverley and Kenneth arrived while we awaited my father's return from the scan. He returned quicker than expected and my mother offered him a sandwich to eat. He took it and tried to wipe his mouth with it because he thought it was a tissue. The doctor eventually returned and spoke to my father with a loud voice. He informed him that it was not a stroke, but a brain tumour the size of an egg. It was pressing on nerve centres in his brain and affecting his movement. The doctor prescribed medication to shrink the tumour and release pressure on his brain. My mother sobbed and. I left the ward, not wanting to cry in front of my father. When I regained composure I joined them again. I had been at the hospital for four hours, so Waverley relieved me and I returned to the accommodation to freshen up. Kenneth took me to a restaurant but I did not feel hungry. As we conversed he commented that he had noticed how cold Kevin acted towards me and that he had heard about the past situation with him. I did not feel comfortable discussing it any further.

The following day I visited my father in hospital and discovered the staff had moved him to a ward. The treatment he received for the tumour was miraculous as he sat in a chair, alert and smiling asking why it took so long for his visitors to arrive. Tania, Ryan, Waverley, her two sons and my mother were there. He looked at all of us in turn with tears in his eyes and expressed how much he loved us. He knew that he would soon be leaving us and became emotional about this.

I met with Kenneth on a few occasions during my visit and he said that he wanted us to have a relationship. He had infiltrated my family by being helpful, offering transport, paying for my father to have a television by his hospital bed, attending their religious meetings and having a bible study. Although Kenneth wanted my attention, all I could think of was my father as in the past I was too distracted by other men who took me away from him.

Kenneth said that my first husband Dan and his third wife visited my father in hospital. His wife was a retired psychiatric nurse who apparently met my parents while caring for my brother Carl in the local residential hospital. Dan and his wife occasionally visited my parent's home which puzzled me as my parents were aware of the violence and abuse I received from him during my first marriage. I asked my mother why they invited him into their home for social evenings and she replied although they were civil to him, they had not forgotten the way he treated me. They took the opportunity to preach to them but unsurprisingly they were unsuccessful in recruiting them. Kenneth said when he mentioned my name at the hospital, it attracted Dan's attention and he questioned him about his connection with me and they reminisced about the past. Apparently Kenneth saw us together in the year we were courting,.

On Ryan's birthday, I arranged a party for him at Waverley's nightclub. Lena provided refreshments and they were both excellent hostesses. I invited Tania and a few friends to join us including Kenneth. Ryan was not keen on attending the party when he heard I had arranged it but Waverley persuaded him to. Ryan sided with his father over the divorce and may have thought that spending time with me would be disloyal to him. He eventually put these feelings aside and enjoyed the evening more than he thought he would. I had recently re-connected with Trent, the man I ran away with at sixteen who was now married with adult sons. He attended the birthday party with one of them. I met Selene for the first time in years and she attended the party with her daughter. Tania said that someone stole money from her bag and although she suspected a person who sat next to it, she had no proof. Apart from that it turned out to be a good evening.

The day arrived for me to return to Cornwall. I packed my belongings, placed them in the car and after having breakfast at the accommodation, I visited the hospital to spend time with my father.

Kenneth arrived soon after, announcing that he had paid more money for the hospital television so my father could watch football matches. He usually transported my mother to and from the hospital but that day she planned to arrive with Waverley. I wanted time alone with my father as he was the most important man in my life, but Kenneth suddenly told him that he wanted to be in a relationship with me and asked for my father's approval. My father was confused and did not know what to say, so I interjected and told Kenneth it was not appropriate to ask him at this time. I added that my father was the main man in my life from now on. Kenneth, feeling a little deflated, left the hospital and my father and I then had time alone. He was worried my mother had not yet arrived, and I reassured him she was shopping with Waverley first. He happily chatted away to me listing all who had visited him and mentioned Aunt Mary had visited with my mother. I paused, and then asked if he was sure it was Mary and not Rosie. He was adamant Mary accompanied my mother. I found this intriguing as it was seven years since Mary passed away. I said no more about it but was delighted that my father may have seen her in spirit.

The nurse brought his lunch and he picked up his comb from the table and tried to use it to eat his meal, but then realised it was not the right tool. I passed his fork to him so that he could eat his food. I sat on the bed beside his chair and checked my phone messages to see if Waverley had contacted me. As I did so, my father held out his hands and said: "Where's my little girl?" I put down the phone and took his hands saying I was there. He put one arm around my shoulders and pulled me towards him for a hug which surprised me. Throughout my life it was I who approached him for hugs and I was still disfellowshipped from their religion. My father leant forward and covered my face with kisses. I stroked his face, looked into his eyes and told him I loved him and promised I would return to the Jehovah's Witnesses. My father grew tired and dozed in his chair while awaiting my mother's arrival. I spent another four hours with him and a nurse arrived to carry out routine checks. The nurses described my father as a real gentleman and whenever they brought his meals, he said: "Thank you my dear". It was time for me to leave, so I kissed my father for the last time and said goodbye.

When I returned to Cornwall, I had frequent contact with my family. Kenneth sent me video messages from my father when he visited after transporting my mother to the hospital. He told me that he liked my mother a lot and gave her plenty of attention that could be flirtatious at times. A few of our relatives were uncomfortable with his behaviour at this vulnerable time. My mother, however, enjoyed the attention. On reflection she would have been looking for someone else to depend on when my father passed away and Kenneth had been there for her. She also knew that he had an attraction to me and I discovered later that he had been told many negative things about my past.

A few weeks later, Kenneth visited Cornwall on the weekend my Morris team was performing at a local event. I suggested that he join us there. Kenneth told Gary, the elder who conducted his bible study about his trip and was warned he would be visiting a land of dark witchcraft and an event that would be Pagan and demonic. I had known Gary since childhood as he was near my age. Gary's father was brother Strong who my parents confided in whenever they had problems. His son however, turned into a self righteous, arrogant adult who also attended university and attained qualifications. We were advised against further education in our teenage years but exceptions were obviously made for him. When Kenneth arrived in Cornwall and attended the event, he discovered our Morris team members were not all Pagan but people with ordinary lives who were musicians and dancers. Our team camped together at a site near the venue and Kenneth conversed with them all. We gathered in one member's large tent on Friday evening to play music, sing songs while drinking our favourite tipple. Kenneth attempted to preach to one of the women, and as the evening progressed he staggered to his tent seriously intoxicated. The woman he conversed with revealed that he emptied a large bottle of brandy that evening! The following morning Clarissa and I visited the shower cubicles and as the queue was so long we decided to share one, to be ready in time for our performance. Clarissa forgot to lock the cubicle door and a young man unexpectedly opened it. He was shocked as we both screamed and a queue of people saw us grab towels to cover our bodies. We returned to the campsite laughing and when we related the incident to the rest of our team, Kenneth was upset that we had shared a shower cubicle. The Cornwall agricultural show and our performance was a success. Kenneth discovered that weekend that it was not Pagan or demonic after all!

Waverley contacted me to let me know that after weighing up options, my father agreed to radiotherapy treatments to try to shrink his brain tumour. The consultant warned there were no guarantees and the outcome could go either way, but he and Waverley thought it worth trying. Unfortunately, my father's health declined further after treatment and when Kenneth returned home and visited the hospital, he sent a video message from my father. He had lost more weight, beginning to look skeletal and asked me to visit as soon as possible. He said that I should return to Jehovah and added without him, we have nothing. I heard my mother laugh and agree with this statement. My father was transferred to a nursing home and at this time I could not return to Kent. The accommodation and the journey was expensive and none of my family offered me a room or even a floor to sleep on. Kenneth visited Cornwall again and I had arranged an evening out with friends on Saturday evening. I invited him to join us and just before midnight, Waverley contacted me to let me know our father had deteriorated further and doctors did not think he would last the night. There were a few times with my father in law we thought he would pass away but he did not. I told Waverley he may last a little longer as the doctors only estimate the time he has left. She contacted me on Sunday morning with the news that my father passed away in the early hours of Sunday morning. Although she accused me of not believing her, I could only go by what I had experienced. She left the nursing home with my mother while he was unconscious after giving the nurses permission to increase his dose of morphine as he was haemorrhaging internally. They assured her it would be the kindest way for him to pass away. Kevin stayed and held my father's hand while praying with him. He said our father responded with 'Amen' at the end of each prayer and he continued until the moment my father released his grip on his hand as he passed away. I commended Kevin for being there and coping at what would have been a difficult time. One of my father's favourite songs *Sunday Morning Coming Down* by *Johnny Cash,* was constantly on my mind. He played it and sang it often, not knowing that he would pass away in the early hours of a Sunday morning. The realisation that my father had gone hit me hard, but at least we had contact and I said what I needed to before his death. All the years of shunning and the damage it caused to our relationship however, remains unresolved. My father was not the type of person to apologise or admit he was at fault, so that also remains unresolved. I hoped his affection towards me was a way of telling me without having to say it. No matter what occurred in our relationship and our lives, he was my father and I loved him dearly. I regret the things I did that caused him unhappiness and distress, but we cannot change the past and I miss and think of him every day.

My car failed its yearly M.O.T. test with no hope of adjustment to make it roadworthy again, Clarissa and I were 'conned' by a man from a local garage who sold us the car. My father had owned his car for ten years, after it was given to him by Aunt Mary's husband. It would not have been worth selling because of its age, so my mother and Waverley offered me the car, Albert wanted it to stay within the family and I accepted their offer. Kenneth volunteered to travel to Cornwall and transport me to Kent for my father's funeral in June of 2015. I could then collect the car before my return. I asked Clarissa to accompany me as I knew there would be many Jehovah's Witnesses who would attend the funeral and I may be shunned. I needed someone to be there just for me to offer support.

CHAPTER 16

MY FATHER'S FUNERAL

When Kenneth transported us to Kent, he placed me in the front seat and Clarissa in the back. She commented that she felt he treated her like a naughty child. Kenneth offered to accommodate Clarissa and I had planned to stay with my mother. When I arrived at the family home however, my mother refused to let me stay there as Waverley had stayed there since my father was in hospital. My mother said she did not want to change the routine. I then had to ask Kenneth if I could stay at his home with Clarissa. He agreed on the condition that I stayed in the main bedroom while Clarissa was in his son's single bed. He added that he would not allow Clarissa and I to share a bed in his home as he would not have fornication under his roof!! We had no plans to behave in this way as nothing was further from our minds, but we did not debate the matter. Kenneth and his son Alan slept on couches in the lounge.

Clarissa and I visited my mother the next day and we arrived in the middle of a discussion with an executor about my father's finances. Waverley, Kevin and Albert were present and I was the only sibling not included in the discussion. My mother carried two chairs into the garden telling Clarissa and I to wait there until they had finished their discussion. They did not speak to me about what was said when it was over. Kevin, Waverley and Albert left and I helped my mother with chores. I cleaned her windows and surfaces of furniture in the kitchen/diner. She had collected many knick-knacks over the years that were covered in thick dust, so I washed them and replaced them. It was timely that Albert went to work, as he did not like things being disturbed in the house. Clarissa helped my mother by working in the garden. She also decided to sort out my father's clothes and we helped her with this. It surprised me that she wanted to give away his clothes so soon, as I thought she may want to keep them for a while. We laid them out on the bed and I emptied the pockets of his jackets. It was distressing to find his used tissues and handkerchiefs. His ties were also knotted so he could put them on easily without having to re-tie them. I found a box of broken watches and recognised one that he wore during my childhood, so I took it with me. My mother asked me to take his suits and shirts to a Cancer Research charity shop. I visited the local hospice to ask where the local charity shop was and became emotional as I explained I had my father's suits with me. They replied that I didn't have to give them away so soon after this death, but I explained my mother had wanted me to take them there. I found the shop and gave them his suits, but decided to keep his shirts to wear them as nightshirts. When I put them on, I think about all the times he fastened the buttons and cuffs. There are a few stains on them from the times he wore them that I find comforting. He once owned a green satin shirt my mother purchased for him as she thought the colour would go well with his copper-coloured hair. He wore it for a while even though it was not the type of shirt he liked. After a few years, I asked him for it and he was surprised and touched that I wanted to wear it.

The next day, I returned to my mother's home and watched Kevin as he searched through my father's shed looking for items he wanted. I sensed that he and Waverley had researched items that would be valuable. He pulled out my father's old 'shove-ha'penny' game board and offered it to me, commenting it would remind me of good times. I guessed he had already researched the value of it, or he would have kept it. Kevin and Waverley are not sentimental people who would keep my parent's belongings merely for the memories. If they were not valuable they would rather dispose of them. This is one of many ways where I differed from them, because to me the memories that items carry are priceless.

In the evening, I stayed with my mother for a while and Clarissa returned to Kenneth's home. I sat at her feet and she brushed my hair and braided it tightly all the way to the end. It shocked me when she took out a pair of scissors and cut off the ends of my hair, claiming that they were not straight. She placed the piece of hair on the arm of her chair and obviously felt she was entitled to do so without asking me. I had reverted to bright blonde hair to please her after all the fuss she made about me colouring it dark brown. I did not however feel comfortable with it. My mother hugged Waverley in my presence and rested her head on my sisters' unnaturally large bosom, commenting that she often liked to rest there. Waverley and I went out for a meal later that evening. She wore a tight dress and as I knew the shape of her body, I could see that she was wearing underwear with padded buttocks as she sauntered through the restaurant. We found a table and I listened to her while she spoke about our family. Waverley had problems shaping her words because of the filler injections she had in her lips. I saw her white-blonde hair extensions, the Botox in her skin, the false nails, teeth veneers, unnaturally huge breasts and padded panties. I realised how completely different we had been since childhood, but now we still were but in a different way. I would not feel comfortable trying to be like her, as I preferred to grow old gracefully. The movie star *Audrey Hepburn* is and always will be my inspiration as she set a fine example, however Waverley's inspiration was a mixture of *Madonna* and *Dolly Parton*..

Clarissa spent the evening with Kenneth and they conversed over a few drinks. As the evening progressed, he told Clarissa that she was the problem that prevented him and I being together. When Waverley and I returned to my mother's home, Kenneth arrived to collect me. He tried to 'turn on the charm' commenting on Waverley's 'cute little onesie' that she wore to stay overnight with my mother. After witnessing his huge ego and his flirtatious spirit with women, there was no way I would consider a relationship with him. Kenneth was aware that he was fairly handsome and he loved attention from women. I also discovered he had a problem with alcohol and often consumed a large bottle of brandy in an evening as he had in Cornwall. The alcohol consumption and flirtatious spirit would be difficult habits for him to control if he planned to join a strict religion like the Jehovah's Witnesses. When Kenneth and I returned to his home, Clarissa retired to her room and I conversed with him in the lounge. He raised the subject of us having a relationship and stated he would expect me to obey everything he instructed. On hearing this, I sat upright, stared into his eyes and replied: "Really!!" Kenneth said he had female friends that he regularly dined with and would continue to do so without any objections. I thought about this for a moment and replied that if there was nothing wrong with him doing this, he should have no objection to me dining out with my male friends either. He did not agree or reply to this. Kenneth thought he would find a submissive female in the Jehovah's Witnesses. He knew that I was raised within it and thought I would make an ideal wife. Kenneth assumed I had not changed from the schoolgirl he remembered and was unprepared for the opinionated, non-submissive person I had become. Kenneth claimed that he had recently given up smoking, however he found convenient excuses for drinking alcohol. Alan, his teenage son, was frequently in trouble with the police and associated with a gang of teenagers who were involved in criminal activities. Clarissa and I noticed that Kenneth was often aggressive towards him and we sensed Alan lacked motherly care and affection in his life. We gave him plenty of affection during our stay and he responded well to it. Alan entered the house one afternoon informing Kenneth that someone wished to speak to him outside. They disappeared for a while and I later discovered a woman he was supposedly dating, heard I was staying at his home. She apparently asked about the situation and told him she was jealous. I was unaware that he had been seeing a woman because he behaved like a single man.

On the day of my father's funeral, Kenneth transported us to the Kingdom Hall of Jehovah's Witnesses. We met Albert and my mother in the car park. She wore her usual light grey suit, commenting that her attire did not matter as my father would know nothing about it. I wore a black skirt and jacket with a royal blue top, as my father loved the colour blue. I was going to wear a hat, but the weather was too warm for it. We entered the hall and my mother sat in the front row with Waverley and her sons. I sat two rows behind with Kenneth, Clarissa and uncle Vernon. Tania and Ryan were in the row behind me. My mother did not want my father's coffin in the Kingdom Hall as she did not want to remember it there each time she attended her religious meetings. My father's coffin remained in the hearse outside the hall during the service. Clarissa's attendance at the funeral caused quite a stir within the congregation as they were all aware of her role as a Village Wisewoman and assumed she 'dabbled' in spiritism. She was the only female who wore trousers as there was no good reason why she should be asked to wear a skirt when it is not in her nature to do so. Gary, the elder who conducted Kenneth's bible study, shook hands with Clarissa. She later revealed that as he did so, he placed one of his fingers between their palms so they would not connect. On reflection, this would have given Clarissa a sign of hostility, but to others it would have appeared a friendly handshake. At first she thought she had not held his hand correctly, but when she tried again, he repeated the action. My father's funeral service was disappointing, as little was said about him, with the exception of his baptism. The elder related the time he made an elaborate dive into the swimming pool and swam to the *brothers*, rather than waiting in line with the others. The elders counselled him on this matter after the event. He mentioned my parent's long marriage, their 'pet names' for one another, and how much he loved his family. I had been shunned for the majority of thirty seven years since I left their religion. Most of the funeral service was about their religion as they seized the opportunity to preach to non-Jehovah's Witness relatives about the 'new system'. They emphasise the promise of resurrection for the dead and seeing their loved ones again if they are recruited. The Kingdom songs used in the service were favourites of my mother's and it seemed all choices for the funeral were more about her than him. On reflection that occurred throughout all of his life with her. A few Jehovah's Witnesses approached me and shook my hand to give their condolences, but it was obvious they did not want to converse for long.

After the service we returned to Kenneth's car and followed the hearse to the local cemetery. As we slowly travelled from Graveton, we passed many places that had significant memories, including the lead factory where my father had worked for many years. As we passed it, I had flashbacks of the picnics we had on the grass opposite the entrance as my mother wanted to be near the factory. When he finished his working day, I ran to greet him when I saw him walk through the gates. Seeing his coffin in the back of the hearse and reliving those memories was a poignant moment. Kenneth followed the procession into the cemetery car park and as we walked to the grave, I caught up with Albert and held his hand. My father was buried in the family plot with my brother Carl. Waverley, who wore a black figure hugging mini dress to the funeral, handed a single rose to each family member to place it in the grave. The undertakers slowly removed my father's coffin from the hearse by the ropes attached to it. The coffin wobbled as they tried to keep it level and I nearly called out to tell them to be careful with him. My family stood in line hugging one another as they lowered his coffin into the grave and my mother was distraught as she clung to aunt Jade. I stood there alone, kissed the rose and said goodbye before releasing it into the grave. I stepped back and stood near my mother who began to tell my relatives what a wonderful support Waverley had been to my father. She said he gave him an abundance of kisses and plenty of help. Although this was true, I had assisted as much as I could during my visits, but she did not mention this. Aunt Jade looked over at me as my mother praised Waverley but I did not know what she thought about that. Jade had hated the Jehovah's Witness religion for years. She had a close relationship with her sister Mary throughout their lives, but when Mary was eventually recruited, she grew closer to my mother. I saw Mary's husband looking at the flowers and thought how lonely he looked without her. I heard that everything in his home was exactly as Mary left it as he had wanted all items to stay as she left them.

We arrived at the local Pavilion hall for refreshments. Surprisingly, most of the Jehovah's Witnesses conversed with me. Kevin took centre stage and offered a prayer before inviting everyone to help themselves to the buffet. A young Indian woman from my parents' congregation approached and sat beside me. She once rented a room in my parent's home, but did not like having to live by their rules. They apparently placed a curfew on her in the evenings if she went out with friends and Albert would walk in and out of his room whenever she used the bathroom. She gave me her condolences and then revealed my father had walked her down the aisle of the kingdom hall and gave her away to the groom on her wedding day. This was not something I wished to hear. She would have known that he did not do this for Waverley and I am sure he would have thought about us that day. It was a thoughtless and tactless piece of information to reveal at my father's funeral given the circumstances. On reflection, Jehovah's Witnesses are not taught social skills and how to behave with others and many of them make tactless and thoughtless statements. Gary's wife picked up a chair, placing it opposite me as she introduced herself. She purposely positioned it so she had her back towards Clarissa. My cousin Carmel and her daughter sat on the next table. They had disliked me for years, believing my mother's version of my behaviour and they were also serious gossips. They stared at Clarissa while sitting at their table, whispering to one another. I had previously warned her about them, so she responded by returning their stare and smiling. Jemima, who was the mother of Josie, my childhood friend, attended the funeral. She was the *sister* who had twelve children and her husband was crippled with muscular dystrophy. Jemima conversed with me, inquiring about my health and the medication I was taking. Puzzled, I replied that I was very well, extremely fit and not on any medication. This surprised her as she seemed to be under the impression I had health problems. On reflection, my mother may have spoken about Waverley and she confused us. Jemima's husband was delighted to see me when I approached him for a hug. Kyle, one of the *brothers* I had known since childhood, said that my father constantly spoke about me. I became emotional on hearing this and replied that my father was the only man in my life that I could trust. I added that I promised him I would return to the Jehovah's Witnesses. Kyle pointed a dominating finger at me and aggressively stated that I should not return for my father, but for myself. Meanwhile, Kenneth was conversing and flirting with the single *sisters* and it was obvious they were attracted to him. Clarissa saw Kenneth converse with Gary and his wife, surprised to see him kneel in front of them when doing so. This did not fit his arrogant personality. After the funeral, I asked him why he knelt before them and he said it was because they were his teachers. He then misinterpreted my question and told my mother I accused him of 'touching knees' with Gary's wife. He accused me of having 'issues' which on reflection was more about diversion and projection of his own 'issues'.

At the end of the day, I was understandably exhausted and hoped I would get a good night's sleep before travelling back to Cornwall. Clarissa and I conversed with Kenneth in the evening as sat opposite us wearing a short bathrobe. He leant back in his armchair with his legs crossed and it shocked me to see that his genitals hung below the short robe. Fortunately Clarissa did not see this as it would have upset her. She retired to bed and Kenneth moved to the couch beside me. I was uncomfortable sleeping in the double bedroom as it had no door. The other doors in the house had huge dents in them as though someone had punched them repeatedly. There were occasions that I awoke in the early hours and saw Kenneth hastily leave the room with a smile. I wondered whether he had been there watching me as I slept. Kenneth drank a lot of brandy that evening and his son Alan put on a DVD movie that did not interest me. I left them both and retired to bed, trying to calm my mind from thinking about all that had happened that day. Kenneth entered the room, removed his short dressing gown and got into his bed beside me. He was naked and a strong odour of brandy emanated from him. He said that he wanted a ten minute hug and then he would leave. As he pulled me towards him I froze, not knowing how to react. I heard Clarissa leave her bedroom to visit the lavatory and I was ready to call out if Kenneth attempted to take it any further. When I did not respond and he knew I was not happy with him being there, he got out of bed and left the room. It was difficult for me to sleep after that and I hoped he would not return. I had a long journey the next day when I returned to Cornwall and that could not arrive too soon.

Kenneth left early the next morning to go to work and while Clarissa and I had breakfast, I told her what occurred the previous night. Alan, his son, was still in the house so we tried to discuss it quietly so that he did not overhear. Clarissa was furious that Kenneth would put me in such a position on the day of my father's funeral. We hurried our breakfast, hastily packed our belongings and left as soon as we could. Kenneth had cleaned my father's car and prepared it for the journey. While doing so, he commented that the car had a different cap on one of the wheel's air valves and smiled about it. It wouldn't have surprised me if he took the original one for his own car and had replaced it with an odd one. It was not the first time I felt I could not get away from Kent fast enough and on the journey back it felt as though I flew! When I drove my father's car to Cornwall, I had mixed feelings. His car comforted me in one way, as I felt that part of him was still with me. I felt the worn material of the steering wheel, remembering exactly where his hands were as he held it. My father had carried the keys in his pockets and there were other items in the car he had used for the past ten years. I was grateful to my family for letting me have his car, however I had not inherited anything else. I did not know about the financial arrangements for some time until Waverley later said that my father's savings were placed in an account for my mother to live on.

When Kenneth realised I did not want a relationship with him, he attempted to create problems between Waverley and I. Someone had told him all about my past and the problems I had within the family. He had spent a huge amount of time conversing with my mother and Albert, but I did not know for certain who had given him the information. Kenneth had blocked Waverley on social media because she also had Gary's wife on her friends list. He said he did not want Waverley reporting details of his life to her. When she confronted him about it, he replied that I had persuaded him to block her and revealed further negative information about our past, telling her the information had come from me. I told Waverley that this was not true, but am unsure if she believed me. It seemed she still viewed me as the 'black sheep' and 'scapegoat', but I assured her I had not returned to the family to cause trouble. On reflection, there are some who refuse to believe a person can change, as this removes them from the 'scapegoat' role and there is no one else to take their place. I later heard that Kenneth was counselled by the Jehovah's Witness committee of elders about his flirtatious spirit with single women at the Kingdom Hall and his arrogant attitude. This did not surprise me, as I had warned him he would find their rules difficult to obey.

A few days after my return to Cornwall, a message was sent to my business website from a client needing help. After exchanging messages I gave her my mobile phone number, She then sent a text message revealing that she was not really a client, but Kenneth's girlfriend. She explained they were dating before I visited Kent and during that time he changed towards her and she did not understand why. She knew of my plan to return to the Jehovah's Witnesses and commented it would put me in a good position for a relationship with Kenneth. I was appalled that she assumed I would enter this religion purely to have a relationship with such a person! I assured her that I felt no attraction towards him and pitied her having feelings for a troublemaker and liar with a flirtatious spirit. She became upset asking why I wanted to upset her by telling her this and accused me of being cruel for telling her the truth. I ended the conversation by giving her my best wishes for the future.

CHAPTER 17

MY RETURN

After returning to Cornwall, I researched where my local Kingdom Hall would be and attended their Thursday evening meeting. I knew the route well as the hall was twelve miles away and situated next to the refuse centre. I parked my father's car in the car park, walked into the hall and sat on a vacant chair. My mother gave me my father's song book that he regularly used and I had the latest translation of their bible given to me by the elders in Fowey congregation. The local hall was full with many of its members conversing with one another. A few approached me to ask if I was visiting while on holiday. It was easy for me to switch back into behaving and dressing as required for meetings. I replied honestly and said I was disfellowshipped. Before they hastily retreated, they said they hoped I would enjoy the evening. At the end of the meeting, I requested to speak to an elder and one of them invited me to their smaller room, joined by another two elders. I explained my situation and the area I lived. They replied that they were not my local congregation as they shared the hall with another. The elders then informed me of meeting times for my local congregation, advising me to attend their meetings as they would be in a better position to assist me.

The following weekend I attended the local congregation's Sunday afternoon meeting. Once again, members of the congregation approached me to introduce themselves and I explained that I was disfellowshipped. It was comforting to be in a place that I knew my father loved to be. At the end of the meeting I asked to see an elder and was once again escorted to their small back room. Three elders were seated opposite me and one of them locked the door, explaining this was done to prevent others from entering the room. This was something new as I did not recall this happening in past meetings with elders. I once again explained my situation. When they discovered I had been out of the Jehovah's Witness religion for twenty seven years, it annoyed them. They did not like to hear that I had a successful life, a career and a busy social life. I told them I lived with a friend who provided me with a home after I separated from my husband. One of the elders asked if I believed their religion was the truth and although I still had nagging doubts, I replied that I did. He seemed surprised by this. They also wanted to ensure I was not 'living in sin' or dating a 'worldly' man. When I replied there was no man in my life he seemed relieved to hear it. I explained that my father had passed away after being a faithful Jehovah's Witness for sixty years and I attended his funeral in Kent only ten days ago. They seemed satisfied with the information I gave and informed me that to be reinstated, I would be required to attend every meeting. I was instructed to enter the hall just before the meeting began, and leave immediately after the final prayer, to avoid any socialising.

Twice a week, I travelled to the Kingdom Hall in my father's car on Thursday evenings and Sunday afternoons while listening to music my father enjoyed. I conversed with him as though he were sitting beside me. I kept the Order of Service from his funeral as it had his photograph on the front, placed inside the cover of his song book. I laid it on an adjacent empty chair so that I had him with me. Most of the congregation members used computer iPads instead of books logging on to the *JW.org* website to access relevant literature for the meeting. This was completely different to the methods I remembered. I did not own an iPad, so I took my laptop computer with me after downloading the relevant literature at home as they did not offer me the Wi-Fi code as I was not yet part of the congregation. When I arrived for the meetings, I did not creep quietly into the hall but walked in with my head held high as I still felt confident in these surroundings. I did not want to sit in the back row, as families were there and the last thing I wanted was the distraction of noisy children. I purchased new skirt suits and ensured my attire was immaculate. A row of mature single women sat just behind me and were impressed by the way I looked and behaved as they commented loudly to one another so that I could hear them. They complimented my singing voice too. I still remembered the old kingdom songs and the new ones were easy to learn. It was comforting to know these women secretly conversed with me to offer encouragement and support, as only elders were permitted to speak to me and did so occasionally. Clarissa was not happy about my return, as she left the Pentecostals after a bad experience, however she understood my reasons and supported my choice. My family were aware that I was returning, but I had not mentioned it to any of my friends in Cornwall.

When the year 2016 began, our Sunday meetings were then changed from the afternoons to mornings, so that the other congregation could enjoy an afternoon meeting for a year.. I found this difficult as I often worked late on a Saturday night. I recall entering the Kingdom Hall one Sunday morning where an elder was involved in a heated conversation with a young man in the foyer. The tall elder towered over the young man who had his back against the wall and the elder's body language appeared threatening. I later discovered this young man was either disassociated or disfellowshipped as he often sat in the back room during meetings away from the rest of the congregation. After attending the meetings for a while, my mother contacted me by phone to praise me. She described my return as a glimmer of light in a world of darkness. I sensed Waverley was not happy about me returning as she saw herself as the 'good girl' who received all the praise even though she was an inactive member. Waverley commented that I would not want any more Christmas or birthday gifts from her and I had not thought about that, but this was the only way I could have contact with my mother to help her out now my father had passed away.

Waverley had hoped that Kevin, being an elder in the Jehovah's Witnesses would help her care for our mother. He suddenly decided to move to Wales soon after my father's passing without telling her. My mother however was aware of his plans as he explained he was 'going where the need is great' for their religion, as he and Mavis had learnt sign language. My mother supported this as she believed they were doing it for Jehovah, but Mavis' family also lived there. Throughout his life Kevin knew he could get away with anything if he claimed it was for the sake of the religion, but in reality, he did not want the responsibility of caring for his mother and knew that when she passed away, he would have to help care for Albert because of his Asperger's syndrome. This decision was also made after I began attending meetings. It seemed Kevin could have been running away from something, as he apparently has not revealed his address to anyone.

While attending the local meetings, elders took it in turn to stand outside the entrance doors and greet each congregation member that entered including those newly interested. When I passed, they silently stared ahead of them. One Sunday morning I arrived at the Kingdom Hall tired and exhausted after working late and an elder at the door glared at me like something he found on the bottom of his shoe! I found the shunning quite difficult in one way, but the positive aspect was that I could attend meetings and leave quickly without anyone prying into my life. There was no strong desire to associate with them and I often remembered the words of Pamela Lovell who hated associating with congregation members, saying that the brothers "smelt of rotting cabbage"!

I visited my mother in Kent and she seemed pleased to see me. I pre-studied religious literature with her and attended her local Kingdom Hall. During our pre-study, whenever a scripture was mentioned in a Watchtower publication, my mother immediately recited the scripture without having to find it. Sixty years of reading the scriptures was imprinted in her memory. Although my mother's hair had turned white, she used a crimson hair dye explaining that Albert insisted on it because he did not want her to grow old. She felt cold temperatures more and wore gloves and thick socks to keep her hands and feet warm. My mother loved wearing colourful clothes, however they were not coordinated well as she would mix prints, for example she wore a floral blouse with a chequered or polka-dot skirt. Her Romani spirit was still in there somewhere! I transported her to the shops in Dartfleet and Waverley gave me instructions to hold her hand so that she doesn't fall and to walk slowly as she only took tiny steps. My mother enjoyed sitting in my father's car as I helped her in and she smiled as I fastened her seat belt. I was about to turn off the cassette player with my father's favourite music, thinking it would be too painful for her, but she said she wanted to listen to it. She thought the car needed new seat covers and gave me money to purchase them. My mother approved of the red leopard print covers I chose, as they coordinated well with the red car. We walked through the town of Dartfleet together and I held my mother's hand at first but soon realised she did not need it. She took her hand from mine rather abruptly and walked faster than Waverley described without falling over. I then realised that she behaved differently with me, but wanted to appear weak and helpless when she was with Waverley who once told me that our mother called out to her in the supermarket with her skirt around her ankles wanting help! She also emptied her bank account while Waverley went overseas for a break. My mother and I visited clothes shops as I was looking for a blouse to wear with one of my suits. When I found one, my mother insisted on paying for it. I thanked her and kissed her cheek which seemed to please her. Many shops displayed Halloween decorations with plastic skeletons in their windows. My mother did not want to see them commenting that we were not supposed to see our skeletons because we are not meant to die. I replied that our bones are a beautiful and powerful framework for our bodies to be admired, but she disagreed.

Albert seemed fascinated by dead bodies and repeatedly described in great detail the appearance of my father as he lay in the chapel of rest. He visited him on five occasions and Ryan accompanied him once. Albert went on to list the relatives he had seen after they passed with vivid descriptions of each one as if they were Museum exhibits.

Although he had not been diagnosed for Asperger's at this time, there were many traits of it in his speech, mannerisms and obsessive fascination for unusual subjects. Albert had controlled the family home all his life, as my parents were relieved he survived after the loss of their still-born son. He disliked Kevin and Mavis visiting, as he said they slammed the cutlery drawer. Albert attached a 'Do Not Slam This Drawer' notice to it, which she apparently ignored. Before their next visit, he emptied the contents of the cutlery drawer on the dining room table, so Mavis would not need to use it. Albert followed my mother around the kitchen and if she touched anything, he would examine it for breakage. Whenever she opened the fridge, he would open and close it again to check she had closed it correctly. When I helped my mother in the kitchen, I noticed that he did not behave in this way. It seemed he only did with those he knew would allow it. He did not know me well enough after all the years we were apart but I expect he sensed I would not tolerate it.

I dined at my mother's home and then we prepared to attend an evening meeting at the Kingdom Hall. I changed into the correct attire and carried the rest of my luggage to the car. As I opened the car boot, I heard a stationary vehicle behind me with its engine running. I did not look around me and continued to place my luggage in the car. When I re-entered the house I glanced out of the lounge window and saw Kenneth's delivery van drive away. He angered me for many reasons, and I was prepared to confront him about his lies to Waverley at the hall that evening. It did not surprise me when he did not attend and his absence gave Waverley a different view of the situation. A few weeks later she sent me a newspaper article about Kenneth who was summoned to court for reckless driving. The article revealed that Kenneth had to appear in court after a car accident because he drove away immediately after the collision. The stories he concocted to avoid prosecution were ridiculous and unbelievable.

My mother preferred to sit at the back of the Kingdom Hall as they provided a row of armchairs for elderly and disabled members. She sat in the far corner saying it was the one that my father preferred. We sang Kingdom songs together and I held her hand as we listened to the prayer. After the meeting ended and everyone socialised, I approached my mother to ask if she needed transportation home. She was conversing with Gary who was aware I stood behind him as my mother told him I was there. He sat in the chair with one foot resting on the knee of the other and continued to stare ahead of him in silence. On reflection, I had no wish to converse with him even if it were permitted. My mother said that Albert would transport her home, so I hastily left the hall.

I spent most of my time at the family home on this visit, assisting with cleaning and transporting my mother when she wanted to go shopping. This was unusual as she had never travelled to the town with Waverley or I when my father was alive, saying she was frightened to travel without him. She was the one who wanted to go and she visited the town frequently after he passed away. I was concerned how she would react to my father's death as she could not bear to be without him when he was alive. Throughout their married life, she instructed him not to travel more than two miles away from her as she would panic. Knowing my father was no longer around and with no belief in a spirit world, I thought the separation from him would result in her losing her mind. My mother however did not panic, or have a mental breakdown, claiming that Jehovah and her faith helped her to cope. On reflection, I wondered if this 'phobia' was more about control of my father than her being genuinely afraid of being away from him. Her reaction after his death revealed the answer. My father restricted her spending in the past as she enjoyed purchasing tacky trinkets. Now that he was no longer around she made the most of the opportunities to purchase anything she desired and visited the shops often. My mother once purchased five mechanical birds that constantly flapped their wings and tweeted when they reacted to sound. She asked me if I wanted one of them and I politely declined the offer!

My visit to Kent went smoothly and uncle Vernon was pleased that I visited him for breakfast each morning. He also accompanied me to the cemetery when I placed flowers on my father and Carl's grave before returning to Cornwall.

CHAPTER 18

REINSTATEMENT

After attending the religious meetings for a period of five months, one of the elders suggested I send a letter to the Governing Body requesting reinstatement. I had followed all their requirements and endured the shunning. On receipt of my letter, the judicial committee discussed the matter and informed me that my reinstatement would be announced at the meeting after their memorial service in March of 2016. At the memorial service I sat in the front row next to brother Pratt. He had been quite aggressive towards me during my first conversation with the committee of elders. Brother Pratt is a Cornish man and when I commented that someone warned me Cornish people took a long time to accept 'incomers', he replied that this was absolute rubbish. Before he sat beside me at the memorial service, he took my hand and shook it while looking at other members of the congregation. The reinstatement had not yet been announced and a twelve year old girl with learning disabilities was eager to speak to me. She approached me with her hand out when she saw him do so and I said that we could shake hands at the following meeting. I felt quite confident at meetings and although I did not feel a great need to associate with the brothers and sisters, I promised my father I would return. A talk was given at one meeting where a *brother* stated a person must love Jehovah God more than their own families. At this time, the love I felt for my father surpassed emotions for anyone else. I contacted my mother to tell her my reinstatement would be announced at the next meeting and took a recording device with me to capture the moment for her. I heard the older *sisters* saying a while ago that they could see no reason why I should not be reinstated. When it was announced, all the congregation members applauded and smiled at me. After the meeting ended, many gathered around me and welcomed me by shaking my hand or kissing my cheek. It was pleasant in one way, but at that moment, I began to feel my freedom slipping away from me.

A *sister* was assigned to conduct my weekly bible study and take me out on the preaching work. Her son was one of the younger elders. The bible studies were not a problem, as although I had been out of the religion for years, it was easy to switch back into the routine. She commented that I read very well and confessed to me that she hated having to give up Christmas as she loved it so much. The elders also commented I was a good student as I regularly did pre-study and attended meetings fully equipped. The preaching work was a different matter, as I had to become accustomed to doing this again.. On the preaching work, I noticed that fewer householders were willing to converse and it was rare to find anyone who answered our knock at their door. The householders who did listen were shown videos by Witnesses on their iPads and they read scriptures from them too. It was a completely different way of working as the preaching was more scripted with specific sentences to use rather than working out your own presentation. This meant all of the Jehovah's Witnesses were now saying exactly the same thing when they preached.

The elders and congregation members wanted to know exactly where I lived. I told them the name of the village and terrace, but not the number of the cottage. Brother O'Cannon tried to guess by describing the house he thought it was. Clarissa's cottage was tucked behind them and she was a well known Village Wisewoman. If they discovered I lived in her cottage it may cause further problems. Although Clarissa trained me in her way of working, I was also a beauty and holistic therapist as well as counsellor, so these were the qualifications I told them about. The group of mature *sisters* got together each week for afternoon tea and invited me. I declined the invitation, explaining that I was working, but I also knew that by spending time with them, they would question me about my life.

One afternoon, I joined a group of Jehovah's Witnesses out on the preaching work. After an hour, we gathered in a large car park for a tea break. Brother Pratt and his wife opened the back of their car and distributed cups of freshly brewed tea to everyone from a camping stove. He passed one to me but did not look at me, even when I spoke to him. There was however a recent talk based on the scripture *Matthew 5:28*: *"But I say to you that anyone who keeps on looking at a woman so as to have a passion for her, has already committed adultery with her in his heart"*. An elderly sister in her eighties reminded me of my mother and I grew quite fond of her. I often conversed with her at the meetings and one evening, I noticed she was not sitting in her usual chair. I glanced around the hall looking for her during one of the talks and brother O'Cannon who sat in the adjacent row, saw me looking around. He stared at me until our eyes met, pointed to his own eyes and then to the platform. This took me back to my childhood when I was constantly told by my parents to listen and keep my eyes focused upon the speaker, but I was now an adult!!

When the congregations members socialised after meetings, I stood at the back of the hall and 'people watched' as I preferred to get to know people by studying body language and interactions. An attractive teenage daughter of an elder followed a handsome married brother around the hall who was new to the congregation. I accompanied him on the preaching work one afternoon and he told me his wife no longer attended meetings. The interaction between him and this young girl reminded me of the relationship between me and Brett. I hoped their situation would not end in the same way as I could see the attraction was mutual. I heard from my mother Brett was diagnosed with cancer in his seventies and after a harsh dose of chemotherapy, he passed away in 2006, three years after the last time I saw him.

Clarissa believed the Jehovah's Witnesses were a cult organisation, but understood my reasons for returning. I arranged to attend a district convention in Exeter but the tickets for the coach had sold out. One sister was not able to go, so I purchased a ticket from her that cost eight pounds. I gave her a ten pound note and she took it from me and walked away without offering the two pounds in change. I did not confront her, but was disappointed she did not offer it to me. I had to be on the coach outside the Kingdom Hall by 6.45am, so I left home at 6.15am. I sat next to a brother who repairs clocks and recognised him because he had fixed my vintage nautical bell clock two years ago. We conversed throughout the journey and I told him humorous stories of my childhood experiences in the Jehovah's Witnesses. They were entertaining for him and anyone else who happened to be eavesdropping. The convention was exhausting and held in a convention hall that was uncomfortably warm. Many tired people had difficulty staying awake and I was one of them. When a person is in this state of falling asleep, the words they can hear will imprint better in the brain, similar to hypnotism. Brainwashing in this way is more successful. I met the elder that I first spoke to when I attended the congregation that shared our Kingdom Hall nine months ago. He claimed he did not remember me visiting or the conversation we had. I then told him I had been reinstated and he kissed my cheek, congratulating me. I wrote pages of notes that day and in the two hour lunch break, I stood back and watched the *brothers* and *sisters* socialising. I was surprised to see a group of teenage girls dressed as though they were attending a nightclub with their tight backless dresses. Their clothes revealed more than mine ever did at their age and mine were frowned upon! The assemblies were more like a 'meat market' where young men and women attended hoping to find a marriage mate. The baptisms were different to how I remembered them as women wore long t-shirts over their swimsuits. One of the few positive aspects of attending meetings or conventions was that I could visit the ladies bathroom and leave my handbag on the chair knowing it would not be touched or stolen.

Certain restrictions were placed upon me by the elders. I was not permitted to raise my hand and offer any comments or answer questions during the meetings. The elders said this restriction would continue for quite a while until they decided to end it. We studied articles and were shown videos at the meetings about losing loved ones in death. One that I cannot forget featured an elderly man dying in hospital and I found this overwhelmingly emotional. One of the sisters held my hand to comfort me. There were many videos using cartoon illustrations and adults as well as children found these amusing. A talk was given about difficulties some brothers faced that did not deter them from serving God. Although my father was extremely ill near the end of his life, he regularly sat on a seat beside the town clock tower with religious publications and preached to passers by.

Another video related the story of a circuit overseer who had an artificial leg. He had told no one about this and one day while he was out on the preaching work, his foot detached from the artificial leg and fell onto the pavement. The *brothers* who witnessed this were horrified and I heard a roar of laughter from male congregation members. They continued laughing for quite a while and all I could think of was their immature sense of humour.

Abstaining from internet pornography was a subject that regularly arose, reminding *brothers* not to give in to temptation. I understood why, as the internet has made pornography easily accessible. One *brother* raised his hand and told the congregation about another *brother* who borrowed an elder's mobile phone to make a call. He found pornographic photographs stored in it. I was surprised the elders let him continue describing this occurrence and the congregation fell silent for a moment until the speaker hastily changed the subject.

At the end of a Sunday morning meeting, it was announced that one of the *brothers* was moving out of the area. He had arranged a farewell buffet and invited the congregation members to stay on after the meeting. I joined the queue at the buffet table and chose a small sandwich, aware that Clarissa had cooked a Sunday dinner. A group of elders were standing in the queue and one of them asked what Jesus would do when waiting in a queue. An elder replied that he would probably have pushed his way to the front and they laughed. I sat upon a chair with my food while everyone socialised. The elder's attractive teenage daughter sat beside me with a large slice of cake in her hand. She commented how much she loved cake and said "you don't get a lovely 'bod' like mine by avoiding it"! I did not respond to this statement hoping that she would move on. She also complimented me on my necklace saying it reminded her of the one in the movie *Titanic*. It was not long before she noticed the handsome married brother and left me to pursue him. I sensed her parents would have problems with her in the near future, as I recognised the signs and remembered my own adolescence. I stayed for a short while and before leaving I waved to all the *brothers* and *sisters*. I could tell by some of their expressions that they were not happy about me leaving so soon. I got into my father's car and let out a sigh of relief.

A few months later, a ministerial servant gave a talk on spiritism. As he read scriptures warning people to avoid such practices, he looked directly at me. I wondered if he had discovered where I was living and with whom. It was obvious that an elder who was the father of the flirtatious teenage girl changed towards me. I stood next to his wife while conversing with her and he spoke to her while ignoring me. When I returned home, I sent mobile phone texts to the woman I was studying with, to find out when our next one would be and received no reply. I sensed something had changed.

A week later, I received a phone text from brother O'Cannon requesting my presence at the Kingdom Hall on Monday evening. He did not explain why, and I thought it may be connected to my mother. When I entered the Kingdom Hall car park, it was empty. The front doors of the hall appeared locked, but when I tried the door handle, it opened. Brother O'Cannon and Brother Pratt were in the back room with their coats on. They invited me to sit opposite them and once again locked the door. I could see no reason for this, as there was no one else present in the building to disturb us. They informed me they had found some websites on the internet that they considered disturbing. Brother Pratt turned his iPad towards me, showing a photograph of myself, Clarissa and her 'Obby 'Oss. They asked if it was me in the photograph and I confirmed it was. I explained I was at a folk music festival. Brother Pratt said: "look at what you are wearing"! I replied that there was nothing wrong with a top hat, sunshades and a long black coat. He asked: "Is this the attire a Jehovah's Witness would wear"? I replied it was unlikely. Brother O'Cannon stated that it was a Pagan festival and I disagreed, repeating that it was a folk music festival. He angrily told me to research my history. Brother O'Cannon also remarked on the difficulty they had finding me on social media and the internet. He accused me of using different pseudonyms to avoid them. I was aware that Brother Pratt's son recently found my social media business page and posted a laughing emoticon on one of my therapy posts. They presented me with more photographs from Clarissa's website and inquired about our relationship. I explained that Clarissa offered me a home rather than see me homeless after my divorce. Brother Pratt angrily and aggressively stated that I was living with a woman who practised spiritism. I disagreed, as spiritism means the practice of mediumship and Clarissa did not use this method in her work. We had a lengthy debate about it and then Brother Pratt presented me with a photograph of a black candle from the website and seemed nervous about the image. I replied that it was a candle that happened to be black, however each person would interpret this image in their own way. He then returned to the subject of my relationship with Clarissa and inquired whether she and I were having a sexual relationship. Another photograph was shown of us standing at the front door of her cottage. I had leant on her shoulder and Clarissa had her arm around me. I replied she was an elderly woman with no interest in sexual relations, but Brother Pratt refused to believe this as on reflection, he was probably near her age. I sensed for some time that he was attracted to me and his voice grew louder each time he repeated the question: "Are you having a sexual relationship with that woman?" This angered me and as I continued to deny it, I became overheated and threw off my scarf and coat in the process. There was however one moment during his accusations and my refusal to back down that we paused for breath, looked at one another and began to laugh. Brother O'Cannon did not find it amusing and commented that the body of elders would need to discuss this situation and my attitude! An older sister at the Kingdom Hall had told me that Brother Pratt was obsessed with sex and constantly raised the subject of David and Bathsheba at the meetings. This had confirmed what I sensed about him. Brother Pratt stated that Clarissa was an evil woman and instructed me to move out of her cottage and never see her again. I replied that she was not evil and had been nothing but kind to me at a time when I needed it most. My Jehovah's Witness family shunned me and refused to help. Clarissa taught me independence, the process of self employment and how to rebuild my life after the divorce.

The elders interrogated me for two hours. Clarissa is well known within her community and the world of media for her work. It was known that I worked with her. The elders discovered this information on the internet after someone in the congregation drew their attention to it. I explained all the events that led to me being with Clarissa and told them about my past which included childhood experiences with the abusive family member who was now an elder. Brother O'Cannon said that they would need to look into the situation because of accusations from the media of not reporting these incidents. I replied that I did not plan to take further action against him, I was purely giving them information about my past. Brother O'Cannon surprisingly revealed that he was once a drug dealer, but had turned his life around and I could do the same. The conversation ended with them informing me they would discuss the situation with the judicial committee. I left the Kingdom Hall relieved to be out of the room, but then discovered I had left the lights on in my father's car. The battery was out of charge, so I had to return to the hall and ask the elders if they had ant 'jump leads' to start my car. Neither of them had, so brother Pratt contacted his son, asking him to bring his 'jump leads' to the Kingdom Hall. I sat with them waiting for him to arrive and brother Pratt commented that he would like a mug of tea. I was aware there were kitchen facilities and when he asked me if I wanted one, I refused as I sensed he would expect me to make it. His son took longer than expected, so he eventually brewed a mug of tea for himself. When his son eventually arrived, they were successful in starting the car. He smiled at me but I was not happy at this time and he sensed something was wrong. I thanked them and drove away as quickly as possible.

On my return home, I told Clarissa what had happened and it angered her. From then on, I stopped attending meetings as I did not want to experience further hostile treatment. I knew the committee of elders would want to see me, but after the aggression from brother Pratt, I had no wish to place myself in this situation again. I wrote a letter to the elders suggesting they read it during their discussion as it explained my situation. I told them about my first violent marriage and how I left my first husband and married a policeman so my daughter and I would be safe. I did not expect my second husband to ask for a divorce and leave me homeless after twenty one years of marriage. I told them how Clarissa was the only person to offer help by inviting me to stay in her home. I could not approach Jehovah's Witnesses as they were shunning me. I added that my mother refused to help me even after reinstatement when she had room in her home to do so. I explained that I was grieving for my father and kept my promise of returning to their religion. I did not think my place of residence should affect this if I followed their rules. I concluded the letter by agreeing to meet with the committee only if they allowed a sister from the congregation to be present. I thought my mother would rather I had slept on the floor of her home than live with someone like Clarissa, as she was fully aware of who and what she was. My mother however, refused to allow me to move into her three bedroom house with her and Albert.

While this situation was unresolved, I visited my family in Kent. After explaining the situation to my mother, she advised me to meet with the elders, agree to everything they said and hang my head in shame! I replied that I could not do that as I was a victim of circumstance and had done nothing wrong. My mother said that she knew this and repeated our conversation to Rosie, who assumed that I had a problem taking discipline from the elders. On hearing this I wrote a letter to her explaining what had occurred and she apologised. Rosie's sister Joan and her husband Arnold offered to accommodate me while I was visiting. Joan and I conversed about many things and the subject of her father arose. She explained that her father left Vivien for another woman and was disfellowshipped. Joan stayed in contact with her father but Rosie shunned him. Joan added that when Vivien discovered his extra marital affair, she attacked him with a broom and this surprised me as I had not thought of Vivien as an aggressive woman however on reflection, I remembered that she was a feisty female! My mother said that when Vivien discovered Brett had made advances to me, she was angry with him for a long time. When he offered to assist her getting out of her wheelchair she threatened him not to touch her. The incident with Brett would have triggered memories of her husband's infidelity. Years later I wrote a letter to Rosie apologising for what happened with Brett and asked her forgiveness. She replied she had forgiven me, quoting a scripture that advised her to do so. Waverley said that Rosie did not blame me for the situation, but it was obvious that my mother had, remembering her comment to my second husband.

Joan and Arnold's children were now adults and remained members of the Jehovah's Witnesses. I had not seen them since they were small and Arnold proudly played a video of his son speaking on stage in another language at a convention. He was an elder who now lived in another country. Joan and Arnold were very hospitable and happy for me to access the internet through their Wi-Fi connection. I would check my email account before retiring to bed, however I could not access the connection for long, as Arnold turned off the Wi-Fi hub before going to sleep. They gave me a spare house key so that I could let myself in if they were out. I was respectful to them and their property during my stay and they told my mother it was a pleasure to have me there. I enjoyed spending time with Joan as many years had passed since I last saw her. I missed Vivien, but Joan's voice and deep brown eyes reminded me of her. I attended a meeting at their Kingdom Hall and the subject of tattoos arose in one of the talks. Joan had seen the large one on my shoulder and her eyes often gravitated towards it when I wore sleeveless tops. She looked at me when the *brother* explained why Jehovah's Witnesses should not have them, but I did not feel ashamed and shrugged my shoulders as it was too late to do anything about it. I kept it covered at meetings and when out in the field ministry. I transported my mother to one of their meetings and met Honour Lovell, a childhood friend I had not seen for many years. The conversations I had with Hattie came to mind, as she had not seen her sister for many years or met her children because of the shunning rule. I found photographs of Honour and her family on social media and sent them to Hattie. She was upset Honour would not have contact with her. As Honour approached us at the Kingdom Hall, my mother said "Here comes MY beauty!" Her annoyance with me was obvious, because my return to the Jehovah's Witnesses had not gone well and she attempted to put me down yet again. I could have walked out of the hall and let someone else transport her home, but I stayed, reminding myself that her comments said more about her than they did about me. This visit was an uncomfortable one in some aspects and when I returned to Cornwall, I knew that more of this awaited me.

CHAPTER 19

DISFELLOWSHIPPED

The elders instructed me to attend a judicial committee meeting, but they refused my request of having another *sister* in the room. After my last experience with them, I did not attend. A few days later, brother O' Cannon and another elder called at Clarissa's cottage. I opened the door to them, while Clarissa watched from the window. Brother O' Canon gave a satisfied smile to himself as they had 'tracked me down' and could give me the news in person. He stated that I was a difficult woman to contact, but I discovered while attending the meetings that Clarissa's window cleaner was a Jehovah's Witness and he was the only one who could have given them my address. They discovered my double-barrelled surname when Clarissa sent the window cleaner a cheque from our joint account and informed him that his services were no longer required.

We had combined our surnames because I had taken on Clarissa's business and she was well known for the work we did. Brother O'Cannon informed me they had reason to believe Clarissa and I were in a sexual relationship as they found tabloid media articles about it on the internet. I stood there and shook my head. This influenced their decision to disfellowship me and by doing so, they had the power to grant reinstatement should I apply to be reinstated in the future. I tried to explain the situation was not what they thought and Brother O' Cannon replied I had two weeks to appeal against this decision. He added that all congregations I had connections with would be informed of this decision. The other elder saw the tattoo on my shoulder and intensely stared at it to let me know he had seen it, but I no longer cared. After informing me that I was disfellowshipped, they walked away. I walked into the cottage and told Clarissa all they had said. She has yet to meet brother Pratt, but when she does, she intends to have words with him! I could see no point in appealing against their decision as I had withheld information about my place of residence and who lived there. I was not in a financial position to move out and they offered no help. I now realise that if I attempted to join the Jehovah's Witness again, there is far too much information from my past that they would use against me and I would always be viewed as 'bad association' no matter what I did.

I visited Kent once again to see my family and visited my mother with Ryan who accompanied me on this trip. She answered the door but refused to invite us in, saying that Waverley was due to arrive to take her shopping. My mother added that as my father's funeral was over and I was disfellowshipped, the shunning would resume. It angered me when she said this in the presence of my son. I explained that the purpose of my visit was to discuss what had happened with the elders in my local congregation. My mother replied with an expression of delight, that the elders had already contacted her and told her what had happened so she didn't need to hear it from me. I doubt she heard the true version of events, but she would believe them without question. I said that Jehovah's Witnesses have no genuine love for people and my uncle Vernon, viewed as an 'outsider' and apostate, had shown more love than they ever had. My mother replied that Vernon tells me what I want to hear. I was determined to tell her some 'home truths' as I refused to become 'the little girl' in her presence as many adults do with parents. I had also returned to dark brown hair which would have angered her. My son stood beside me not knowing how to react and because I raised my voice, she warned me to control my anger as she was having to control her own temper. I was no longer afraid of her threats. I had an honest answer for everything she directed at me and she eventually walked into the house slamming the door behind her.

My mother told Waverley that I was angry when I arrived at her door and was shouting at her. She said my voice became louder and louder while I was running down the elders and the religion. I replied there was more to it than that. Waverley took me out for the evening and we visited the Inn that her friend Lena managed. Lena prepared a wonderful buffet meal and gave us special treatment. I drank more vodka than usual that evening and threw myself into having a good time to forget about the afternoon debate. A couple joined us who were both Jehovah's Witnesses. I had known them since my teenage years and they also attended my father's funeral. I met Kyle's daughter who was not in the religion (Kyle was the one who lectured me at the funeral). They were friendly towards me which helped enormously after the day I had.

I also visited Tom and Amy Sheldon who were always so welcoming. They gave me unconditional love even though they did not always agree with my choices in life. Amy once commented that I was like another daughter to them as they had known me for a long time.

Although Ryan travelled to Kent and stayed with me the atmosphere between us was uncomfortable, I later discovered he was an informant for a group of former 'friends' who created a 'vendetta group' against Clarissa and I. Ryan also sided with his father after our divorce and had given the impression he wanted to be with me, with the intention of reporting my personal information back to them. To be sure of this I gave him a piece of information that no one knew. The main instigator of the vendetta put this information out on their internet blog two days later. I knew then that I could no longer trust him. He was manipulated by his father Patrick who promised him a considerable inheritance. This ruined the close relationship we once had. I had to be extra careful when conversing with Ryan about revealing any information that would be useful to the group. Tania had experienced problems with him also and after giving many chances, she cut off all contact with him. I am unsure whether his thought processes are caused by traits of high functioning autism that have become more prevalent in him as an adult, or whether there is another underlying mental health issue. I do acknowledge that the vendetta group are not totally to blame as Ryan had chosen to behave this way.

CHAPTER 20

COUNSELLOR

I joined various social media groups and conversed with former members of cults. I then researched organisations and their methods of mind control, discovering there are many counsellors in America who assist former cult members, but few in the United Kingdom.

I was advised by a Counselling Organisation to enrol in Crisis and Trauma Counselling to help former cult members. After attaining a Diploma at Distinction level, I studied two books: *Combatting Mind Control* and *Releasing the Bonds* by *Steven Hassan*. My past experience is extremely useful as I understand the difficult experiences former members have to cope with. I heard that many who were shunned after leaving their religion, lacked social skills as they are not taught how to function in the outside world. They had problems dealing with life outside of their religion and this sadly resulted in suicide. I hope that by providing this service I can help save lives of those who feel that they have no one to turn to.

I visited Kent once again with Clarissa to spend time with Waverley and Uncle Vernon. I decided against visiting my mother and Albert after her reaction on my last visit. I spent time with Tom and Amy Shelden and other friends who were pleased to see me. On the day I planned to travel back to Cornwall, Waverley invited Uncle Vernon and I for a hearty breakfast in a carvery restaurant. She also invited Albert as he is a huge man who would not refuse an invitation for a meal. My mother then decided to accompany him so that she could monitor any conversations that occurred between us. Uncle Vernon sat opposite me and Waverley sat between my mother and I. I did not converse with her for quite a while, but eventually I 'broke the ice' by complimenting the rings she wore. I listened to the stories of how she acquired each one. Her wedding ring was tight on her finger years ago and she could not remove it, but as she grew old and frail, her finger was smaller and the ring was loose. My mother said that she lost her marcasite engagement ring a while ago, so I advised her to wear another ring my father purchased for her above the wedding ring so that she did not lose it. We finished our breakfast and left the table. I spoke to Waverley and Vernon about my journey to Cornwall and although my mother did not speak, I noticed in my peripheral vision that she gazed up at me in awe as she stood beside me. We left the restaurant and as we walked towards the car park, my mother gave me a religious pamphlet entitled 'Return to Jehovah'. I took it but informed her I already had a copy. I added that I regularly looked at the JW.org website and the schedules for each meeting which pleased her. I did this however to keep updated with their teachings and read the subjects they were studying. I also checked monetary donations they were requesting from their members.

My family stood in line outside the restaurant and I said farewell to each one in turn and kissed them. I kissed my mother's cheek and she held my arms momentarily, but I felt the pressure of her pushing me away so that we did not hug. This was the last time that Uncle Vernon and I saw her, so I am grateful that Waverley arranged this meeting as it was a better memory of the last time I saw her than the previous occasion. I heard that the Jehovah's Witnesses would visit her often after my father's death but this became less frequent after a month or so. My mother however, always made excuses for them.

CHAPTER 21

BEREAVEMENT

Two years after this visit, when I had my weekly phone conversation with Uncle Vernon, he said that Aunt Jade had visited my mother and was concerned about her breathing, as she would gasp for breath even after walking short distances. Waverley contacted me soon after this to tell me my mother had fallen down the stairs and seriously injured her leg. She was admitted to hospital and Waverley could not visit her because of Covid restrictions. Waverley kept in regular contact by telephone and she gave me the number. I did not contact my mother as I was unsure of her reaction and did not want to upset her. The medical staff gave her a thorough check up, as she had avoided medical check ups for some time. The blood around her heart had thickened, so they prescribed blood thinners and sent her home when her leg injury had improved. Three days later, my mother had a lot of chest pain, took painkillers and then suddenly passed away because a blood clot entered her heart. Albert telephoned the ambulance service and when they arrived, the medical team were unable to revive her.

My father had passed away at eighty two years of age, and my mother followed him five years later at the age of eighty seven. They gave sixty years of their lives in faithful service to the Jehovah's Witness religion, convinced they would never grow old or die in this present 'system of things'. My mother's funeral service was conducted on an internet site. The elder who conducted the funeral service, suggested that all siblings write a few lines about our mother that he could read out. It was obvious by his expression and tone of voice that he resented reading the words I had written. I had written that 'my mother had musical and creative talents that myself and my children inherited from her' but he left me out of the sentence and only included the children. Whether it was he that changed this or Waverley when she wrote it down, I do not know. I had injured my knee and was unable to drive three hundred and forty miles to attend the burial after the service, but had sent flowers. Clarissa refused to transport me there as she was in the vulnerable category during the Covid pandemic. Waverley said I could have travelled on the train, but limping around train stations and wearing a mask for twelve hours of travelling would not have been easy. I made the decision after asking myself if my mother would have done the same for me and I knew what the answer would be. In one way I was sad about this as she was my mother, however we had not parted on the best of terms and she continued to shun me. My brother Albert stopped answering my mobile phone texts.

Albert has had a traumatic time emotionally as he lived with my parents for forty six years of his life and was then alone in the family home. Having traits of Asperger's syndrome, he is obsessed about seeing his parents again and wants Armageddon to occur as soon as possible so they will be resurrected. He refuses to have contact with Uncle Vernon and I, terrified that if he does, he will not survive Armageddon nor see his parents again. Albert makes allowances for Waverley as an 'inactive'

Jehovah's Witness, as he has learnt from my parents she is useful and would help him financially. The elders turned a 'blind eye' to Waverley's lifestyle and she in turn, continued to care for her parents and Albert. It is surprising what they will tolerate to offload responsibility!

Many who I remember in my parents' generation from their congregation have now passed away. I reconnected with Hattie Lovell after she became disfellowshipped and discovered that the elder she married was physically violent towards her. She asked the elders for help, but they blamed her and advised her to be a better wife. Hattie wanted a divorce, but the only way she could do this was by committing adultery. The elders and members of the congregation blamed her for the marriage ending, while comforting and pitying her former husband. Hattie's mother Pamela passed away only a few months after my father and her father Troy passed away a few months after my mother. Hattie had invited her father to live with her and she cared for him until he died. Troy no longer attended meetings and her sister Honour had no contact with them until the last few weeks of his life. Her parents were inactive Jehovah's Witnesses and Honour could have had more contact with them but chose not to. Meanwhile, she was visiting old people in the nursing homes and singing to them, displaying photographs on social media of her hugging them all while offering no help to her father. Despite this, she later arranged for Troy to have a Jehovah's Witness memorial service via the internet. It was surprisingly one of the most personal funerals I attended within this religion. There were family videos and footage of Troy playing his music with bands and it described his career, the celebrities he mixed with and the lucrative lifestyle his family had. I doubt that all the Jehovah's Witnesses who knew him approved of his lifestyle and the content of this memorial service. Honour had described him as a strong Jehovah's Witness and this was untrue as in the last few years of his life it was Hattie, the disfellowshipped daughter who gave him the love and care he needed. If I had not been shunned by my parents I would have done the same, but having Waverley as the dutiful daughter, had enabled them to shun me.

CHAPTER 22

CONCLUSION

Within the last five years I have intensively researched and studied the effect that religious cults can have on its members. While doing this research I discovered that the Jehovah's Witness religion has many traits of a cult from a check-list known as the *B.I.T.E. method* by *Steven Hassan*. This is Behaviour Control, Information Control, Thought Control and Emotional Control. Jehovah's Witnesses may not be one of the worst, but they practise these rigid rules and restrictions, severely affecting the lives and mental health of its members.

As I mentioned in the earlier part of my book, one of Jehovah's Witnesses called at my parents home during a time of crisis after Carl was admitted to a residential hospital. My mother was distraught and seeking answers to life's problems as well as something to believe in. This is a well known sales technique, for example, a sales person selling brooms will repeatedly call at homes, as eventually the day will come when a household's broom will wear out or break and they are there to provide another.

My mother needed a positive hope for the future and thought that Jehovah's Witnesses had given it to her, promising that she would not grow old or die. They taught their members that Armageddon was 'just around the corner' and my mother thought that she would be saved and live forever on a paradise earth. They also promised her that Carl would be cured of his autism and enjoy a normal life with her. I sense that my father agreed to join as it gave them a new hope for the future and would also help him 'tame' my mother's wild and free spirit. Now that I understand this process, I can see why my parents were recruited, however the fault does not lie with them, but with the governing body who run the organisation.

My study of family dynamics helped me understand more about my own. My mother favoured her sons and would do anything to protect them, that included sacrificing other relationships. My sister was the industrious one and good at making money, therefore she would be the one capable of caring for them in their old age. By placing her in the role of the 'golden child' throughout her life and turning a blind eye to anything she may have done wrong, she would be expected to help them later in life, to pay them back for having this favoured position.

I was the outspoken child and from the day I disclosed my abuse, I was placed in the role of 'black sheep' and 'scapegoat'. There is a history of mothers and daughters not getting along in my maternal family line and instead of learning from this, my mother treated me in the same way my grandmother allegedly treated her. My father allowed her to have her way in most things and our lives revolved around her needs. He also wanted our family to look good in the eyes of others and decided not to 'rock the boat'.

Kevin was the firstborn, the 'blue eyed boy' and for years he thought he was the favourite child, but when he realised Waverley had this role, he decided to move away and leave the responsibility to her. Albert was the youngest and was 'wrapped in cotton wool' by my parents. Now they are no longer around he only allows Waverley to care for him as she promised my parents she would. The role of the black sheep set me free in many ways from this corrupt situation.

After researching Christian and Pagan religions, I believe that Paganism versus Christianity seems to be more about a 'battle of the sexes'. Paganism has female deities and women were revered as powerful life-givers. Some time later, Christianity arrived and to gain followers they instilled fear by creating a 'scapegoat' Devil out of Pagan imagery, the most popular being the Greek God Pan. Men controlled the Christian organisations with their wives and families under their control and in total submission. I have concluded that Paganism versus Christianity is more about a 'battle of the sexes'. In all my years of researching the occult, I personally have found no 'demons' nor had any frightening experiences. This caused me to wonder if religions create a fear of the occult, as when a seeker does discover the truth, it empowers them to the extent they no longer need religion. Leaders then lose control and power over their people. Unfortunately there are a huge amount of 'power hungry' manipulative people in this world obsessed with titles, self-importance and controlling the lives of others.

Many have remarked on the strength of character I had at the age of sixteen to ask to be disfellowshipped from a religion I was born into. I was a headstrong teenager who wanted my freedom to the extent that I did not consider or realise the consequence of this decision or how it would affect my life in years to come. I have often wondered about the life I would have had if I had not left, but I doubt it would have been a happier one. My mother assured me that if I married a 'spiritually strong' *brother* my life would have been happy, but after reconnecting with Hattie who married an elder and was physically abused, I could see this was not so.

Taking risks in life opened my mind to many possibilities and although it has been a 'roller coaster', I have had some astounding life experiences. As I left the Jehovah's Witnesses at a young age, I did not think their teachings would affect my life When I researched the long lasting effects religious cults can have on children raised within them, the indoctrination at such a young age does have a profound effect on one's life. When a person is courageous enough to leave a cult and enter the outside world, with no knowledge of social skills and how to survive within it, life can be incredibly challenging. This has serious repercussions on all aspects of their lives.

Unfortunately, my children had learnt the art of shunning from my parents as they witnessed how I was treated by them. They are now adults and were not raised within a religion, but they have shunned me many times. That is, however, their choice and I continue living my life and staying in contact with one or two family members and those who have proved to be genuine friends.

I am not, nor will I ever be a submissive woman which is a requirement within this type of religion. If a woman shows signs of confidence and are not intimidated by the elders and are knowledgeable about anything other than the organisation's indoctrination, they will not want her associating with other females within the congregation. This will result in a swift excommunication.

I have written this book with the intention of reaching out to former cult members who are shunned by their families and friends. You can get through this, learn how to cope and have a fulfilling life. Remember you are a strong and special individual and the powers that be and your ancestors still love you and believe in you. Do not let the opinions of other humans shape your reality or control you. Become the strong and powerful person you are meant to be. Remember my words and my story. I will end this book by sending you my understanding, strength and love.

Useful Resources

Silentlambs – www.silentlambs.org

Former Jehovah's Witness Forum – www.jehovahs-witnesses.com

Steven Hassan – www.freedomofmind.com

Caring for Cult Victims – www.cultinformation.org

Religious Cult Counselling – www.takingthehelmcounselling.co.uk

Hope Valley Counselling – www.hopevalleycounselling.com

Understanding Cults – www.psychologytoday.com

Catalyst Counselling – www.catalystcounselling.org.uk

Printed in Great Britain
by Amazon

22309627R00175